T0343921

Still shouting at 50

As Index marks its half-century, **JEMIMAH STEINFELD** writes about staying true to the manifesto that started the magazine

"Our need today is for organs of consciousness that could help us to know and to care about other members of the same intellectual community, much as Christians once were vigilant for other Christians in times of religious persecution."

THUS WROTE THE poet Stephen Spender in the founding manifesto of this magazine. As Spender outlined, Index came into being after Pavel Litvinov, a Soviet physicist and dissident, called on the international community to help those being censored in the USSR. The year of our first publication was 1972. The Cold War was not yet a chapter in a history textbook, nor was apartheid. Spain, Portugal and Greece were still under military dictatorships. Mao Zedong was the leader of China.

The challenges were great and our mission was to concern ourselves with all because censorship was not a one-sided issue. "The problem of censorship," Spender wrote, "is part of larger ones about the use and abuse of freedom."

Since 1972 we have done our best to live up to the ideals of the founding manifesto. We have covered the wars, the revolutions and the protests. We have smuggled writings out of prison and published material banned elsewhere. We have provided a forum for critical debate and waded into the thorniest issues of the day. And we have dealt with the complexity of technology, both a blessing and a curse. Our articles have rippled across the world in myriad ways, influencing statesmen and laymen alike, and providing a refuge for the persecuted.

To mark our half-century we have created a birthday issue. It is not a celebration in the conventional sense. By all means, our refuge should no longer exist. But in 2022 the battles remain as large. We need to continue to shout. And we want to celebrate the brave and brilliant people who got us to this place – and do a little back-patting too over our role in documenting abuses and sometimes lessening them.

And so to our anniversary special. We have asked editors from the five decades to reflect on their time at Index and we've selected pieces from our archive to accompany them. This was no easy task. As Spender wrote, the "material

by writers which is censored in Eastern Europe, Greece, South Africa and other countries is among the most exciting that is being written today". How right he was. We have therefore not tried to choose the best – a mission impossible. Instead we've picked articles that capture a moment in time and reflect our rich, varied history.

At the same time, we've invited journalists around the globe to revisit articles published in our first year and consider them from the vantage point of 2022, such as Susan McKay's look at the contentious role of the BBC in Northern Ireland then and now. In our culture section, Nick Harkaway reimagines the early days of Index, a fantastically fun accompaniment to Martin Bright's deep-dive into the real Index origin story.

Moving to today, Indian journalist Aishwarya Jagani brings you an alarming tale of women who found themselves on an auction site and we publish letters from prison by the Hong Kong media mogul Jimmy Lai. As for the future, Sir Tom Stoppard considers mob justice and its ramifications.

"In being concerned with the situation of those who are deprived of their freedoms one is taking the side of openness," wrote Spender in the manifesto. Onwards we march. ✖

Jemimah Steinfeld is editor-in-chief of Index on Censorship

51(01):1/1|DOI:10.1177/03064220221085925

Marking a milestone from the start

About our 50th anniversary cover

There's no easy way to encapsulate 50 years of Index – and censorship – in one single image. So we went back to the start. While the first cover of Index was not the most dynamic, its sparseness fitted the theme. Censorship is, after all, about omission. We used this template to showcase our new content. A cover that highlights how far we've come and how little has changed.

CONTENTS

CREDIT: (cover) Index on Censorship

The Index

51(01):04/05|DOI:10.1177/03064220221084506

A round-up of events in the world of free expression from Index's unparalleled network of writers and activists.

Edited by
MARK FRARY

The Index

ELECTION WATCH

GUILHERME OSINSKI looks ahead to votes around the world

1. Hungary, 3 April

After almost 12 years in power, Hungary's Prime Minister Viktor Orban (above) will see his fate being decided in new parliamentary elections this April. Orban leads a government that stands for national sovereignty, traditional Christian values and controversial policies including anti-immigration and anti-LGBTQ rights.

Another ingredient that promises to heat things up is that on the same day that voters choose a new parliament, the country will hold a referendum on LGBTQ issues. Four key points will be addressed. One of them wishes to find out if Hungarians support sexual orientation workshops in school without the parents' approval.

To retain his job, Orban has to defeat a well-established alliance formed by the Democratic Coalition, the Socialist Party, liberals and the centre-right Jobbik. If run democratically, we should expect a tight outcome in this election race.

2. Philippines, 9 May

Under the wing of President Rodrigo Duterte since June 2016, the Philippines has seen a series of human rights violations in the country. The murder of journalists has become a trend, with more than 20 killed since Duterte's first day in the president's chair.

Now, a general election might bring new freedom to the country. With Rodrigo Duterte not eligible for a re-election campaign, the 67.5 million Filipinos registered to vote will choose a new president, vice president and 12 senators.

So far, polls suggest that the Philippines' new leader will be Ferdinand "Bongbong" Marcos (below), son of Ferdinand Marcos, a dictator who took over the country for 21 years between 1965 and 1986. It's expected that a significant number of pro-democracy groups will urge people not to vote for Marcos, who is believed to represent the legacy of his father.

3. Colombia, 29 May

Colombia's president, Iván Duque, who has run the country since 2018, won't be able to contest for a new term – one term is the limit – but he would struggle to win anyway. According to a December 2021 poll, only 25% of Colombians had a positive view of Duque's presidency.

Threats and attacks against indigenous, Afro-Colombian and other community activists, which were happening frequently during Duque's presidency, are expected to feature in debates between candidates.

Gustavo Petro, former Mayor of Bogotá and defeated by Duque in 2018, represents the left-wing. Another contender is Ingrid Betancourt (above), who was captured by the Revolutionary Armed Forces (FARC) in 2002 and kept hostage for six years. Recently she said: "I am here to claim the rights of 51 million Colombians who are not finding justice because we live in a system designed to reward criminals".

In 2021, many people hit the country's streets demanding more attention from the government on fundamental rights such as education, healthcare, poverty and police violence, issues that should be central themes in the election. ✘

CREDIT: [Election Watch] (Betancourt) Christian Roar Pedersen, (Marcos) Christian Roar Pedersen, (Orban) Flickr/European People's Party; [Inks spot] Nabil (illustration of Crabman); Crabman (Mohammed VI)

YOU MAY HAVE MISSED

A round-up of important news on free expression from around the world

The right to protest threatened

In early January, the UK House of Lords voted down a series of measures in the government's Police, Crime Sentencing and Courts Bill, many of which were introduced at the last minute without the chance for debate, writes editor at large Martin Bright. These included the power to stop and search anyone at a protest (or simply passing by a protest) without the need for reasonable suspicion. The new measures would also have allowed the courts to ban people from attending protests in future even if they hadn't been convicted of any offences in the past. These are what are technically described as "precautionary powers", usually reserved for counter-terrorism and serious crime rather than peaceful protest. In addition, police would have been able to intervene if protests were judged to be too loud. Despite its failure at this stage of the legislative process, the government has made it clear it intends to reintroduce these draconian proposals.

Academic forced to leave Greece

A prominent Turkish-Armenian academic has had to leave Greece after being labelled an "undesirable foreigner" in what he sees as punishment for creating a database of how placenames have changed over time.

Sevan Nişanyan, born in Istanbul in 1956, is a linguist and compiler of the hugely comprehensive Etymological Dictionary of the Turkish Language.

In 2012, he wrote a blog post about free speech arguing for the right to criticise the Prophet Mohammed, which incensed Recep Tayyip Erdogan and was later jailed for more than 16 years on trumped-up charges.

In 2017, Nişanyan escaped from the low security prison where he was being held and travelled to Greece, where he claimed asylum.

Last December, he was denounced by the Greek police as a national security threat. His supporters say his name was added to Greece's "list of undesirable foreigners". At a recent press conference, Nişanyan claimed the reasons for the inclusion of his name on the list is considered a state secret.

He suspects it is related to his creation of the Index Anatolicus, "the authoritative source on the name changes to 53,000 Turkish places".

Nişanyan has now been forced to leave the country against his will. ✖

Ink spot

Moroccan satirical artist facing expulsion from Denmark

ABDELALI ACHAHBI, KNOWN as Crabman, is a 35-year-old Moroccan from Sale, north of Rabat, with a degree in art, computer programming and animation.

His 3D animated short films on the political situation in Morocco, human rights, and King Mohammed VI, part of the Alwati dynasty, have earned him a large social media following. However, his caricatures of the king have seen him receiving threats from Moroccan social media users accusing him of being a traitor for portraying him as the "Commander of the Faithful" and self-proclaimed descendant of the Prophet Mohammed.

Achahbi has lived in Denmark for 12 years but his recent request for asylum has been turned down.

The government says it was rejected because of problems in the application procedure: his asylum request was filed in Herning, his town of residence, in April 2020, but the government only received it 10 months later. Achahbi provided a duly stamped receipt proving it was the Herning police who held up the request.

If Achahbi is forced to return to Morocco he faces arrest, imprisonment and possible torture for his caricatures as others in the country have discovered to their cost.

The Index

PEOPLE WATCH

MARK FRARY highlights the stories of human rights defenders under attack

Kakwenza Rukirabashaija

UGANDA

On 28 December 2021, writer and journalist Kakwenza Rukirabashaija was dragged from his home and detained without charge following his posting of critical tweets of Ugandan President Yoweri Museveni. Rukirabashaija was held incommunicado for more than 48 hours, according to Frontline Defenders. The writer subsequently posted images on Twitter showing signs of torture.

Rukirabashaija has not been charged with any crime and has now fled Uganda in fear for his life.

Miguel Mora

NICARAGUA

On 5 February, Miguel Mora of Nicaraguan cable news channel 100% Noticias was found guilty of "undermining national integrity" and conspiracy. He has been sentenced to 13 years in prison.

Mora, a presidential candidate of the Democratic Restoration Party, was the last of six political prisoners jailed for violating the Sovereignty Law. He was found guilty based on evidence from an interview he had conducted and four tweets. During the trial, Mora said, "I have not conspired against anyone, I am innocent."

Baktash Abtin

IRAN

Baktash Abtin, a film director and a member of the Iranian Writers' Association, has died from complications relating to Covid which could have been avoided had he received medical care earlier. Abtin had contracted the disease while in Tehran's Evin prison. He had been sentenced in 2019 to five years' imprisonment on charges of "illegal assembly and collusion against national security" and one year for "spreading propaganda against the state", in relation to his joint authorship of a book on the history of the IWA.

Tamana Zaryabi Paryani

AFGHANISTAN

Tamana Zaryabi Paryani, who has taken part in protests in Kabul recently, has been seized by armed men who entered her apartment and who claimed to be part of Taliban intelligence.

Footage of Paryani desperately screaming for help was subsequently shared on social media. A Taliban spokesman said the footage was a "manufactured drama" and would not confirm her arrest but later tweeted that "insulting the religious and national values of the Afghan people is not tolerated anymore".

Maintaining human rights scrutiny during security-related crises

DAVE ELSEROAD, head of advocacy at the Human Rights House Foundation, on keeping up scrutiny of Russian human rights violations

Today, the attention of much of Europe and the wider world is fixated on Ukraine. Armed conflict presents numerous challenges, not least of which is that security issues can often push human rights issues off the international agenda. It is within this context that Human Rights House Foundation and members of the network of Human Rights Houses are pushing to maintain international scrutiny of the human rights crisis perpetrated by the Russian authorities. Our partners at HRH Crimea highlight that Russian authorities, which exercise effective control over Crimea, have established a framework that "fundamentally contradicts international human rights law". Vostok-SOS, a member of the Educational HRH Chernihiv, reports on-going violations in the eastern Ukrainian region of Donbas. HRH Tbilisi raises cases of human rights defenders targeted by de facto authorities in South Ossetia. Additionally, at the end of 2021, HRHF issued a "Crisis Point in Russia" report outlining on-going repression against human rights defenders and organisations in Russia.

The security situation in Eastern Europe must not prevent scrutiny of Russia. The international community has tools available, including putting Russia on the formal agenda of international and regional human rights bodies, but must strategically employ them. The crisis is a domestic and international crisis. We must therefore maintain our focus accordingly.

THE LATEST FROM OUR CAMPAIGNS

Index on Censorship works on a number of active campaigns around the world. Find out more at **INDEXONCENSORSHIP.ORG**

China's long arm

Uyghurs silenced in Europe

A landmark report published on 10 February by Index highlights the shocking extent of Chinese attempts to repress Uyghurs living in countries across Europe, including the UK.

The report, compiled over months of detailed research and gathering of personal testimony, shows how the "long arm" of the Chinese Communist Party is silencing ethnic Uyghurs. Countless Uyghurs who have managed to escape China in search of freedom and security, have instead found themselves threatened and silenced by threats to friends and family still living in China.

From being persecuted in China, they find themselves hounded in Europe. Meanwhile, Uyghurs in Xinjiang are increasingly being pressured to inform on friends and relatives living abroad. This intelligence-gathering drive by the CCP is part of a concerted effort to compile a "global register" of information to assist the authorities in China to clamp down further on them.

As the Uyghur Tribunal recently

concluded, genocide, human rights abuses and torture are taking place against the Uyghur population of China.

Jessica Ní Mhainín, policy and campaigns manager at Index on Censorship, said: "This report shows the shocking reach of the Chinese government's "long arm", and also shines a light on the depths to which they will stoop in their concerted campaign against the Uyghur people.

"It has been widely accepted that there is a genocide taking place against Uyghurs in Xinjiang. What today's report from Index on Censorship demonstrates is that the CCP is now taking this campaign into countries around the world.

"Most of the approximately 12,500 Uyghurs that reside in the UK and EU still have friends or family members in Xinjiang. Speaking out or reporting CCP-backed threats could put their loved ones at an increased risk of internment, torture or worse."

You can read the report China's Long Arm: How Uyghurs are being silenced in Europe at **indexoncensorship.org/uyghurseurope**

2021 Tyrant of the Year announced

Our Tyrant of the Year 2021 was announced in January. There was fierce competition, with many rulers choosing to use the cover of Covid lockdowns to crack down on their opponents. More than 11,000 people voted in our poll and the "honour" went to Turkish President Recep Tayyip Erdogan.

We can think of a few reasons why Erdogan claimed the top spot. He refuses to release civil society leader Osman Kavala, imprisoned since 2017 despite being acquitted twice. Student LGBTQ+ artwork and campaigning on International Women's Day has led to arrests in the country.

He has, perhaps ironically, become the first European leader to withdraw from the Istanbul Convention on violence against women. Kurds have continuously seen their rights to freedom of expression curtailed, and finally opposition politicians such as the Democracy and Progress Party's Metin Gurcan have been jailed for criticising the president.

While Erdogan topped this year's poll, two other names pulled in plenty of votes: China's Xi Jinping came in second with Syria's Bashar al-Assad following closely in third. ✖

The Index

World In Focus: Kazakhstan

In January, Kazakhstan saw protests over fuel prices turn violent. The president since 2019, Kassym-Jomart Tokayev, called in support from Putin's Russia to restore order

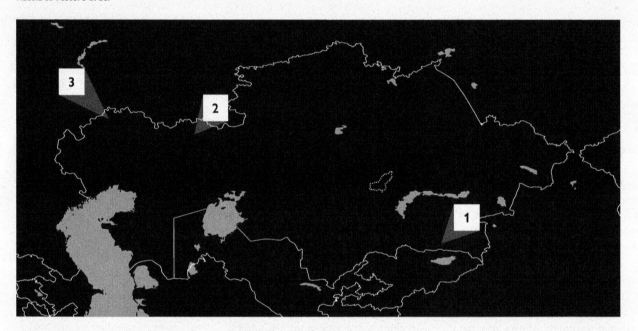

1 Almaty

On 5 January, Almaz Kaysar, a photo correspondent with independent news site Vlast, was filming a column of demonstrators in Almaty. The journalist was wearing a press vest but he was surrounded by six aggressive young men in masks with sticks. They expressed suspicions that he worked for the KNB intelligence agency and wanted to capture the faces of the protesters in order to bring them to justice. At first, some protesters tried to protect the photographer, but the number of people against the filming increased. In the end, Kaysar's smartphone was pulled out of his hands and smashed on the ground. He was forced to take off his press vest and continue his work incognito.

2 Aktobe

On 9 January, police in Aktobe in the west of Kazakhstan carried out a search at the home of Ardak Yerubaeva, a reporter who works for independent Kazakh news site Orda.

The police said the search was the result of social media posts that Yerubaeva had published on her accounts.

Journalist Askar Aktleuov reported that she was taken from home without explanation and her son left at home. "We believe that this may be due to the coverage of the protests on 4, 5 and 6 January," he said.

After two hours of questioning, Yerubaeva was eventually released without charge.

3 Uralsk

As soon as the mass protests of January 2022 began in Kazakhstan, journalists started to be chased and silenced by special forces. Human rights defender and journalist Lukpan Akhmedyarov was one of the targets.

Working for a newspaper in the city of Uralsk, in the northwest of Kazakhstan, Akhmedyarov was approached and arrested on 7 January after leaving his office. Accused of engaging in the demonstrations, he was sentenced to 10 days of administrative arrest. His lawyer argued that he was at the protests performing his work duties as a journalist, covering the events, but the court did not accept this.

Akhmedyarov was kept at the Uralsk Special Detention Center of the Department of Internal Affairs, before being released on 17 January. He claims he was a victim of psychological pressure and ruthless treatment during his detention.

TECH WATCH: THE LATEST MUST-HAVE IS CYBERSECURITY LAWS

MARK FRARY on chilling new cybersecurity legislation

N RECENT TIMES, authoritarian regimes have increasingly enacted draconian cybersecurity laws in order to silence their opponents. In 2019, Vietnam introduced new legislation that requires internet providers to remove content that was critical of the country's Communist authorities, leading Reporters Without Borders to call it "a totalitarian model of information control". Last year, Zambia's new Cyber Security and Cyber Crimes Bill generated controversy for its extra-territorial reach and threat to freedom of expression.

In a joint statement 10 organisations, including Transparency International Zambia, said, "It provides several avenues for abuse of the cyber space by state organs which threaten the constitutionally guaranteed freedom of expression and right to privacy."

However, a new cyber bill set to be introduced in Myanmar by the military regime might be one of the most draconian ever to make it into law. The legislation has been discussed since 2019, two years before the coup. A draft was circulated just after the regime of General Min Aung Hlaing took over but was dropped after widespread criticism. A new draft was circulated in January this year and its provisions promise to be even more harsh.

Free Expression Myanmar (FEM), which has seen the draft, says the military could permanently block the whole of Facebook on the grounds that it included just one post criticising a military leader. The new rules would also criminalise the use of virtual private networks (VPNs) and those who use them can be fined 5 million kyat (around £2,000) or face three years in prison.

Internet service providers are also required to retain names, internet addresses and ID numbers for three years and must be handed over upon request by the authorities. And the 2022 draft includes a range of provisions that could seriously undermine the financial systems that are commonly used by members of the public to finance groups that oppose the military.

FEM said, "Any block that prevents an organisation from raising funds can be a violation of the right to freedom of association. If the organisation is blocked because of its political message, this is a violation of the right to freedom of expression too." ✖

BELOW: Access to the internet in Myanmar is under threat

Free speech in numbers

406 MILLION

The number of monthly active users of Spotify almost two years after Joe Rogan moved his podcast to the platform

753%

Percentage growth in sales of the graphic novel Maus in the last week of January after it was banned by a Tennessee school district.

1,540

The number of people killed by the junta in Myanmar since the coup in 2021
Source: AAPP

409

The number of days between activists being arrested at the flame lighting ceremony in Greece for protesting against China holding the Winter Olympics and their case being heard in Greek courts

7.5

Years to which Uzbek blogger Fazilhoja Arifhojaev has been sentenced for commenting on a social media post on whether it was appropriate for a Muslim to congratulate non-Muslims on their religious holidays

 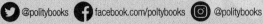

SPECIAL REPORT

"Identity politics has thrown up a phenomenon, a battleground
which is not political so much as psycho-social, an intolerance
between individuals, and it's about language"

SIR TOM STOPPARD ON THE SHIFT AWAY FROM VALUING FREE SPEECH AS UNIVERSAL| HUMPTY DUMPTY HAS MAYBE HAD THE LAST WORD P22

CREDIT: Yuri Timofeyev/AFP/Getty

Dissidents, spies and the lies that came in from the cold

Index started at the front line of an ideological war, writes **MARTIN BRIGHT**

THE STORY OF Index on Censorship is steeped in the romance and myth of the Cold War.

In one version of the narrative, it is a tale that brings together courageous young dissidents battling a totalitarian regime and liberal Western intellectuals desperate to help – both groups united in their respect for enlightenment values.

intelligence services) were keen to demonstrate that the life of the mind could truly flourish only where Western values of democracy and free speech held sway.

But in all the words written over the years about how Index came to be, it is important not to forget the people at the heart of it all: the dissidents themselves, living the daily reality of censorship, repression and potential death.

The story really began not in 1972, with the first publication of this magazine, but with a letter to The Times and the French paper Le Monde on 13 January 1968. This Appeal to World Public Opinion was signed by Larisa Bogoraz Daniel, a veteran dissident, and Pavel Litvinov, a young physics teacher who had been drawn into the fragile opposition movement during the celebrated show-trial of intellectuals Andrei Sinyavsky and Yuli Daniel (Larisa's husband) in February 1966. This is now generally accepted as being the beginning of the modern Soviet dissident movement.

The letter itself was written in response to the Trial of Four in January 1968, which saw two students, Yuri Galanskov and Alexander Ginzburg, sentenced to five years' hard labour for the production of anti-communist literature.

The other two defendants were Alexey Dobrovolsky, who pleaded guilty and co-operated with the prosecution, and a typist, Vera Lashkova.

Ginzburg later became a prominent dissident and lived in exile in Paris, Galanskov died in a labour camp in 1972 and Dobrovolsky was sent to a psychiatric hospital. Lashkova's fate is unclear.

The letter was the first of its kind, appealing to the Soviet people and the outside world rather than directly to the authorities. "We appeal to everyone in whom conscience is alive and who has sufficient courage... Citizens of our country, this trial is a stain on the honour of our state and on the conscience of every one of us."

The letter went on to evoke the shadow of Joseph Stalin's show-trials in the 1930s and ended: "We pass this appeal to the Western progressive press and ask for it to be published and broadcast by radio as soon as possible – we are not sending this request to Soviet newspapers because that is hopeless."

The trial took place in a courthouse packed with Kremlin supporters, while protesters outside endured temperatures of 50 degrees below zero.

The poet Stephen Spender responded to the letter by organising a telegram of support from 16 prominent artists and intellectuals, including philosopher Bertrand Russell, poet WH Auden, composer Igor Stravinsky and novelists JB Priestley and Mary McCarthy.

It took eight months for Litvinov to respond, as he had heard the words of support only on the radio and was waiting for the official telegram to arrive. It never did.

On 8 August 1968, the young dissident outlined a bold plan for support in the West for what he called "the democratic movement in the USSR". He proposed a committee made up of "universally respected progressive writers, scholars, artists and public   ➔

In another, it is just one colourful episode in a fight to the death between two superpower ideologies, where the world of letters found itself at the centre of a propaganda war.

Both versions are true.

It is undeniably the case that Index was founded during the Cold War by a group of intellectuals blooded in cultural diplomacy. Western governments (and

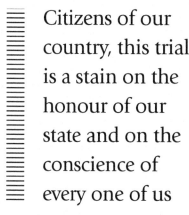

Citizens of our country, this trial is a stain on the honour of our state and on the conscience of every one of us

ABOVE: The Prague Spring, Czechoslovakia, 1968

→ personalities" to be taken not just from the USA and western Europe but also from Latin America, Asia, Africa and, ultimately, from the Soviet bloc itself. Litvinov later wrote an account in Index explaining how he had typed the letter and given it to Dutch journalist and human rights activist Karel van Het Reve, who smuggled it out of the country to Amsterdam the next day. Two weeks later, Soviet tanks rolled into Czechoslovakia to crush the Prague Spring.

On 25 August 1968, Litvinov and Bogoraz Daniel joined six others in Red Square to demonstrate against the invasion. It was an extraordinary act of courage. They sat down and unfurled homemade banners with slogans that included "We are Losing Our Friends", "Long Live a Free and Independent Czechoslovakia", "Shame on Occupiers!" and "For Your Freedom and Ours".

The activists were immediately arrested and most received sentences of prison or exile, while two were sent to psychiatric hospitals.

Vaclav Havel, the dissident playwright and first president of the Czech Republic, later said in a Novaya Gazeta article: "For the citizens of Czechoslovakia, these people became the conscience of the Soviet Union, whose leadership without hesitation undertook a despicable military attack on a sovereign state and ally."

When Ginzburg died in 2002, novelist Zinovy Zinik used his Guardian obituary to sound a note of caution.

Ginzburg, he wrote, was "a nostalgic figure of modern times, part of the Western myth of the Russia of the 1950s, '60s and '70s, when literature, the word, played a crucial part in political change".

Speaking 20 years later, Zinik told Index he did not even like the English word "dissident", which failed to capture the true complexity of the opposition to the Soviet regime. "The Russian word used before 'dissidents' invaded the language was 'inakomyslyashchiye' – it is an archaic word but was adopted into conversational vocabulary. The correct translation would be 'holders of heterodox views'."

It's perhaps understandable that the archaic Russian word didn't catch on, but his point is instructive.

As Zinik warned, it is all too easy to romanticise this era and see it through a Western lens. The Appeal to World Public Opinion was not important because it led to the founding of Index. The letter was important because it internationalised the struggle of the Soviet dissident movement.

As Litvinov later wrote in Index: "Only a few people understood at the time that these individual protests were becoming a part of a movement which the Soviet authorities would never be able to eradicate." Index was a consequence of Litvinov's appeal; it was not the point of the exercise and there was no mention of a magazine in the early correspondence.

The original idea was to set up an organisation, Writers and Scholars International, to give support to the dissidents. It was only with the appointment of Michael Scammell in 1971 that the idea emerged to establish a magazine to publish and promote the work of dissidents around the world.

Spender and his great friend and co-collaborator, the Oxford philosopher Stuart Hampshire, were still reeling from revelations about CIA funding of their previous magazine, Encounter.

"I knew that [they]... had attempted unsuccessfully to start a new magazine and I felt that they would support something in the publishing line," Scammell wrote in Index in 1981.

Speaking recently from his home in New York, Scammell told me: "I understood Pavel Litvinov's leanings here. He understood that a magazine that was impartial would stand a better chance of making an impression in the Soviet Union than if it could just be waved away as another CIA project."

Philip Spender, the poet's nephew, who worked for many years at Index, agreed: "Pavel Litvinov was the seed from which Index grew... He always said it shouldn't be anti-communist or anti-Soviet. The point wasn't this or that ideology. Index was never pro any ideology."

It has been suggested that Index did not mark quite such a clean break – it was set up by the same Cold Warriors and susceptible to the same CIA influence. In her exhaustive examination of the cultural Cold War, Who Paid the Piper, journalist Frances Stonor Saunders claimed Index was set up with a "substantial grant" from the Ford Foundation, which had long been linked to the CIA.

In fact, the Ford funding came later, but it lasted for two decades and raises serious questions about what its backers thought Index was for.

Scammell now recognises that the CIA was playing a sophisticated game at the time. "On one level this is probably heresy to say so, but one must applaud the skills of the CIA. I mean, they had that money all over the place. So, I would get the Ford Foundation grant, let's say, and it never ever occurred to me that that money itself might have come from the CIA."

He added: "I would not have taken any money that was labelled CIA, but I think they were incredibly smart."

By the time the magazine appeared in spring 1972, it had come a long way from its origins in the Soviet opposition movement. It did reproduce two short works by Alexander Solzhenitsyn and poetry by dissident Natalya Gorbanevskaya (a participant in the 1968 Red Square demonstration, who had been released from a psychiatric hospital in February of that year). But it also contained pieces about Bangladesh, Brazil, Greece, Portugal and Yugoslavia.

Philip Spender said it was important to understand the context of the times: "There was a lot of repression in the world in the early '70s. There was the imprisonment of writers in the Soviet Union, but also Greece, Spain and Portugal. There was also apartheid. There was a coup in Chile in 1973, which rounded up dissidents. Brazil was not a friendly place."

He said Index thought of itself as the literary version of Amnesty International. "It wasn't a political stance, it was a non-political stance against the use of force."

The first edition of the magazine opened with an essay by Stephen Spender, With Concern for Those Not Free. He asked each reader of the article to say to themselves: "If a writer whose works are banned wishes to be published and if I am in a position to help him to be published, then to refuse to give help is for me to support censorship."

He ended the essay in the hope that Index would act as part of an answer to the appeal "from those who are censored, banned or imprisoned to consider their case as our own".

Since Index was founded, the Berlin Wall has fallen and apartheid has been dismantled. We have witnessed the "war on terror", the rise of Russian president Vladimir Putin and the emergence of China as a world superpower.

And yet, if it is not too grand or presumptuous, the role of the magazine remains unchanged – to consider the case of the dissident writer as our own. ✖

Martin Bright is editor-at-large of Index

51(01):14/17|DOI:10.1177/03064220221084569

 Only a few people understood at the time that these individual protests were becoming a part of a movement which the Soviet authorities would never be able to eradicate

PICTURED: The BBC
Northern Ireland HQ,
Broadcasting House,
in Belfast

Sound and fury at political 'bias'

When, in 1984, Margaret Thatcher tried to silence both republican and loyalist voices in Northern Ireland, the BBC thwarted her. Whatever happened to such feistiness? **SUSAN MCKAY** reports from Belfast

THE BBC WALKS a tightrope between communities in Northern Ireland today – as it has done for more than half a century, before and after the conflict.

In February, the Democratic Unionist Party's former leader Arlene Foster, a host with the right-wing channel GB News, interviewed Jeffrey Donaldson MP, the party leader. Donaldson had just pulled the party's first minister, Paul Givan, out of office, forcing the resignation of Sinn Fein's deputy first minister, Michelle O'Neill, since, confusingly, theirs is a joint office. He blamed the Northern Ireland protocol which, under the Brexit deal, creates a kind of border in the Irish Sea.

Foster asked him about figures he had given on its cost to the Northern Irish economy, noting that "your opponents… including the BBC in NI", had challenged them. She may have heard John Campbell, BBC NI's respected economics and business editor, who had raised serious questions about Donaldson's figures.

Donaldson ignored Foster's loaded remark but the BBC was quick to reject her claim. "Our journalism is fair and impartial," its statement said. "That is the BBC's job. We are not in opposition to anyone."

Northern Ireland was meant by its founding fathers to be a unionist state and the BBC was compliant with its role as the voice of the Stormont government, which meant that when it came to the injustices experienced by the minority nationalist community it was silent. The civil rights movement and the violent conflict that followed forced it to change. "There is no shared frame of reference on the question of Ireland," wrote Anthony Smyth in his 1972 essay for Index on Censorship.

Today, almost a quarter of a century after the Good Friday agreement brought about a devolved power sharing regime, the DUP claims unionists are now discriminated against by the institutions of state, including the BBC.

The DUP has often complained when the BBC features voices it perceives to be insufficiently respectful of its politics. A perpetually angry unionist rump made up of hardliners whose votes the DUP covets have recently taken to calling some journalists (including this one) "anti unionist activists". Its spokespersons declare support for the Defund the BBC campaign. The BBC, they say, is biased.

Mention the BBC in Northern Ireland and one name will immediately come up: Nolan. Everyone has an opinion. It tends to be a love-hate thing. The Stephen Nolan Show, which airs on BBC Radio Ulster on weekday mornings, boasts that it is the "biggest show in the country", a claim the BBC defended when a local commercial station challenged it, though it does not provide figures.

The head of a manufacturing trade alliance recently told the Northern Ireland Affairs Committee at Westminster that NI's public sector was insular, overly preoccupied with the local and so afraid "that they are going to end up on the Nolan Show" that they will do nothing "that has a bit of risk attached to it".

Nolan is a big fish in the small pond of NI broadcasting. He cultivates the notion that he is an outsider, jokes about how the "sixth floor", meaning the BBC bosses, are devastated by his success, the brash working class Protestant boy from Belfast's inner city Shankill Road. Yet he is one of the BBC's top earners, with a salary above £400,000 a year. He and his team are capable of a journalism that is forensic, ruthless and effective. He wins awards. His interview in 2014 with Iris Robinson, then a DUP politician, over her view that homosexuality was an "abomination" was transformed by Conor Mitchell into a powerful opera.

However, some, including marketing executive Tim McKane, argue that Nolan gives valuable and profile building primetime exposure to certain minority voices while rarely giving a platform to others. McKane asked the BBC last year for figures on the number of times Traditional Unionist Voice leader Jim Allister had been interviewed and was told that no such figures were kept. Allister is a kind of Northern Irish Nigel Farage. His party's sole elected representative at the NI Assembly at Stormont, he has always opposed the Good Friday agreement, refers to the EU as a "foreign power" and champions the cause of bringing down the devolved power sharing institutions. His popularity is rising.

Claims and counterclaims about bias in public bodies are significant in

ABOVE: Stephen Nolan's BBC Radio Ulster show boasts that it is the biggest in the country

a post-conflict society still afflicted by sectarian hostilities – the reconciliation aspired to in the Good Friday agreement is far from being fully achieved. When I asked BBC NI how it dealt with this, I was referred to the Impartiality and Editorial Standards Action Plan, which is based on recommendations from the Serota Review into the BBC's overall governance and culture. This, I was told, "focuses on impartiality [and] editorial standards" and "represents the BBC's biggest and most significant push to ensure its programmes and content are fair, accurate and unbiased and truly reflect the broad public which it serves." No information was offered as to how this was measured in the complicated context of Northern Ireland. There is no NI representative on the BBC's governing body.

If the BBC in NI has been making efforts to diversify, it is not apparent. At both managerial and journalistic levels there is still a predominance of white men who look in the mirror and see – white men. Some women who work there describe a boys' club ethos →

Almost a quarter of a century after the Good Friday agreement, the DUP claims unionists are now discriminated against by the BBC

→ in which sexism and ageism collide. A number of court cases are pending. Ivy Goddard, project leader of the Inter Ethnic Forum, said that while "small changes" had been made in recent years, there were still, despite extensive lobbying, few faces and voices from minority communities, which include thousands of people.

Angry male callers dominate online phone-ins. When a senior male presenter, speaking at a recent conference, dismissed claims that women's perspectives were not heard enough, one activist pointed out that if she wanted to talk about the right to choose abortion, she had to do so while arguing with Jim Wells, a DUP politician who is a fundamentalist Christian who once compared abortion to the Holocaust.

In 1984, when Margaret Thatcher prohibited the voices of spokespersons for republicanism and loyalism from being broadcast, BBC NI boldly thwarted her command, using actors of the calibre of Stephen Rea to do voiceovers. The ban ended in 1994. There is little sign of such feistiness now.

In 2017, BBC NI co-funded the documentary No Stone Unturned about a 1994 sectarian massacre by loyalists in Loughinisland. The documentary, by the Belfast based Fine Point Films, was directed by the internationally renowned Alex Gibney. It provided strong evidence of state collusion and controversially named the chief suspect. After a falling out over editorial issues, BBC NI failed to show it. Nationalist politicians were among those who demanded to know why, when the film was being screened in cinemas and was receiving huge attention in Ireland and abroad, the BBC in NI ignored it. The BBC said it would make its own decisions.

After the conflict in NI ended – more or less – many of the international media left. With the local newspaper industry struggling, the BBC's relatively well-paid jobs are highly prized. It has some excellent journalists, some multi-award winning programmes. But investment in NI programming is falling.

Ofcom's Media Nations report last year noted its hours of first-run content dropped by 6% to 568 hours, representing a drop of 30% in spend. Ofcom also reported that some 90%

ABOVE: The BBC used actors to voice the words of Sinn Fein's Gerry Adams, left, and Martin McGuinness when the Thatcher government tried to silence figures on both sides of the divide

of people in NI, the highest proportion in the UK, are "very" or "quite" interested in news. News and current affairs programmes from the BBC's Belfast and Derry bases reach 30% of the population, while its news coverage reaches half. It faces considerable competition from Ulster Television's news output. It relies on older people – in 2019, among the under 24s, there was a 23% drop in numbers using it.

The BBC's Belfast press office declined Index on Censorship an interview. It was "a bit of a transitional period, with a new interim director and head of news", I was told. And it was dealing with the licence fee issue [it is to be frozen]. Everyone was too busy. ✖

Susan McKay is an Irish writer and journalist whose latest book is Northern Protestants – On Shifting Ground

51(01):18/20|DOI:10.1177/03064220221084572

CREDIT: PA Archive/PA Images

How do you find 50 years of censorship?

HTEIN LIN, MYANMAR artist and former political prisoner (1998-2004), has created this painting for our 50th anniversary in the style of his 'How do you find…..?' series. Through the series he has previously observed London, Amsterdam and other cities through his Myanmar eyes, identifying, connecting and adapting cultural references.

In this piece, the 50 is printed on Shan mulberry leaf paper using the monotype technique he developed during his six-and-a-half years in prison, painting with his fingers on scraps of plastic and printing onto white prison uniform. Tucked into the cells in the

numbers are iconic images of censorship and the censored: Xi Jinping and Pooh Bear, Myanmar writer and prisoner Win Tin, George Orwell, Anna Politkovskaya, Václav Havel, and Ma Thida, friend, Myanmar writer, former prisoner, and current Chair of PEN's Writers in Prison Committee. Dr Li Wenliang, silenced for exposing the early days of Covid, Liu Xiaobo, Nelson Mandela, Aung San Suu Kyi and Alexei Navalny rub shoulders with Donald Trump and a Charlie Hebdo cartoon.

Around the figures, festooned with barbed wire, flutter the icons of social media

and internet shutdown, and more traditional images of censorship such as redaction, book burning, arrest and murder.

Lin continues to live and work in Myanmar and remains committed to freedom of expression. He is a founding member of the Association for Myanmar Contemporary Art (AMCA) whose planned launch date of 1 February 2021 had to be postponed because of an unexpected military coup. ✖

51(01):21/21
DOI:10.1177/03064220221085914

'Humpty Dumpty has maybe had the last word ...'

The battlefront over freedom is still between the individual and the state, says **SIR TOM STOPPARD**, but identity politics has thrown up a phenomenon which is about language – and words can, and do, hurt

HOW QUAINT IT sounds now. *I disagree with what you say, but I will defend to the death your right to say it.* Could you have imagined a time when this shop-worn profession of faith in Enlightenment values would split the community? Try it like this - *I disagree with what you say, and I will defend to the death my right to silence you* – and ask yourself which is the heterodoxy now. (Whose death, by the way? Voltaire meant his own, but the anonymity conferred on the trolls of our age has made the perfunctory death threat the coinage of dispute; not to speak of the death threats which are far from perfunctory but, rather, the dangerous edge of a pathological egoism.)

How did this happen? When did it? Obviously, not overnight, and not before "the end of history" which was first a catchy book title and then a complacent catchphrase for the triumph of the west over the Soviet system. To put it like that sounds as if I'm suggesting a connection, but the connection is only with my own

> I don't want to criminalise every fool who says there were no gas ovens

perspective on the centrality of "free expression", and with a memory I have from, at a guess, forty-plus years ago. The occasion was a lunch, a public airing for the magazine and what it stood for, at a time when, as far as I was concerned, the permanent foreground was the suppression of free speech in Russia and the Soviet bloc.

I was a speaker, and I dusted off an old quotation from Cecil Rhodes – "You are an Englishman, and have consequently won first prize in the lottery of life." Rhodes's statue was in no danger then but his reputation had been knocked off its pedestal long before, and the approved attitude to such a sentiment was to mock Cecil Rhodes for it. But, I told the lunch, I could not bring myself to mock. If my life had not been diverted when I was eight, I would very likely be living in Czechoslovakia where I had friends persecuted for what they spoke and wrote.

As far as I could see, tolerance of dissenting opinion was the sign and *sine qua non* of a free society; indeed it was the freedom on which the structures of freedom rested.

Yet, it turns out, I couldn't see as far as I thought I could.

Back then, all the way to – it seems – the day before yesterday, I saw the battlefront as one between the individual and the state. It is still that, of course, all over the globe, but identity politics has thrown up a phenomenon,

ABOVE: The Czech-born playwright Sir Tom Stoppard, a long-time supporter of Index on Censorship, pictured in Prague in 2009

a battleground which is not political so much as psycho-social, an intolerance between individuals, and it's about language. Words speak louder than actions. Sticks and stones will still break your bones but the idea that words can't hurt you has been repealed. People are

being hurt by words, and consequently are picking up sticks and stones, not in the form of death threats (mostly) but (frequently) in the form of hounding the transgressor out of his or her livelihood.

From Alice in Wonderland to Nineteen Eighty-Four and until the last Trump, the appropriation of language is the declared bedrock of authoritarianism and there is no mystery about it. But personally I always had faith in the ultimate commensurability of language and

reality. When the German Democratic Republic put out that the Berlin Wall was to keep people out it made me laugh. Reality would take care of itself.

With words, I'm a hardliner. Language will evolve naturally, but diktat is not natural to it. But with language itself, I'm a libertarian. I don't want to criminalise every fool who says the moon landing was faked and there were no gas ovens. Reality will take care of them too. But no one, not even Lewis Carroll, saw identity

politics coming. Humpty Dumpty has maybe had the last word. *When I use a word, it means just what I choose it to mean – neither more nor less,* and that includes pronouns. Will reality take care of it now? I doubt I'll find out but perhaps my children will. ✖

Sir Tom Stoppard is a Czech-born British playwright and screenwriter

51(01):22/23|DOI:10.1177/03064220221085931

The article that tore Turkey apart

KAYA GENÇ looks back at an Index article which revealed a dark period in Turkey's recent history – and led to its author's imprisonment

THE YEAR 1995 was a testing one for Index and its new contributor Yaşar Kemal, Turkey's greatest living novelist at the time. In January, German weekly Der Spiegel had published The March of Lies, an article in which Kemal detailed the oppression Kurds suffered in Turkey during the 20th century. With the burning of villages and the summary execution of civilians, the anti-Kurdish assault intensified in the 1990s – something Kemal condemned in his essays.

Using Turkey's stringent anti-terrorism law, a prosecutor charged this towering figure of Turkish literature – known as Turkey's Faulkner – with propagating separatism. The court cleared Kemal on 2 December but, in the background, more serious trouble was brewing.

In its January 1995 issue, Index published Kemal's The Dark Cloud Over Turkey, another seminal essay →

RIGHT: Guards patrol the streets of a small town in Silvan, a town in South East Turkey in 1993

→ that made waves in the country, creating fury in the upper echelons of government, dividing intellectuals and leading to its author eventually being sentenced to 20 months in prison.

Overnight, the case turned Kemal into a pariah in Turkey and introduced Index to the country's dissidents.

Burhan Sönmez, PEN International's new president, followed it closely. "When Yaşar Kemal published his Index piece in 1995, I was a young lawyer," he told Index. "The 1990s were among the darkest periods in Turkish history – the pinnacle of the Kurdish civil war, where intellectuals were frequently murdered. Each day I'd go and receive dead bodies of lawyers, journalists and intellectuals from hospital morgues. I became a first-hand witness to each sentence Kemal has written in his Index piece."

Police assaults during this time left Sönmez with brain trauma and he went into exile in the UK, receiving long-term treatment with the help of London's Freedom from Torture Centre.

Around the same time, Ece Temelkuran, a celebrated Turkish columnist and author, started as a court reporter for the left-of-centre Milliyet newspaper.

"I was 23, interviewing mothers of imprisoned figures, writing a book about them," she recalled. "It was a charged era. On the one hand the government was killing Kurds and subjecting them to forced disappearances; on the other there was this core group of intellectuals who supported each other. In his Index piece, Kemal mentions hesitant voices about the Kurdish issue. There were also powerful voices coming from opinion leaders – an institution in those years."

Elif Shafak, Turkey's most widely-read female novelist, also retains vivid memories from 1995. "I was in college," she said. "It was a very turbulent, tense period with severe human rights violations across the country. Yaşar Kemal was an author

I widely read and deeply respected. I admired him not only as a remarkable novelist but also as a public intellectual and a defender of human rights and minority rights. Almost every week he would be attacked in Turkey's mainstream newspapers and magazines by ultra-nationalists or Islamist and authoritarian columnists, and yet he kept writing – he kept speaking up for his values."

His case, said Temelkuran, the columnist, "wasn't about freedom of expression. It was about the freedom of expressing views on the Kurdish issue".

Since the 1960s, intellectuals in Turkey have been divided, she added, "between those brave enough to discuss the Kurdish issue and others who ignore it. Kemal could have talked about the freedom of expression in a universal framing. There is a big difference between saying these things about Kurds and expressing them without referencing Kurds".

This indifference was the source of Kemal's anger, and the Turkish media's refusal to acknowledge the Kurdish issue became the crux of his Index piece. During the 1990s, Kemal argued in The Dark Cloud Over Turkey, the government tried to "drain the pool to catch the fish" by declaring all-out war on Kurds as the world watched.

"Only the people of Turkey have been kept in ignorance. Newspapers have been forbidden to write about the drainage," he complained. Why were they silent?

 These concealers of truths were "ostriches" who refused to remove their heads from the sand

"Maybe there was no need for censorship. Maybe our press, with its sense of patriotism and strong nationalist sentiment, chose not to write about it, assuming the world would neither hear nor see what was happening."

These concealers of truths, Kemal wrote, were "ostriches" who refused to remove their heads from the sand while the "country is awash with blood".

In the wake of the Index case, readers came to Kemal's rescue. They passionately defended him in book clubs and private conversations. But nationalists, from the left and the right, denounced him, using the conviction as proof of his "heinous character".

Even secularists found Kemal's characterisation of Turkey as a "racist, oppressive regime" that has been "rotted from the root" hard to swallow.

In the pages of Cumhuriyet, the leftist newspaper where Kemal published legendary long-form reports in the 1960s, he was scolded for crossing a line.

In fact, he passionately believed in the republican project and wanted it to be true to its Anatolian roots.

"Anatolia has always been a mosaic of flowers, filling the world with flowers and light," he wrote. "I want it to be the same today. If the people of a country choose to live like human beings, [to] choose happiness and beauty, their way lies first through universal human rights and then through universal, unlimited freedom of thought."

The Index case taught a lesson to young writers following Kemal's case.

"If you pay too much attention to human rights," Sönmez said, "you become a target in Turkey." Temelkuran reached a different conclusion. "Yes, Kemal was sentenced in the Index case, but defining himself solely through this sentence and presenting himself as a victim would make him a bad writer," she said. "Kemal's literary identity was superior to his political identity."

In 2012, 17 years after his conviction, Kemal contacted Sönmez, who had published his second novel, Sins and Innocents, in Turkish.

"Some newspapers dubbed me 'the new Yaşar Kemal'. He must have seen those and bought my book before sending along a note to give him a call," he said.

Over the phone, Kemal bellowed: "*Kuro!* Aren't you a Kurd? Why don't you speak Kurdish with me?" (Kuro is "boy" in Kurdish.)

"I liked that he talked to me as if I was a boy, and I switched from Turkish to Kurdish, which delighted him."

Kemal gave a hearty laugh and asked Sönmez to visit him the next day. In Kemal's house, overlooking the Bosphorus, they spent the day talking about books.

Kemal's masterpiece, Memed, My Hawk (1995), tells of injustices inflicted on a Kurdish boy and the shattering silence surrounding it. Memed joins a band of brigands to exact revenge, and Kemal turns his adventures into a modern epic.

Sönmez said his interest in the art of novels began with that book. "I must have been 13 or 14 when I first read it."

During the meeting, the master told his disciple: "Here is what we have in common. We both process the imaginary world of an invisible language, Kurdish, inside a visible language, Turkish." Kemal told him they were bilingual, "because our language was banned and we had placed it somewhere different in our subconscious".

"When we used Turkish, we developed different imagery," said Sönmez. "Kemal said he noticed this in my Sins and Innocents. To hear this from a master as a young writer, of course, filled me with pride."

Temelkuran had a chance to meet Kemal in 2005 when the novelist's partner brought her to his apartment. "I learned that he was reading my articles. He was a madly funny man," Temelkuran said.

If you pay too much attention to human rights you become a target in Turkey

When she wrote the first chapter of her first novel, Kemal asked to send it along. After reading it, he said: "This doesn't work." When Temelkuran went to Beirut, rewrote the first chapter and sent it back, he said: "This works."

Shafak also had a chance to visit the master. "Years after reading his work as a student, I had the privilege of visiting him and his wife several times in his house in Istanbul," she said. 'I listened to him talk so candidly about what it feels like to be a novelist and a defender of human rights in a country as troubled and troubling as our beloved motherland, Turkey."

Kemal died in 2015, aged 91.

Nowadays, Shafak fears, Turkey's political situation has returned to the suffocating era of the 1990s.

"I wish we could look back on the 1990s and say, 'At least we've made considerable progress since then.' But I am afraid there is no progress to speak of. Turkey has been sliding backward into ultra-nationalism, Islamism, populist authoritarianism.

"Anything and everything you write might easily offend the authorities – from politics to history, from memory to gender and sexuality. Words are so heavy. It isn't easy to be a novelist in Turkey. Anyone who speaks up and stands against the clampdown on civil society and the demise of democracy is, today just like yesterday, immediately labelled as 'traitor'."

I was in secondary school when Index published Kemal's essay. Reactions of people around me crystallised their characters: the reporter

who took a French course with me in Istanbul's French Institute telling fellow students Kemal was a sellout, "a tool of the Western imperialism"; the nationalist brother of a school friend banging on about "heinous intellectuals", unaware of his bigotry and ignorance. Instinctively, I took Kemal's side.

Now, I see that moment of silent solidarity as my entry into the struggle against censorship in Turkey.

Later, I learned about the support network formed by the publisher Erdal Öz, the novelist Adalet Ağaoğlu and hundreds of other intellectuals who rushed to courts to defend Kemal. Together, they've formed a new form of friendship, previously unimaginable, that remains alive today.

Shafak says she saw why Index mattered while watching Kemal's plight in her student years. "I have enormous respect for Index and its fight for freedom of expression," she said. "The role of Index was always vital throughout the decades but, to be honest, it has become all the more urgent and needed today. We see so many attacks against pluralism, democracy, diversity and freedom of speech everywhere, often accentuated by social media platforms.

"In country after country, journalists, writers, poets, cartoonists, editors and publishers are being targeted. At a moment like this, global solidarity is crucial. We need to connect beyond borders."

Shafak has written for Index and also judged its awards, and said it had always been "an incredibly inspiring journey", adding: "I see Index as a sanctuary. As writers and readers, we need Index on Censorship just like we need oxygen to breathe." ✖

Kaya Genç is an author and contributing editor (Turkey) for Index. He is based in Istanbul

51(01):24/27|DOI:10.1177/03064220221084507

Of course it's not appropriate – it's satire

Pieter-Dirk Uys, one of South Africa's foremost satirists, tells **NATASHA JOSEPH** about making up swear words during apartheid and the threats facing comedy today

THE SECOND PAGE of Pieter-Dirk Uys's newest book, One Man Shows: The Black and White Years (published in 2021), is topped with a small grey box of text.

Under three words in bold – "Disclaimer and Warning" – it reads: "The scripts in this collection, from 1981 to 1994, have not been altered to reflect today's values and current sensibilities. They are an authentic record of what was performed at the time. The words are specific here to their social context. Deeply offensive terms were used ironically and satirically to expose racism, sexism and hypocrisy and to reflect the prejudices of society at the time. Offensive depictions and harmful terms have therefore been purposefully retained for historical accuracy. To alter the words and scripts would not only give an untrue and false account of the performances but would render the satire and political import of these scripts incomprehensible."

After a long career as an author, actor and activist, it's clear that Uys has as little interest in being censored, or censoring himself, as he did during the long, cruel and strange years of apartheid.

He was born in 1945, three years before the racist system became formal government policy. By the 1970s and 1980s, he was often at loggerheads with the country's notorious Publications Control Board (later the Directorate of Publications). Uys created theatre, and the board scoured it for evidence of, among other things, compatibility with "certain standards of indecency and obscenity". Inevitably, it found Uys's work decidedly lacking in decency.

Index visited Uys at Evita se Perron in the small Western Cape town of Darling, about 85km outside Cape Town. The venue was once Darling's railway station; today, it is a tearoom, restaurant, book shop, museum and theatre – its name taken from Uys's best-known character, Evita Bezuidenhout.

Several boards in the museum display some of the letters Uys received from the censors in relation to plays such as Selle Ou Storie (Same Old Story – many of his plays were written and staged in both English and Afrikaans) and Karnaval (Carnival). One undated letter warns that Karnaval cannot be staged for audiences aged between two and 18 and that two words – both racial slurs, one used to describe black South Africans and the other a pejorative for people of mixed race – must be excised.

It adds that those changes may not be enough to save the play from punitive action when staged: "The committee sounds the warning that the director of the proposed public entertainment may illuminate certain parts of the text with offensive and obscene gestures."

Some creators may have been deterred, but Uys still describes the Publications Control Board as "the great love of my life, a love that made

ABOVE: The satirist Pieter-Dirk Uys

me world-famous in Cape Town". Censorship galled him, of course. It also, he says today, pushed him to think more creatively – to invent words that sounded rude but didn't exist in any language and so escaped the censors' red pens. And it taught him a crucial lesson: make your enemies look ridiculous.

Which is not to say he wasn't frightened, at first.

"The reality about censorship ... I had to run for my life," he told Index over two South African delicacies, rooibos tea and koeksisters. "People kicked me out of their houses. They threw tins of cat food at me – I learned

CREDIT: Stefan Hurter

to catch the tins and feed my cats."

His first communication from the censors arrived while Selle Ou Storie was in rehearsals in Johannesburg in 1974 or 1975. A "guy with a suit on, with two policemen guarding him, made me sign for a brown envelope".

"None of us smiled. None of us laughed."

He was horrified – not for himself, but for the cast. "It was a play with characters, people … I had to tell them that we couldn't perform," he said. "Immediately they saw themselves as criminals. I didn't mind if it was for me, I can handle that. But when you've got people with you declared as criminals in the country, that's pretty grim."

Then something remarkable

happened: "Eventually, we couldn't help laughing – it took [only] a few weeks, thank God."

When Karnaval was later banned, Uys and the cast perused the board's letter to see how many swear words had been misspelled. "We photocopied those pages and hung them up in the men's toilet of the Space Theatre [in Cape Town]."

It was a cheeky gesture, and it made the censors look absurd. That's what Uys wanted. The alternatives, fear and anger, weren't for him.

"To be frightened means they have won. To be angry means they have definitely won, because then they know your passion and how you can actually be silenced. And it doesn't travel. Anger doesn't travel. People shouting about it doesn't travel, especially not on stage. Protest theatre was very important for the struggle [against apartheid], but terribly bad for the theatre.

"I'm not talking about The Island or Sizwe Banzi is Dead [both by Athol Fugard, John Kani and Winston   →

 It taught him a crucial lesson: make your enemies look ridiculous

"To be frightened means they have won. To be angry means they have definitely won"

→ Ntshona] – those were great theatre plays. But [most] protest theatre just became predictable, and it played to empty houses. The stage, the theatre, is no place for protest. The theatre is there to make you find your protest.

"I want to offend everybody, because that means I've rattled their cage. I give them an alternative to their politics, and they think, 'He can't say that. Can he say that? Why can he say that? Gosh, we never thought we'd laugh at the things we don't want to think about.'"

Absurdity and anarchy

One person who certainly doesn't approve of Uys's approach to his craft is his alter ego, Evita.

"Evita has no sense of humour. She'll never offend. She's a diplomat."

She really was, once upon a time. Part of Bezuidenhout's elaborate back story involves 10 years spent as South African ambassador to the independent – and fake – "homeland", the Republic of Bapetikosweti. Her signature bouffant was recently tamed into a sleek short style in honour of her 85th birthday and necessitated by South Africa's Covid-linked ban on visits to the hairdresser. But she remains as demure and studiously inoffensive as she was when she first appeared as a character in Uys's one-man show, Adapt or Dye, in 1981.

She was born of two things, in Uys's telling: "Absurdity and anarchy."

He said: "I've had to find words [over the years] to explain my actions. I didn't have any words to even explain why I was doing things, I just did them instinctively. I had to produce anarchy – including sexual anarchy – because I was doing a middle-aged Afrikaans lady, who was definitely a mouthpiece for saying things that I could not, would not – or that you did not want me to – say."

Evita gave Uys a direct line to senior apartheid officials. She once wrote to the then minister of police imploring him to "lock up Pieter-Dirk Uys because he's a communist, a terrorist and he wears women's clothing". The politician replied, addressing his correspondent as "Dear Mrs Bezuidenhout" saying: "We'd love to lock him up, but the jails are full of all the others."

Another lesson for Uys: "He had a sense of humour." And a reminder: "Don't underestimate the enemy."

"They are charismatic," he said. "They have a sense of humour. The man who has to ban the play is not the man who makes the decision to ban the play."

"The censor has become the citizen"

The end of formal apartheid in 1994 didn't mean Uys – or Evita – ran out of material. Evita interviewed a number of recently unbanned politicians from the now governing African National Congress (ANC) for a TV show called Evita's Funigalore.

"When one thinks [that] 28 years ago [these politicians] came out of the darkness of the horsemen of the apocalypse, we did these interviews and they just dazzled with their optimism and their love for the country and their sense of humour – my God! That's gone. Cyril [Ramaphosa, the current president of both the country and the ANC, who was among Evita's 1994 interviewees] is in such a state of not knowing where to stand."

The Publications Control Board and the Directorate of Publications are long gone, so does that mean an end to censorship? Uys said: "The censor has become the citizen. In my day, the censor was one mind, two minds, maybe three – politicians, religious people as well, moral people. But it wasn't that everyone had an opinion, and the power to crucify."

In the months before Covid, he staged a show in Johannesburg and gave free tickets to university students who had written requesting them. He took aim at former president Jacob Zuma and the group walked out. He found them afterwards at the bar and asked about their departure. They replied: "You can't make fun of black people, you're white." He left them to settle the bar tab and sent a letter to the university asking that it pay for the tickets. It did.

One of the students he spoke to alone at the event said: "You can't go there. You can't go there."

He replied: "You're going to lose your freedom of speech." He mimed pulling a zipper across his mouth. "Your mouth is going to disappear."

But South African satire and comedy is in good hands. At an awards ceremony a few years ago, he met a number of "young black comedians who don't give a fuck" about what is or isn't appropriate. They still keep in touch.

"That's my optimism. I hope these young people or middle-aged people are not punished by their shadows." ✖

Natasha Joseph is a freelance journalist based in Cape Town

51(01):28/30|DOI:10.1177/03064220221084438

ABOVE: At an African National Congress rally in 1994, Evita Bezuidenhout in her apartheid national dress presents the future president of South Africa Nelson Mandela with some *koeksisters* (a South African sweet delicacy)

CREDIT: Benny Gool

The staged suicide that haunts Brazil

In October 1975 the high-profile journalist Vladimir Herzog was murdered in Brazil. His family are still waiting for an apology and for the treatment of journalists to change, writes **GUILHERME OSINSKI**

VLADIMIR HERZOG, BORN in Yugoslavia, arrived in Brazil with his parents on 24 December 1946. He established himself as a journalist and worked for TV Cultura where he became editor in chief. On 24 October 1975 he went to the DOI-CODI headquarters of the political police to be interrogated. There, he was tortured to death. The police made it look like suicide, with Herzog found hanged in his cell. It took decades for the cause of his death to be revised on his death certificate.

When Herzog, known to his friends and family as Vlado, was killed Brazil was in the grips of a bloody military dictatorship that had begun in March 1964 and would only end in 1985. Index wrote about it from the start of publication in 1972. In the first issue of the magazine, Christopher George wrote an article entitled Press Freedom in Brazil. He reflected on the government of Getúlio Vargas, between 1930 and 1945, when the media was kept under close supervision, and which he believed had left its mark on the Brazil of the 1970s. A law passed in 1967, the "law to regulate the liberty of expression of thought and information' he described as "extremely restrictive". He wrote: "The present law, apart from providing more than sufficient scope for restrictive interpretation, offers no protection at all to journalists in cases where they

seem genuinely to be on the right side of it. For critics of an army-dominated government that equates opposition with insubordination, not even its own law is protection against the jackboot."

Herzog's tragic and unjust fate altered Brazilian society, leading to a series of protests that helped end the dictatorship. Ivo Herzog, Vlado's eldest

son, was only nine years old when his father was killed. Now chairman of the board of the Vladimir Herzog Institute, an organisation created to celebrate his father's life and legacy, Herzog told Index he believes that justice in relation to Vlado's murder has not yet been achieved.

"We continue to fight for international justice. There was a decision by the Inter-American Court [of Human Rights] in 2018 and Brazil has not yet complied with the recommendations," he said. "The two main points that have not yet been accomplished are that the circumstances of my father's death and of others who have died in a similar way be investigated. And the second part that has not yet been carried out by the Brazilian state is a public apology with the presence of the armed forces to ask for forgiveness for what happened at that time." →

Herzog's tragic and unjust fate altered Brazilian society, leading to a series of protests that helped end the dictatorship

RIGHT: Vladimir Herzog at his desk at TV Cultura, October 1975

ABOVE: Vladimir Herzog pictured in April 1960 in front of the Alvorada Palace, the official residence of Brazilian presidents

→ For Herzog, the Brazil of today has not changed in relation to the one he knew in the military regime. He remembers neighbouring Argentina, which also faced a dictatorship between 1966 and 1973.

"There was a rupture there, crimes were investigated, and those responsible were judged and arrested. There are dozens of monuments. Brazil did not have this rupture and perpetuates a culture of violence with origins dating back to the colonial period."

Many of the events that happened during the dictatorship are still frequent in the country today, especially when it comes to journalistic freedom.

"Press freedom in Brazil has always been an unresolved issue," said Herzog. He added that the country is so disparate that there is more than one Brazil.

"I am here in São Paulo, in theory a city as cosmopolitan as London. But when you go to the countryside of the North, Northeast, it's really lawless land. So you have journalists who try to denounce issues of land grabbing, mining, and they are threatened and often murdered."

Index has reported on the dangers that those covering deforestation, for example, have experienced over the past few years. Herzog himself recalls the murder of journalist Tim Lopes in 2002, who was tortured and whose charred body was found in a Rio de Janeiro favela while he was reporting on child abuse and drug trafficking.

Stories of torture and pain towards journalists feel like a never-ending cycle and are present in the minds of many Brazilians. One of them is Amelinha Teles, who worked in the underground press during the dictatorship.

"I was a press activist in Rio de Janeiro and São Paulo. We did everything from cleaning the photolith [equipment used for photos] to doing a [page] layout," she told Index. She also regularly tuned into the radio. "I listened to radio from Moscow, the BBC from London," she added, remembering just how difficult it was to hear what was said as the military would interfere with radio transmissions.

Teles, who was arrested and tortured in 1972, never forgot the anguish she felt day-to-day while carrying out routine tasks.

"It was a daily strain. News of deaths, arrests, heated ideological and political debates. You had to work in a clandestine office with your fellow press mates."

Despite the risks, Amelinha still bought the printing materials herself.

"I couldn't buy everything in one place. [I'd use] false documentation, false address. I couldn't give any clues that I was from the press. I had to lie and it was very difficult, but it was the only way to survive," she said.

She echoes many of the things Herzog told Index, saying that Brazilian journalists today continue to face censorship and lack of freedom, despite very different political and historical contexts.

You have journalists who try to denounce issues of land grabbing, mining, and they are threatened and often murdered

"Journalists are threatened, attacked. There is a lot of fake news, distortions. To practise journalism today you have to have a lot of courage. President Jair Bolsonaro himself threatens and offends female journalists in a humiliating and cruel way."

José Ferreira Lopes, popularly known as Dr Zequinha in the city of Curitiba, adds that Brazil's president doesn't need to arrest or kill journalists to intimidate them.

"He undermines their work and is aggressive with them, protecting only those journalists who defend him," the politician told Index. Ferreira Lopes was also arrested and tortured during the dictatorship and had to live in hiding.

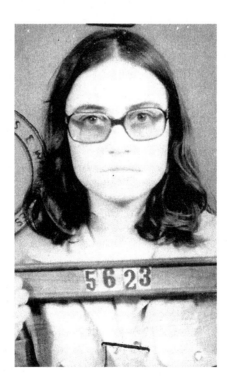

ABOVE: Amelinha Teles at the police station when she was arrested in São Paulo, February 1973

He still vividly recalls his days in prison.

"I was put in a closed cubicle where intense sounds were alternated with absolute silence. So you ran out of memory." Ferreira Lopes likened it to an MRI scan and said that when he recently had an MRI he automatically remembered those days in prison.

How can Brazil leave this past behind and improve its treatment of the press? For Vladimir Herzog's son Ivo, the Institute named after his father is instrumental. It currently works on three fronts. One of them is the Vlado Proteção coalition, whose function is to give visibility to crimes against journalists and provide legal advice and protection. In addition, the institute has run the Vladimir Herzog award since 1979 and the Young Journalist award since 2009, to fulfill the goal of strengthening journalists who cover human rights issues.

"The threat of murder is as serious as the murder itself, because the threatened journalist ends up not doing the story. He censors himself," said Herzog.

Teles believes it is important for Brazil to use the press to remember its history and to help alleviate the pain of the past. She said she made a proposal to the National Truth Commission in 2013 (which investigates human rights violations that happened between 1946 and 1988) for newspapers to commemorate Vlado on the anniversary of his death every year.

"His case is known, but there are others that no one talks about," she added. ✖

Guilherme Osinski is the editorial assistant at Index and the 2021/2022 Tim Hetherington fellow

51(01):31/33|DOI:10.1177/03064220221084567

Greece haunted by spectre of the past

Almost 50 years after the fall of the colonels, journalists are being forced to be careful about what they say. TONY RIGOPOULOS reports

PRESS FREEDOM IS in peril again in Greece, the cradle of democracy, nearly half a century after the repressive days of the colonels' dictatorship came to an end.

Since coming to power in 2019, the liberal-conservative New Democracy administration, under Prime Minister Kyriakos Mitsotakis, has moved gradually to silence its critics – setting off alarm bells among press watchdogs across Europe.

The public broadcaster ERT and the state news agency ANA have been put under the prime minister's supervision and, last year, the state passed a law criminalising the dissemination of false information that could "undermine public confidence in the national economy, the country's defence capacity or public health".

The daily paper Efimerida ton Syntakton (EfSyn) revealed last year that an independent journalist

covering the refugee crisis had been put under surveillance by the National Information Service.

The murder of veteran TV crime reporter Giorgos Karaivaz, close to his home, shocked journalists across the country last April. The case remains unsolved.

TV stations, newspapers and several websites belong to a handful of entrepreneurs with interests linked to the ruling party – thus limiting press freedom and reducing pluralism. One of them, Evangelos Marinakis, a shipowner who also owns football clubs Olympiakos in Greece and Nottingham Forest in the UK, has evolved into a media tycoon who controls a major TV station, newspapers, websites and the country's only press distribution agency.

Since ND took power, reporters and photographers have been subjected to bullying and harassment. In November 2020, while covering a demonstration to commemorate the student uprising in 1973, I was detained by police, manhandled and verbally abused.

According to a Friedrich Naumann Foundation for Freedom report, in 2007 Greece ranked 30th among 180 countries but plummeted to 70th place in only three years and fell to 99th in 2014. Under the left-wing Syriza government (2015-19), the ranking remained low, but the country slowly climbed to 65th place in 2019, only to roll back to number 70 in 2021.

Since the fall of the military dictatorship in 1974, Greece has gone through a painful process of

> ## A reporter covering the refugee crisis was put under surveillance by the National Information Service

ABOVE: Publisher Kostas Vaxevanis has been targeted by the Greek government for his investigative journalism. And his newspaper is facing a blizzard of lawsuits from the state

CREDIT: Nikolas Georgiou/ZUMA Wire/Alamy

democratisation. The 1990s were marked by the creation of private TV and radio broadcasters mimicking European and US channels. TV stations were relatively pluralistic, despite being owned by entrepreneurs with interests often linked to the ruling political parties

Journalist labelled 'gangster' by PM

Documento, one of the leading investigative newspapers in Greece, has come under sustained attack from the New Democracy government

KOSTAS VAXEVANIS, 55, its publisher – who was given a freedom of expression award by Index in 2013 for revealing the "Lagarde list" of wealthy Greeks with undeclared accounts in Switzerland – has been publicly denounced by the prime minister, Kyriakos Mitsotakis, as "a gangster" and a "member of the underworld".

Vaxevanis told Index that the attack came after his newspaper's revelations about offshore companies belonging to the PM's family, irregularities in his tax return documents and the participation of his close friend and adviser Nikos Georgiadis in a paedophile ring in Moldova.

In January this year, Vaxevanis, who had revealed crucial aspects of the Novartis pharmaceutical scandal in Greece, was accused by a special court of "collusion to abuse power" and being a "member of a criminal organisation".

At the same time, Documento and its journalists are facing more than 80 lawsuits, most filed by powerful state officials.

"The prime minister, representing a Balkan Trumpism and eliminating my presumption of innocence, called me and other journalists 'members of the underworld' and 'gangsters'," he said, "revealing who is behind my persecution and dictating to the justice system that it must eliminate me."

Since Mitsotakis came to power, Documento has suffered big cuts in private advertising and was deliberately excluded from a state advertising campaign about Covid-19 measures.

After the murder of TV crime reporter Giorgos Karaivaz in April last year, the paper reported that a contract had been taken out on Vaxevanis in the Greek underworld. As a result, three suspects were arrested and Vaxevanis given police protection.

– New Democracy and PASOK. Press freedom was considered a cornerstone of the Greek republic, but things started to shift rapidly after the debt crisis broke out in 2010. Since then, Greece has been struggling with "ghosts from the past".

So if the question is whether or not media freedom in Greece has improved since the dictatorship, the answer is obviously "yes". But a modern liberal country setting the bar of media freedom just above the level of a violent military dictatorship that ended 48 years ago, and only slightly surpassing it, cannot be considered a democratic conquest. It sounds more like an embarrassing defeat. ✖

Tony Rigopoulos is a journalist based in Athens. He is an editor at the investigative newspaper Documento and editor-in-chief of koutipandoras.gr

51(01):34/35|DOI:10.1177/03064220221084570

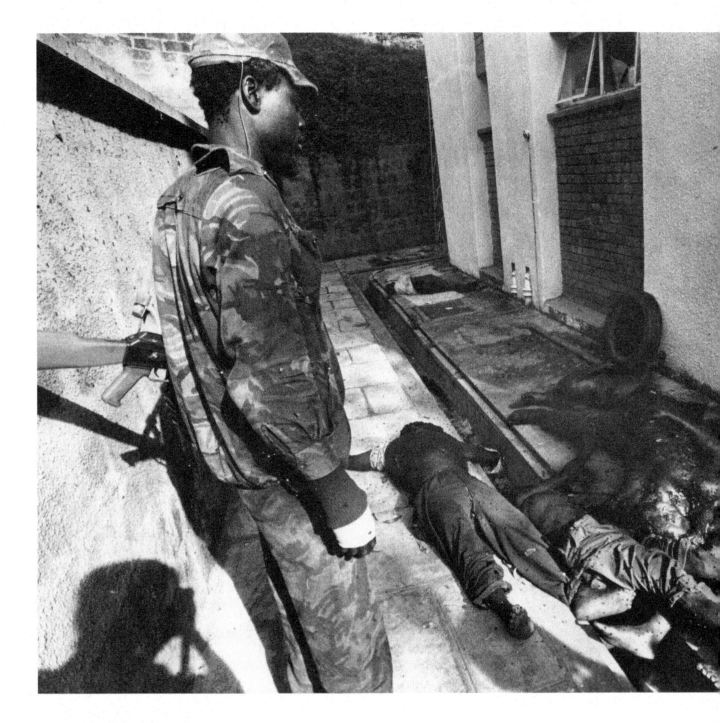

CREDIT: Rolls Press/Getty

Ugandans still wait for life to turn sweet

More than 40 years after the overthrow of Idi Amin, **ISSA SIKITI DA SILVA** in Kampala hears the frustrations of people today about Museveni's cruel regime

THE QUEEN'S CLOCK Tower in the Ugandan capital Kampala might have been demolished, but the place where the monument stood bears testimony to Idi Amin's eight-year reign of terror. This is the spot where, in September 1977, Amin's firing squad executed 12 senior government officials suspected of plotting to overthrow him.

LEFT: The bodies of prisoners massacred by Idi Amin's secret police at the State Bureau HQ during the fall of Kampala in April 1979

very young, due to celebrate 15 years of independence. I was disappointed by our political leaders and felt like leaving the country. But I told myself that maybe one day the human rights situation will improve and our children and grandchildren will enjoy total freedom and stop living in fear in their own land."

Like Simon, Vincent, a vendor in Usafi Market, grew up hoping that Amin's successors would ensure that Uganda would never see such terror and that life would become sweet. But he, and the rest of the country's 45 million people, were to be disappointed.

"It became worse and it is getting worse," Vincent told Index. "Honestly, what the people want is not to be offered stashes of cash and bags of maize but to be free to speak out when things are not going well and to cheer and vote for politicians of their choice.

"Why detain, torture or shoot someone just because that person didn't vote for or support the ruling party? We will never have good leaders in this country. All of them look to me like a bunch of killers and profiteers, period."

Vincent said he was too young to have lived under Amin but one of the dictator's henchmen was a family friend and neighbour who used to confide in his father.

"Our father told us many horror stories. He was very close to the guy. I think that he used to tell him each and every brutal crime they were committing, many of which went unreported."

Officially, 300,000 were killed under Amin, whose rule ran from 1971 until 1979, but Vincent believes the real figure was much higher.

In October this year, it will be 60 years since Uganda gained independence from the UK, but have its people ever experienced any kind of freedom and democracy?

"What will we reap after six decades of so-called victory over colonialism?" asked a 58-year-old construction worker along the bustling Kampala Road. "If you want my honest opinion, I will tell you that there is no difference between what the previous leaders did and what the current ones are doing," he said, declining to give his identity, or even mention the name of the current president – Yoweri Museveni – afraid that government spies might be listening.

"Those ones [Amin's cronies] tortured and executed their countrymen," he said. "They arbitrarily arrested people and sentenced them on fake charges and never allowed criticism of their policies. Besides, they stole public money. The current ones are doing the same thing, even worse, and going as far as banning the NGOs for baseless reasons."

In August 2021, a government-controlled body suspended the activities of 54 NGOs for allegedly operating illegally and not filing tax returns.

A human rights report by the US State Department last year said that significant human rights issues in Uganda – ruled by Museveni, now 77, since 1986 – included extrajudicial killings by government forces, forced disappearances, torture, life-threatening prison conditions, unjustified arrests and prosecutions of journalists, censorship, site blocking and criminal libel laws.

Other restrictions are placed on freedom of expression and assembly, as highlighted by Human Rights Watch in its 2021 World Report.   →

Nearly 45 years later, Simon, 74, a retired teacher, vividly remembers it.

"I don't like talking about it because it was shocking and horrific. I kept praying that Amin would one day be captured and put on trial for all the crimes he was committing," he told Index.

"I will never forget that day, never. I was only 29 and the country was still

Abuse of the novelist, and many similar cases, give Uganda a deplorable human rights image

→ At the end of last year, the satirical writer and novelist Kakwenza Rukirabashaija was arrested, held incommunicado and tortured for allegedly using his social media pages to insult Museveni's son, General Muhoozi Kainerugaba. Rukirabashaija, who was named International Writer of Courage by PEN last year, is best known for his novel The Greedy Barbarian, which tackles corruption in a fictional country. He was arrested twice in 2020 and detailed that treatment in his latest work, Banana Republic: Where Writing Is Treasonous.

"In Africa, when you write fiction, especially political fiction, such as the political allegory Animal Farm by George Orwell, the leaders will always think that one is writing about them," Rukirabashaija wrote.

His abuse, and many similar incidents have given the country a deplorable human rights image, which the Museveni regime has done nothing to counter.

Sylvia Namubiru Mukasa, CEO of Legal Aid Providers Network, told Index that human rights and freedom of expression were deteriorating. "Increasingly we are having a violation of freedom of expression for all Uganda and this is happening with impunity."

For Alice, a retired civil servant, women's rights are today's big issue. "Amin ill-treated women and considered them like tissues, something you use here and throw away right on the spot. Forty-three years after he was overthrown, the situation of women in Uganda remains static," she said.

"Women's rights and gender equality remain sensitive and contentious issues. I am not afraid to say that no significant progress has been made since 1979 apart from enacting laws that have proved difficult to implement."

The Museveni regime is also trampling over environmental rights, according to Ritah, an unemployed graduate. "I am too young to have lived under the Amin regime but my

ABOVE: President Yoweri Museveni, 77, has ruled Uganda with an iron fist since 1986. His regime has been accused of multiple human rights abuses

father told me that his government never allowed a forest to be savaged to make way for the so-called economic development," she said.

"What we are seeing today is complete madness and a serious lack of respect for the environment. What kind of government tortures both humans

What kind of government tortures both humans and nature?

and nature? As things stand, I am afraid that we will have nothing left as forests and ecosystems by 2050."

She said the country needed a change of leadership as soon as possible to start cleaning up the mess of 60 years of political, social and economic chaos. "As a country, we are hanging by a thread. Look at what this regime has done to our young people: drug and alcohol abuse, gambling, violent crime due to high levels of unemployment."

Another unemployed youth, a supporter of NUP, the party of opposition leader Bobi Wine, alleged that jobs were being given along political and ethnic lines. "Supporters of the ruling party are being favoured and given well-paying jobs while others, like us, are being overlooked because we are not one of them," he said.

Uganda's youth unemployment rates are believed to be among the highest in Africa, at about 70%, and about 400,000 young people join the job market each year to compete for about 9,000 jobs.

The youth, who now works as a boda-boda (motorbike taxi) driver, added: "[It's the] same thing if you are not from the president's ethnic group. You get nothing if you don't belong to that part of the country.

"You begin to wonder what this guy [Museveni] and his comrades spent so many years in the bush fighting for? Human rights violations? Tribalism? Nepotism? Corruption? All these scourges are featuring in his regime.

"We are doomed. His son is due to take over after he dies or becomes incapacitated. Life will go on as if nothing has happened. His backers – the USA, the UK and China – must see the people's tears and tell him to retire peacefully before it's too late." ✖

Issa Sikiti da Silva is an Index on Censorship contributing editor based in west Africa

51(01):36/38|DOI:10.1177/03064220221084508

How much distance from Mao?

China historian **RANA MITTER** looks back to 1972 when Mao was in power and asks just how far free speech has come in the 50 years since

ABOVE: Protesters fill the streets of Hong Kong to fight for their democratic rights, October 2019

F IFTY YEARS AGO, US president Richard Nixon visited China, opening a door that had been closed since the revolution of 1949. He went at the height of the Cultural Revolution, when China's leader, Chairman Mao Zedong, had declared war on China's "old customs" and urged teenage Red Guards to attack and humiliate the country's intellectuals and teachers. At this time, China's freedom of expression was almost non-existent, with screaming propaganda posters the most prominent expression of political debate.

The country that Nixon visited has changed immeasurably in the half-century since then, yet one thing remains constant, although its forms have changed. Now as then, China has one of the most comprehensive systems of censorship anywhere in the world. Today, it is the only one of the world's top 10 economies that has a pre-emptive system of censorship that extends from the printed word to the internet.

In 1972, China's economy and society were closed, as was much of its publishing industry. Although Nixon had visited in February of that year,

there was no sense that the Cultural Revolution was coming to a close. Instead, the radical faction of the leadership, whose senior members later became known as the Gang of Four, pushed hard for a new campaign that targeted Confucius, the philosopher whose teachings had underpinned Chinese society for much of the past 2,000 years. The attack on Confucius

was also meant to be a dig at the reform-minded premier, Zhou Enlai, and it showed that the scholarly and philosophical traditions of China, much of them tied up with the use of writing, were still a target for the revolution.   →

战无不胜的毛泽东思想万岁！

LONG LIVE THE INVINCIBLE
THOUGHT OF MAO TSE-TUNG!

ABOVE: A billboard outside a hotel in Shanghai
during the Cultural Revolution, which lasted from
1966 until Mao's death in 1976

→ The Cultural Revolution ended
shortly after Mao's death in 1976, and
the Gang of Four were arrested. Mao's
successor, Hua Guofeng, loosened
censorship as a way of showing that
a new era had arrived. In 1977, Lu
Xinhua published a short story titled
Shanghen (The Scar), the first of a series
of works by various authors that told of
the traumas of the Cultural Revolution.
The stories' impact was immense, and
a whole genre known as Scar Literature
emerged in response. It ushered in an era
of immensely widened boundaries.

Of course, China's apparatus of
repression remained very real, as the
dissident Wei Jingsheng found when he
was sentenced to prison for his advocacy
of a fully democratic system in China.
But the opening of thought in China in
the 1980s was also real. One prominent
example of it was the television series
River Elegy, broadcast to tens of
millions of viewers on national television
in summer 1988, which made a case
for China's modernisation, rejecting a
"peasant emperor" (a clear reference to
Mao) and the "yellow river" of Chinese
tradition in favour of the "blue ocean"
that led out towards the USA.

The liberal trend was abruptly cut
off after the massacre of protesters by
People's Liberation Army troops in the
centre of Beijing in June 1989. But in a

Of course,
China's apparatus
of repression
remained very real

way that seems remarkable in retrospect, there was a second, less extensive but very notable opening in the mid-1990s to late-2000s. China's leaders were still feeling vulnerable as the shadow of Tiananmen Square had isolated the country on the international stage; if future bids to enter the World Trade Organization and host the Olympics were to succeed, China would have to show a more open face to the world – and, for a while, it did. This was a time when US president Bill Clinton and Jiang Zemin, general-secretary of the Chinese Communist Party, debated democracy live on Chinese television, and when scholars could write about issues such as pluralism, democracy and constitutionalism.

Censorship was still evident, but there were ways round it. Sometimes, edgy books were published in provincial centres far from Beijing, such as the 1997 novel Tiannu (Wrath of Heaven), which lightly fictionalised corruption at the heart of the Beijing municipality. It was published not in Beijing but in Inner Mongolia, and although it was banned eventually, plenty of copies, including dodgy reprints, were to be found all over China.

Today, censorship is harsher and more effective. What changed? In one sense, there is much more space to manoeuvre in 2022 than could have been imagined in 1972. The all-encompassing control of Beijing over writing and publishing, and the almost total closure of China to the outside world, along with the lack of any true commercial publishing world, and the heavy restriction on education, meant that pathways around censorship were hard to find in the 1970s.

Now China has many paths for self-expression and far more frank speaking slips under the net than is sometimes realised. But it is undoubtedly more restrictive than, say, in 1992. One reason is the changing nature of China's leadership. Periods of loosening of censorship in the past often coincided

with the sense that the outside world still had knowledge that China had to draw on, possibly including even political reform. (In the late 1990s, learning from Singapore on governance and the USA on finance was a popular combination.) After the financial crisis of 2008, China's leaders cooled on the idea of learning from the West, or of allowing the free flow of information from there.

Although this trend did not begin with Xi Jinping, his accession to power in 2012 accelerated the trend; unlike his predecessors Jiang and Hu Jintao, Xi has shown no signs (at least in public) of wishing to balance factions or to allow small liberal traces in an authoritarian setting.

Another friend of the censor has been technology. Digitisation has made it much easier to distribute writing widely. It has also made it simpler, in many cases, to shut it down. State control over commercial social media (Weibo, Bilibili, Youku et al) provided the capacity to remove, for instance, all mentions of tennis star Peng Shuai from social media in late 2021 after she was reported to have accused a senior Chinese politician of having pressured her into a sexual relationship.

Censorship is not just about political scandals, of course. Entire sectors of publishing can be shut down overnight because they violate the CCP's ideas about appropriate social values: online fanfic is a frequent victim, as Megan Walsh shows in her excellent book, The Subplot, on Chinese reading habits in the 2020s.

Hong Kong's experience since the National Security Law was imposed in 2020 has shown that censorship can take different forms: "one country, two systems", to use the official term for the difference between the mainland and the territory. There is certainly more direct censorship: films in particular are to be subjected to new laws that ban "subversive" ideas about China – regulations that did not exist up to now. But far greater pressure comes from a

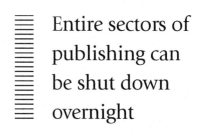

Entire sectors of publishing can be shut down overnight

broadly-defined law that bans violations of "national security" by writers, journalists, artists and even, it appears in one case currently going to trial, children's story writers.

Repeatedly, writers and artists have asked the authorities to define clearly what the new "red lines" are. The authorities respond with answers both bland and tautologous, that freedoms remain intact except where "national security" is violated, but without ever defining it. That, many observers would note, is the point. Mainland China, even at its freest, was always subject to authoritarian control. Hong Kong, until 2020, was used to only partially democratic politics but one of the freest media and publishing environments in the world. It remains to be seen how a population reacts to having its freedoms removed, as opposed to not being granted freedoms they never had.

In 2013, a symbolic moment happened when celebrated film director Feng Xiaogang, nicknamed "China's Spielberg", declared at a movie award ceremony that "censorship" was a torment. Except that viewers in China didn't hear him say the word, instead hearing a bleep – because the television feed was censored. In the years since then, Feng has repeatedly battled the censors and also topped the box office. For in today's China, in a way that Mao could never have foreseen in 1972, commerce and censorship coexist in an uneasy embrace. ✖

Rana Mitter is professor of history and politics of Modern China, University of Oxford

51(01):40/41|DOI:10.1177/03064220221084568

Looking back to when we looked forward

They say hindsight is 20/20, something that could be applied to the magazine. With 50 years of history it stands to reason that some articles where we've made bold declarations and predictions have dated while others feel eerily prescient. We've chosen two from the archive – one concerning the internet in China and the other on climate change – which show this dichotomy. And we've invited great thinkers to look at them today and share their own wisdom.

51(01):42/43|DOI:10.1177/03064220221084528

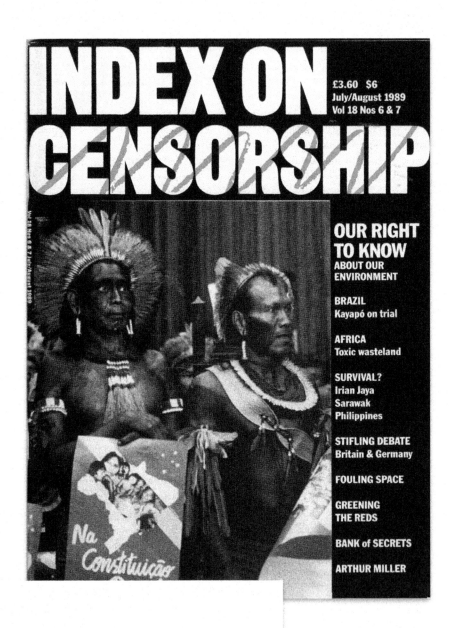

INDEX ON CENSORSHIP

£3.60 $6
July/August 1989
Vol 18 Nos 6 & 7

OUR RIGHT TO KNOW
ABOUT OUR ENVIRONMENT

BRAZIL
Kayapó on trial

AFRICA
Toxic wasteland

SURVIVAL?
Irian Jaya
Sarawak
Philippines

STIFLING DEBATE
Britain & Germany

FOULING SPACE

GREENING THE REDS

BANK of SECRETS

ARTHUR MILLER

Na Constituição

GOD'S GIFT TO CHINA

LIU XIAOBO

PRAISE THE LORD AND KEEP ON BLOGGING

Today, there are more than 100 million Internet users in China. The Chinese Communist government is ambivalent in its attitude towards the Internet, and is showing many signs of awkwardness. On one hand, their lame-footed reforms require high economic growth and the main benefit of the Internet is that it is a tool for making money. On the other hand, dictators are afraid of open information and free expression and, therefore, are afraid of the political effects of the Internet. In recent years, particularly, the Internet has played a major role in the awakening of ideas on rights and the defence of civil rights among the Chinese people. This has seriously worried the current government. In the interests of maintaining its ideological control over the people, it places great importance on controlling speech and blocking information on the Internet. It invested huge amounts of capital in the Golden Shield project [a highly sophisticated and all-embracing surveillance system built with the aid of western telecoms compa-

Our summer 1989 issue bore an image of two indigenous Kayapo people captioned "Our Right To Know About Our Environment". Decades before Al Gore's Inconvenient Truth we have been talking about how the climate crisis and censorship feed off each other. The multi-award winning novelist, essayist, poet and activist **MARGARET ATWOOD** responds

WE ARE ENTERING a new era of book banning and censorship – not in totalitarian and authoritarian dictatorships alone, as was once the case, but in the United States, erstwhile champion of Freedom of Expression and home of the First Amendment. One focus is the realm of public education:

books concerning race, gender fluidity, the Holocaust, and the history of the United States, as well as those long-term targets, evolutionary science and feminism, are in the crosshairs. But if climate science is not prominent on this list, it soon will be. One-time Florida Governor Rick Scott – now a Republican Senator – forbade state employees to use the terms "global warming" and "sustainability," presumably because it might be bad for business. It's hard to sell a piece of real estate that is predicted to be underwater soon.

The climate crisis will spur natural disasters – as it is already doing. Floods, fires, high winds, sea-level rises, crop failures, and the spread of destructive species will cause famines, homelessness, an increase in wealth inequality, and mass migrations, or an attempt at them.

These in turn will generate social unrest. Autocracies will have no trouble shutting down the bad news and exterminating or interning those causing them headaches. But how will democracies respond? Like Rick Scott – close your eyes, wipe out words, pretend it isn't happening, thus preparing the ground for future death and destruction? Regulate the news, in ways that are considered good – as in wartimes? Create ecotatorships, in an attempt to stem or reverse the catastrophic effects of climate change by severely regulating material spaces? Open the Free Expression doors and fall victim to foreign "content farms" and bot operations, run by those who wish to weaken or obliterate democracies? Hard choices! I'll pop back in via seances in a hundred years or so to see how it all worked out. ✖

Copyright © O.W. Toad 2022

Nobel Peace Prize laureate Liu Xiaobo, who died in 2017 having spents years in prison for his peaceful promotion of democracy, wrote an article in Index in 2006 called God's Gift to China. In it he said "the effect of the internet in improving the state of free expression in China cannot be underestimated". Charlie Smith of internet censorship watchdogs **GREAT FIRE** comments

IN CHINA, CENSORSHIP has existed for as long as one has had opinions and a free will to voice them. The internet only makes censorship more efficient in public and private spaces. Today, not only are netizens unable to access most foreign internet services, but self-censorship is widely practised on domestic platforms. Civilians have begun to shy away from talking about sensitive topics, because they have long known that even if they try to share them with others, they will be blocked

or even convicted. Fewer and fewer people have the courage to speak up and fewer and fewer people know the truth. This trend is not optimistic.

Xi Jinping's rise to power has accelerated China's re-entry into the ultra-left ideology of the Cultural Revolution period, with increasing online censorship and media control. Peng Shuai's #MeToo post was censored within 20 minutes. Wukan's citizens now live in fear of reprisals, when they are not living behind bars. The 709 crackdown and the Umbrella movement illustrate that the internet may not be God's present to China. Many great academics, writers, human rights defenders and lawyers, activists, artists and free thinkers have been jailed because of their activities online. Many of them were co-signatories of Charter 08, a manifesto calling for more rights.

Is it possible to see stars from the bottom of a well? Yes and no. Before the internet, Liu writes, "since the government was monitoring the

telephones of sensitive people, we had to ride our bicycles in all directions of Beijing". With the current version of the internet, the government has the ability to monitor virtually everybody's communications. But what is today's equivalent of riding around on a bicycle? With such vast resources of control available to the government, opposition may seem impossible. Perhaps we just don't know what the future oppositional tools will look like. Just like Liu embraced the opportunities of computers early on, we need to keep looking for new developments that enable political evolution.

In the end, it's all about people standing for their values, every day, for a long time, which brings real change. Ideas cannot be jailed, cannot be tortured and do not suffer. Only people can. And too many have. It's time for us to change the way we use the internet. Our ideas will be our present to China. And the internet will only be the wrapping paper. ✖

50 tech milestones of the past 50 years

When Index was first launched in 1972, a computer weighing 32kg helped take the last of the Apollo astronauts to the Moon. Within five years, computers as powerful as that were in people's homes. Today's smartphones would seem like magic to our Seventies forebears.

50 years is a long time in geopolitics but an even longer time in technology, which has played a pivotal role in the landscape of freedom of expression. **MARK FRARY** maps out the 50 technology milestones that we have passed since our launch.

ABOVE: Jobs and Gates: Dominating the world since the 1970s

1973

MOBILE PHONE
Motorola unveils a prototype of its DynaTAC handset. It is 23cm tall and weighs 5.5kg. Recharging takes 10 hours and then you can speak for only 35 minutes.

1973

INTERNET
Vint Cerf and Bob Kahn create the TCP/IP internet protocol to allow networks of computers to be interlinked.

1975

DIGITAL STILL CAMERA
Kodak's Steve Sassoon demonstrates the digital still camera, cutting out the lengthy development process of film.

1975

MICROSOFT
Programmer Paul Allen and high school friend Bill Gates spot the potential for writing software for the new wave of microcomputers that have begun to appear. The company goes on to dominate the software market and is one of the key players in democratising access to computing.

1976

APPLE
Steve Jobs, Steve Wozniak and Ronald Wayne set up what is now the world's largest company by market capitalisation. The company's first product, the hand-built Apple I microcomputer, sells fewer than 200 units.

1980

24-HOUR NEWS CHANNELS
The launch of CNN heralds the start of 24-hour news channels and changes the media landscape forever.

Professor Stephen Cushion, of the Cardiff School of Journalism, Media and Culture, tells Index: "No longer was TV news scheduled at set times of the day – news was continuous and in real time, changing the pace of the news cycle and shining a light on parts of the world often left in the dark. In doing so, news

technology writer Harley Hahn calling it "the largest global forum for uncontrolled freedom of expression".

1981

IBM PERSONAL COMPUTER
IBM recognises the need to enter the microcomputer market and launches the PC, which goes on to sell millions of units.

1986

LISTSERV BULK EMAIL
Listserv, the world's first automated email management system, launches. By 2022, more than 300 billion emails are sent every day, informing recipients about Nigerian get-rich-quick schemes as well as freedom of expression abuses.

1987

ANTI-VIRUS SOFTWARE
The first computer viruses had emerged in the 1970s. The first dedicated software to tackle them comes with the release of Ultimate Virus Killer for the Atari ST computer and John McAfee's VirusScan.

1989

GLOBAL POSITIONING SYSTEM
The world becomes a better-known place with the launch of a constellation of satellites, allowing people to know their location with unprecedented accuracy.

1989

WORLD WIDE WEB
At Cern, scientist Tim Berners-Lee unveils a proposal for the World Wide Web to avoid the "problems of loss of information about complex evolving systems". By 2022, his single web server has grown to more than a hundred million.

1990

ELECTRONIC FRONTIER FOUNDATION LAUNCHED
Following a series of US Secret Service raids over the distribution of documents that showed how the emergency 911 system worked, the Electronic Frontier Foundation is founded to work on civil liberties issues raised by new technologies.

1991

PRETTY GOOD PRIVACY
Increasing surveillance of electronic communications inspires US computer scientist Philip Zimmermann to create Pretty Good Privacy (PGP), a means of signing, encrypting and decrypting electronic messages and other data.

Zimmermann tells Index: "Before the emergence of telecommunications technology, people found it easy to have private conversations. But electronically mediated conversations had much greater risk of interception.

"Today, the need for protecting our right to a private conversation has never been stronger. If an autocracy inherits

BELOW: The first iteration of the World Wide Web, running on Berners-Lee's desktop

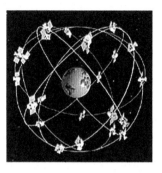

ABOVE: An early render of the GPS constellation

or builds a pervasive surveillance infrastructure, it becomes nearly impossible for political opposition to organise, as we can see in China. Secure communication is necessary for grassroots political opposition in those societies."

1994

BLOGGING
Student Justin Hall publishes brief posts diarising his views and sharing relevant links at **Links.net**. The term "weblog", later shortened to blog, is coined three years later.

1996

VIRTUAL PRIVATE NETWORKS (VPNS)
The virtual private network or VPN, a secure pipeline carrying ➔

channels have encouraged greater speed and immediacy in routine reporting, but this has come at the expense of journalistic balance and accuracy."

1980

USENET
The forerunner of modern social media networks, Usenet, launches. Messages are categorised within newsgroups in nine major hierarchical subject areas, including computers, humanities, social discussions and controversial topics.

The structure of Usenet – held on a distributed network of computers rather than a single, centrally administered server – means it has very few rules about what people can post, leading to

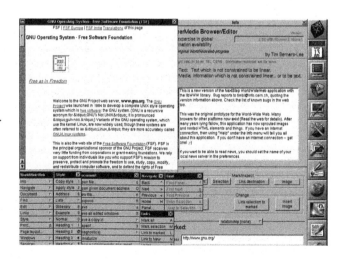

➜ data from the internet to and from a private network, is invented, enabling users to shield their identity, location and activity.

1996

GOOGLE
Stanford University PhD students Sergey Brin and Larry Page unveil an internet search tool called BackRub which uses the number of links between pages to rate their relevance and popularity. It is later renamed Google.

1997

WIFI
The US Institute of Electrical and Electronics Engineers outlines the 802.11 standard, freeing internet users from cables.

1998

THE GREAT FIREWALL
China implements the Golden Shield Project to control access to the internet, a part of which eventually comes to be known as the Great Firewall.

Charlie Smith, one of the founders of the Greatfire project, which monitors and challenges internet censorship in China, told Index: "The Great Firewall

BELOW: Facebook founder Mark Zuckerberg

ABOVE: An early beta version of the search engine Google

has proven to be effective largely because the control is not complete. There is no need to stop all discussion of sensitive topics, just to stop such discussions from spreading too widely. Compared [with] the days of fax machines, the internet continues to be a powerful tool for writing open letters and gathering signatures. The government doesn't need to stop such initiatives from taking place. What they do need to do, and are doing, is to control the extent to which such initiatives are disseminated."

1999

USB DRIVE
The idea of *samizdat*, the secretive copying and distribution of censored works, gets a boost with the invention of USB drives. These thumb-sized storage devices have been used ever since to share data and files, and have even been dropped by balloon into North Korea to share news

and entertainment from beyond its borders.

2001

BOTNET
The existence of the first botnet, a network of connected devices used to steal data, overwhelm websites and send spam email, is revealed.

2001

STELLAR WIND
In the aftermath of 9/11, US president George W Bush approves a plan by the National Security Agency to create a secret warrantless surveillance programme to monitor the email, telephone conversations, financial transactions and internet activity of US citizens.

2001

WIKIPEDIA
The community-written and edited free encyclopedia is launched. As of 8 February 2022, there are 6,450,327 articles in the English version of Wikipedia, containing more than 4 billion words.

2002

THE ONION ROUTER (TOR)
The concept of "onion routing" is launched, pushing internet traffic through multiple servers and encrypting it each step of the way.

2003

SKYPE
Skype brings internet telephony to a wide audience for the first time. After its launch, it is widely used

by political dissidents, including during the Arab Spring protests.

2004

FACEBOOK
The Facebook, as it is endearingly known at the beginning, is launched as an online version of the printed "face books" of Harvard college students. By 2022, it has 2.9 billion monthly active users.

2005

BODY-WORN POLICE VIDEO CAMERAS
In the UK, Devon and Cornwall police become the first to trial the use of body-worn video cameras in a move that the government says will "cut down on paperwork and help prosecute criminals". Their use becomes widespread but campaigners argue that they are used in situations, such as peaceful protests, which infringe the right to freedom of expression.

2005

SECURITY IN A BOX (SIAB)
Front Line Defenders, Tactical Tech and a global network of activists, trainers and digital security experts launch a comprehensive package of digital security tools and tactics to help human rights defenders.

2005

REMOTE SENSING IN HUMAN RIGHTS
The use of remote sensing technology – the imaging of the Earth's surface by satellite – in documenting human rights atrocities takes a leap forward with the launch of the Geospatial Technologies and Human Rights Project.

Micah Farfour, special adviser for remote sensing in the Evidence Lab at Amnesty International, says: "Fifty years ago, the first

ABOVE: Steve Jobs introduces the iPhone

Earth-observing Landsat satellite was launched with 60-metre resolution, scanning much of the surface every 18 days. Today, the Earth land surface is scanned almost daily with a minimum of three-metre resolution.

"This dramatic increase in the frequency, along with higher spectral resolution, has allowed human rights organisations clearly see remote areas of the world to document and corroborate abuses, near-real time."

2005

YOUTUBE
The video-sharing platform launches. By 2022, it has more than two billion users but questions remain over its commitment to freedom of expression and how it censors offensive and illegal content.

RIGHT: The US National Security Agency whistleblower Edward Snowden

2006

TWITTER
The "microblogging" service that forces us, initially at least, to sum up our thoughts in fewer than 140 characters is launched. By 2022, it has more than 200 million daily active users, but they no longer include Donald Trump, Naomi Wolf or David Icke.

2006

WIKILEAKS
Julian Assange launches a site specialising in "the analysis and publication of large datasets of censored or otherwise restricted official materials involving war,

spying and corruption". By 2022, it has published more than 10 million documents but Assange remains at the centre of a long-running extradition case to the USA.

2007

IPHONE
Apple founder Steve Jobs unveils the iconic smartphone.

2008

TEMPORA GCHQ SURVEILLANCE
Taking advantage of the fact that much of the world's internet traffic passes through the UK, the country's GCHQ spy service starts trialling a programme called Tempora that eavesdrops on emails, messages and phone calls in a manner that is not targeted at particular individuals but at anyone who may prove to be of interest.

2009

BITCOIN
The pseudonymous Satoshi Nakamoto publishes a paper outlining a "peer-to-peer version of electronic cash that would allow online payments to be sent directly from one party to another without going through a financial institution".

2010

NSO GROUP
Israel's NSO Group is founded,

promising to provide "technology to help government agencies detect and prevent a wide range of local and global threats". Later, its Pegasus phone monitoring tool is implicated in spying on individuals of interest, including murdered journalist Jamal Khashoggi.

2011

ARAB SPRING AND SOCIAL MEDIA
The spread of anti-government uprisings from Tunisia to Bahrain is largely credited to the use of social media platforms. Governments respond by shutting down internet access.

2011

WECHAT
Chinese communications giant Tencent launches the super app WeChat, which includes messaging, social media and payments. By 2022, it has more than a billion monthly users.

2013

EDWARD SNOWDEN REVELATIONS
Edward Snowden makes stunning revelations about the use of illegal government surveillance such as the NSA's Prism and GCHQ's Tempora (see above).

Ben Wizner, director of the ACLU Speech, Privacy and Technology Project, tells Index: "When Edward Snowden's disclosures first came to light in the summer of 2013, President [Barack] Obama defended US surveillance practices by insisting that they had been approved by all three branches of the government. That was true – but it was also the problem.

"Once those programmes were exposed, and the public had the chance to weigh in, all three branches of the government changed course and agreed that historic reforms were necessary. This has been the pattern through our modern history: the only →

→ significant reforms we've seen to intelligence programmes have occurred after government employees broke the law and shared with the media information that never should have been withheld from the public in the first place."

2014

SIGNAL

The secure messaging app of choice among many dissidents and human rights activists launches. It is the first messaging app to offer end-to-end encryption. By 2022, it has more than 40 million users.

2015

EYEWITNESS TO ATROCITIES APP

The International Bar Association and LexisNexis launch the eyeWitness to Atrocities app, allowing users to document and report human rights atrocities in a secure and verifiable way so the information can be used as evidence in a court of law.

2015

TROLL FACTORIES

Russian whistleblower reveals the existence of troll factories, including the Internet Research Agency, where employees flood social media and the comments sections of publications with pro-Vladimir Putin propaganda and anti-Western sentiment.

Hi, I'm Charli D'Amelio, I do TikTok dances.

ABOVE: TikTok is the latest social platform to reach huge audiences

2017

TIKTOK

Chinese company ByteDance launches a short-form video entertainment app called Douyin, which launches on international markets as TikTok.

Chris Stokel-Walker, a media lecturer at Newcastle University and author of the book TikTok Boom, says: "TikTok has had an impact on human rights, highlighting issues where they previously haven't been broadcast. That's particularly welcome given the challenges that TikTok was known to have as it moved out of a China-led setup to a more Western one, when early content moderation guidelines required censorship of issues and events controversial to China."

2017

UWAZI

The NGO Human Rights Information and Documentation Systems launches Uwazi, open-source database software for curating, annotating and sharing document collections between human rights defenders. By 2022, it hosts more than 150 databases.

2018

CAMBRIDGE ANALYTICA

87 million Facebook users discover that their personal data has been harvested by this British political consultancy for use in Facebook advertising campaigns. The company counts Donald Trump and the Vote Leave campaign in the UK's recent Brexit referendum among its clients.

2018

GENERAL DATA PROTECTION REGULATION

Countries in the European Union make it much harder for organisations to target people with marketing with the introduction of the General Data

ABOVE: Cambridge Analytica whistleblower, Christopher Wylie

Protection Regulation (GDPR).

Jim Killock, executive director of the Open Rights Group, says: "GDPR stops discrimination and protects equality. The introduction of GDPR has helped protect the rights and freedoms of workers, immigrants, refugees, asylum seekers, LGBTQIA+, victims of domestic violence, patients, children and mothers."

2018

PROJECT DRAGONFLY

The existence of Google's Project Dragonfly, a search engine designed to operate with China's strict censorship rules, becomes known. After criticism of the tech giant, the project is terminated.

2021

CCTV MILESTONE

The number of closed-circuit television cameras surpasses one billion, with the UK one of the biggest users.

"The UK is sleepwalking into a surveillance state of unprecedented proportions. There are an estimated six million CCTV cameras in the UK, a per capita coverage exceeded only by China. Further, we have the most totalitarian electronic surveillance infrastructure of any democracy in

history," said Silkie Carlo, director of Big Brother Watch.

"This total surveillance environment is redefining the right to privacy in the technological era and will have a chilling effect on the right to free expression and free assembly."

2022

TRUTH SOCIAL

TRUTH Social is launched in February by former US president Donald Trump, just over a year after his ban from Twitter. The platform, which is said to have raised $1 billion in investment, says it will be a "social media platform that encourages an open, free and honest global conversation without discriminating against political ideology".

THE FUTURE

New technology is a double-edged sword. It has the power to democratise access to information and gives a voice to people who have previously been silenced. Yet it also gives authoritarian governments greater power to track those who speak out against them and the tools to censor their words and restrict their freedom of expression. ✖

Mark Frary is associate editor at Index on Censorship

51(01):44/48
DOI:10.1177/03064220221084443

IMAGINE THE WORLD

26 MAY–5 JUNE 2022

hayfestival.org/wales

@HAYFESTIVAL #HAYFESTIVAL2022

HAY
FESTIVAL
HAY-ON-WYE

Censoring the net is not the answer, but ...

Young people must be safeguarded, says **VINT CERF**, one of the fathers of the internet, and perpetrators of excesses better policed

CALLS FOR CENSORSHIP of the internet come from many sides. This is not surprising, given that its openness has facilitated the propagation of misinformation and disinformation with the potential to disrupt safety around the world.

Often lost in this debate are the enormous benefits that the open internet has conferred and continues to offer. The discovery and sharing of useful information on the world wide web is, in part, responsible for the rapid development of defences against Sars-Cov-2 (Covid-19).

Major economic growth is directly attributable to internet-based businesses able to develop global markets. In the midst of the pandemic, billions of people were able to work from home, learn from home and avoid risky face-to-face gatherings.

The internet was born out of the initial need of the US Defence Advanced Research Projects Agency (Darpa) to facilitate the sharing of computing resources and research among institutions in the USA, the UK and Norway. Despite its military research origins, the internet was incubated in an academic research environment. Its first users were network engineers and computer researchers. Their applications ranged from electronic mail and remote access to time-sharing and file transfer. Significant work was undertaken in pursuit of artificial intelligence applications such as speech understanding and image analysis.

Not long after the internet became operational in 1983, the US research agencies Nasa, the National Science Foundation and the Department of Energy built their own networks using the internet's TCP/IP protocol suite and interconnected them through the expanding internet. Then research and education networks in other countries also implemented these protocols, connecting to what was becoming a global network.

Commercial service began in the USA in 1989. In 1991, the world wide web protocols were layered on top of TCP/IP and spawned countless websites and new applications. Soon after, a wireless local network technology called Wi-Fi was developed.

With the arrival of the smart iPhone from Apple in 2007, the internet and world wide web became accessible from anywhere you could get a wireless mobile or Wi-Fi signal. The original three internet networks are long gone, and others as well, but the internet is less a thing than it is an architecture.

New networks will come, such as we are seeing with massive investment in low earth orbit satellites. An interplanetary internet is in development by the space-faring nations of the world.

Research to develop a quantum internet is a new focus of attention to make feasible large-scale quantum computing. The open internet design continues to fuel its expansion and evolution.

The early years of the internet were forged in an atmosphere of academic information sharing and set the stage for the open internet from which we have benefited for decades. The freedom of the web has led to myriad applications in education, commerce, entertainment and government services, and the evolution of social media.

Often lost in the debate are the enormous benefits of the open internet

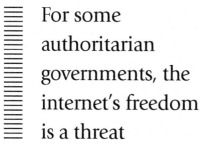

For some authoritarian governments, the internet's freedom is a threat

content of the internet. Demands are made of platform providers (mostly offering web-based services) to filter access to the content of the internet – in other words, to censor the system.

For some authoritarian governments, the freedom of the internet is a threat and the hazards of the online world provide an excuse for excessive monitoring of the users of the internet and censorship of content. Even in democratic countries, the risks of using online services have spurred efforts to impose content regulation on social media providers, web search services and even general internet access providers.

Censorship is not the best, or the only, response to the harmful behaviour we see on the internet. Applying critical thinking to what one sees and hears allows us to reject bad information. Cross-border co-operation to track down and apprehend people and organisations engaged in harmful behaviour is needed.

The creation of safe spaces for younger users is another reasonable response. For that case, monitoring, control and filtering may be justifiable. It is vital, however, to recognise that our young people grow up and must be prepared to encounter hostile conditions, misinformation and other risks as they navigate the online world and benefit from its richness and capacity for innovation. ✖

Vint Cerf, a US computer pioneer, is one of the fathers of the internet

We have discovered, however, that the virtuality and apparent anonymity of the web has a downside. Like-minded people flock together in so-called cyberspace. Nowhere is this more apparent than in social media spaces. Negative views are reinforced. Trolls revel in stirring up emotions. Nations use these media to incite political turmoil. Revolutions are co-ordinated on mobile phones and their myriad apps.

To make matters worse, the software that animates millions of applications is vulnerable to hacking. Email users receive "phishing" messages intended to trick them into giving up passwords or money or both. Ransomware attacks hold companies and institutions hostage for ransom under threat of loss of vital information.

Botnets are created by co-opting vulnerable internet devices and using them to generate spam or denial-of-service attacks against internet infrastructure. Citizens, businesses and academic and government institutions are at risk. A common response to these hazards is to attempt to regulate the

51(01):50/51|DOI:10.1177/03064220221084578

ESSEX BOOK FESTIVAL

1 - 30 June 2022
100 Events | 40 Venues
200 Writers & Artists

From Climate Change
to AI, Rebellions to
Metamorphoses, join us
for a month of challenging
conversations,
adventurous writing
and dynamic debates
in over 40 venues
across Essex....

essexbookfestival.org.uk

YEARS OF INDEX ON CENSORSHIP

Our pick of some of the most interesting articles
from five decades of Index on Censorship and
reflections from former editors of the magazine

1 9 7 2 | 2 0 2 2

HUMAN RIG[...]
IN THE USA

Helsinki watchers and US PEN report:
Undesirable aliens • Discriminated minorities

WEST GERMANY

Censorship does (not) exist [...]
The problems of a political satirist

£1.50/$3.0[...]

ARGENTINA
Foul play in education

ARTHUR MILLER ON POWER
TOM STOPPARD: MAD SCENE

Life under padlock
Vaculik, Kohout, Kliment

Ngugi Wa Thiong'o
President Marcos & the media

on censorship

index
3/1973   50p

........Dietrich A. Loeber
SAMIZDAT UNDER SOVIET LAW.
Frene Ginwala THE PRESS IN
SOUTH AFRICA...........
[...] CHANG TSUNG-CHI[...]

1 9 7 2 | 1 9 8 1

1972-1981

An arresting start

Index's first editor, **MICHAEL SCAMMELL**, recounts
the time he was detained in a Moscow airport
after a trip to meet artists from the USSR

ABOVE: The book associated with the exhibition that Scammell organised at the ICA in London

THE LIFE OF an Index editor isn't normally exciting, but there are occasional exceptions to the rule. Early in my tenure, a year after founding Index, I set off for Moscow with two goals in mind.

One was to meet and interview the renowned author Aleksandr Solzhenitsyn, who had suffered repression and censorship his whole life; the other to meet the banned sculptor and painter Vadim Sidur, whose work had never been shown in his native country, and discuss the possibility of exhibiting it in London.

I called on Sidur first, because I knew him from an earlier visit and had published an article about his sculptures in The Observer. After a suffocating Russian bear-hug, he showed me his latest work and we talked about a possible exhibition. With Index behind me, I thought I had a better chance of arranging something than when I was alone.

As it happened, Sidur's basement studio was a popular meeting place and we went out to meet another guest, Klara, whom I also knew from my earlier visit. She offered to take me to Peredelkino, an authors' dacha retreat on the edge of Moscow, to show me [author Boris] Pasternak's famous house and introduce me to his neighbour, the novelist Lydia Chukovskaya, who had once harboured Solzhenitsyn when he was hiding from the police.

Before going to see Chukovskaya, I met many well-known dissidents – including the writers Andrei Sinyavsky, Yuli Daniel and Evgenia Ginzburg, and Pavel Litvinov and Larisa Bogoraz, the pair who composed and distributed Appeal to World Public Opinion, the article which resulted in the foundation of Index.

In Peredelkino, I also met Lev Kopelev, a friend of Solzhenitsyn from their time together in a prison camp and the prototype of Rubin in Solzhenitsyn's novel The First Circle. Kopelev told me Solzhenitsyn was being sheltered by the cellist Mstislav Rostropovich in the Moscow suburb of Zhukovka, not far away, and if I took a local train there he would introduce me to Solzhenitsyn.

This seemed too good to be true and, in high spirits, I went to the Belorussky station the next day and bought my ticket. Four suspicious-looking men lingered on the platform, but I told myself not to be foolish: they couldn't possibly know who I was and were looking for someone else.

At the last stop before Zhukovka, however, I was disabused. A policeman boarded the train and ordered me to get off. As a foreigner, I wasn't allowed to travel more than 15km from Moscow's centre and was breaking the law. Crushed and afraid, I returned to Moscow and immediately contacted my friends to tell them what had happened.

Two days later, my time was up and I left for Sheremetyevo airport. Before I could even reach the ticket counter I was surrounded by border guards and whisked away to a private room. I was told to strip naked while the guards painstakingly searched my clothes and emptied my suitcase. They carefully confiscated a roll of photos I had taken and my diary of the visit, then one of them let out a triumphal cry. Chukovskaya had given me a note to take to Soviet biologist and dissident Zhores Mevedev, which I had had tucked into a packet of tea for safety. I →

Four suspicious-looking men lingered on the platform, but I told myself not to be foolish: they couldn't possibly know who I was

→ didn't know what was in it, but learned much later that she was sending him power of attorney over her royalties in the West so he could buy her medicine that was unavailable in the Soviet Union. The search was followed by an interrogation lasting almost three hours, and I had to wait three more hours to catch a plane to Prague, my next stop.

A couple of months later, a Soviet newspaper published a scurrilous article asserting that I was a "sinister criminal" and "an agent of anti-Soviet groups abroad". My 16 pages of handwritten notes were said to be coded, which wasn't true, and a small brass icon given to me as a gift was deemed "contraband". The story was taken up by the British and American press and I was interviewed by the BBC and wrote articles for The Guardian and Index analysing the methods of Soviet propaganda and their influence in the West.

Luckily, I also had my revenge. Later that year, I got permission from Solzhenitsyn's Swiss lawyer to

Before I could even reach the ticket counter I was surrounded by border guards and whisked away

co-publish in Index – with Harper & Row – Solzhenitsyn's Letter to the Soviet Leaders, translated by one of our contributors, Hilary Sternberg. Solzhenitsyn was expelled to the West soon afterwards and I met him for the first time at his lawyer's office in Switzerland. Later still, after extended negotiations, he agreed with my plan to write his biography and even to help to a limited extent, although he would not endorse it.

My work at Index continued, and in the next few years I became acquainted with more and more artists whose work was banned in the Soviet Union. Many of them had been expelled or had managed to move to the West voluntarily. In 1976, with the help of two Russian art specialists as judges, Index was able to stage a major exhibition, Unofficial Art from

the Soviet Union, at the Institute of Contemporary Art in London. Nearly half the artists represented were there, but here comes the sad part. The artist who had first alerted me to the calamitous situation of painters and sculptors in the Soviet Union, Sidur, was not there, nor were his sculptures.

The sculptures, even maquettes, were too heavy to smuggle, and even the lithographs that I already possessed had to be withheld, owing to a tragic misunderstanding between us that I didn't learn about for many years and wasn't fully resolved until the Soviet Union collapsed. ✖

Michael Scammell was one of the founders of Index and the magazine's first editor from 1972 until 1980

51(01):55/56|DOI:10.1177/03064220221084532

ABOVE: Aleksandr Solzhenitsyn, writer and outspoken dissident who exposed the horrors of the gulag, lost his Soviet citizenship in 1974

It was the year that Index was born: 1972. Huge swathes of Europe were behind the Iron Curtain while other countries across the continent were in the grip of military dictatorship. Index's mission was clear: to give voice to the voiceless, to metaphorically liberate those not free to talk. And in our first issue, Greece was a pressing concern

1972-1981

The clockwork show

Published to be read alongside George Mangakis' magnificent "Letter" from inside a Greek prison, this essay by an anonymous intellectual at large discussed the prison of the mind for those technically free

A GREAT DEAL HAS been said and written about the facts of the Greek dictatorship. Therefore I prefer to write about the psychology of the situation; the feelings and attitudes, the long-ranging impact of this harrowing experience. I can only speak for myself and others like me; and it is not for me to say how typical we are. I cannot speak for the prisoners, the tortured, the exiled: they need no arguments, they are their own arguments. 1 cannot speak for the indifferent, the unscrupulous, the cynical: they have no problem.

The question that is often asked of us is how the dictatorship affects one's personal life. Has it really made all that difference? Is there real hardship, and real oppression?

In the first year of the dictatorship, quite a few people may have answered this question with: 'As long as you mind your own business, you can live quite happily and peacefully'.

Apart from the fact that there do exist, after all, quite a large number of people who are not content, who are not able to reduce their lives to 'minding their own business', it seems to me that not even this contention is true. It is not enough to mind one's own business. After these last few

years, most people have found out that sooner or later, no matter what their position is, some demand will be made, some sign of submission or conformity will be required of them.

It may be something apparently trivial, like being ordered to put out the flag on the anniversary of the coup; or something not so trivial, like being ordered to send one's child to a propaganda rally; or like having to make a 'voluntary' subscription to a Public Loan, or a contribution to various Funds.

There are other more pressing tests: a summons to sign some official statement needed for propaganda or security reasons, to co-operate in some state project, to sit on some state committee. Finally, there are the crucial tests, like whether to shelter a friend from the security men, help someone to escape, take part in subversive activity.

And so the moment of choice comes, sooner or later, for each and everyone. If the demand is a trivial one, it may seem easy enough to decide either way. One accepts, saying: 'after all, it is only a formality'. Or one refuses, knowing the risk of punishment is not very great. In both cases, however, an entire, irreversible process of personality-change slowly

begins. The first 'yes' brings a twinge of – can one call it shame? Not yet, perhaps. Uneasiness – which is soon gone, however, and buried away.

The first 'no' also brings a twinge, an uneasiness, but of a different kind. Not fear, only a slight anxiety: has my action been noticed? Will it be held against me? Written down in a file?

The second choice will inevitably be more painful, which does not mean more difficult. On the contrary, the decision will be taken more quickly, because there is a precedent; a pattern of behaviour has been formed. But it will be more painful because the issues will be clearer (they will grow clearer with each new choice; it will become less and less easy to fool oneself, either way). And so, one enters the magnetic field where the pendulum swings. It is simple enough, in my mind: it swings between shame and fear. Both are ugly, corrosive and degrading emotions. But they are not clear-cut. There is not that comfort: choose and have done. For shame does not exclude fear. The little man, the obscure clerk, the man in the street who has signed all he has been asked to sign, who has attended innumerable, dreary, cretinous propaganda sessions, who →

ABOVE: Coup leader George Papadopoulos dancing the traditional Sirtaki with the Royal Guard in 1968, on the anniversary of the revolution of 21 April 1967, which created the colonels' dictatorship

→ has swallowed humiliation, bullying and blackmail, still does not feel safe. He still worries about his job. He still knows there is no guarantee for him, and no appeal if the worst does happen.

Fear, on the other hand, the fear of those who have said 'no', does not always exclude shame. There is always shame for not doing enough; for not risking more; for not going the whole way. And for feeling fear.

So fear and shame work on each other, reinforcing each other even while conflicting. Which of them is worse, under the circumstances? In some ways fear is more unbearable, its attacks are more acute, while they last. And it has a companion, which is suspicion. The person who has said 'no' in one way or another experiences blessed moments that are free of fear; but suspicion will fill in these gaps. It will always

be present, tainting relationships, contacts, communications. I don't want to go into the detailed description of the workings of fear, they have been written about extensively: the wellknown ring at the door at dawn, which one knows is not the milkman, etc. It is enough to say that fear feeds upon itself, grows large with its own irrationality, twists the very root of one's life. In the end, one's whole personality rests upon a void, a gaping, sucking hole – which is fear, eating away at one's entrails. However, the long-term effect of shame has a more deteriorating effect than fear, even—or especially—when it is not acknowledged. Constant exposure to fear may lead to a nervous breakdown, or severe mental disturbance, while constant co-habitation with shame leads to a total decomposition of

character. Of course, there are ways of overcoming both shame and fear. The first is overcome by self-interest, callousness, spurious reasoning, habit sometimes, or complicity. Fear is overcome by total dedication. Not everyone can use these remedies. For those who cannot, and I should think there are many, the pendulum swings. Fear – shame; and in the middle, hatred. Hatred of those responsible for this state of affairs, which sometimes helps to cover shame: it is a convenient way to soothe a bad conscience. It can also help to overcome fear, it can be cleansing and fortifying; if one hates hard enough, there is no room for fear.

In either case, though, living with it for a long, unrelieved period can do severe damage, especially when there are no real outlets for it. And one wonders, what can come of a nation fashioned by shame, fear and hatred? If one cares at all, then, for the people among whom one lives—I don't want to use words like nation, country, motherland—simply, the people among whom one lives, it is difficult to remain indifferent. It requires a singular lack of imagination not to see the kind of life that is being shaped here. Education, literature, and to a lesser degree the fine arts, are the most obvious victims. Teaching in Greek schools was conventional and retrograde enough before the coup, with a very few exceptions. Now dogmatism, rigid uniformity, narrow paternalism are more than ever dominant in the attitude of the school to the child. Experimental and progressive methods are distinctly discouraged. Compulsory education has been reduced from nine to six years, and school hours in secondary education have been reduced to six hours a day. Some of this already inadequate teaching time is further curtailed by regular and compulsory attendance at church services, although the school curriculum includes at least 2 hours of religious teaching per week. Expenditure on education appears to have earned the singular distinction of being practically the only major item of public expenditure to have been consistently reduced since the colonels took over. Textbooks are shabbier and drearier than ever, and frequently biased. Some history books breathe not a word about the

existence of dictatorships in Europe: they ingeniously refer to General Franco's Concordat and to Portugal's Guild Republic. Science books explain away scientific phenonena with phrases like: 'Our good God has made things in such a way that. . .' Children are gradually becoming expert in the art of lying and pretending at school. They know very well that certain subjects and words are taboo, only it is no longer the four-letter words that have to be whispered, as in the old innocent days, but words like 'dictatorship' and 'junta' and 'Patata'—their nickname for Pattakos. The children often dare each other to tear out the title page of their text books, which usually bear the junta's omnipresent emblem. The universities, of course, get their own share of brainwashing. In a speech addressed to the philosophy students at Jannina, Mr. Ladas, General Director of the Ministry of the Interior, assured his young audience that philosophy began and ended in Greece. He went on to refute any objection about other countries having also produced philosophers by loftily concluding that even if they had, it would not have been much use, since the Greeks had already said all there was to say.

These are only tiny examples of what is being done to the minds of the young, to the minds of all of us. In literature, pressure is not so blatant because writers do not lay themselves open to pressure, by the simple process of not publishing. Books are printed privately for the most part, with the inscription: 'not intended for commerce', and circulated by hand or by mail among friends. In other words,

writing has become a strictly private, ingrown affair, no longer a means of wider communication or a civilizing factor. The art of the cinema in Greece, anaemic enough as it was, has been given lethal injections of conformism by means of encouragements such as the State prize (a very generous prize) which is awarded every year to the best Greek film on a 'national subject'. Greek films on such subjects, rabid with chauvinism, have already flooded the market.

Artists who have chosen silence become frustrated, atrophied, often bitter, while those who have chosen to carry on regardless become aggressive, insensitive, somehow out of touch, perhaps as a result of their growing sense of isolation. Here again, shame and fear perform their ugly counterpoint. What kind of art will grow out of this climate? Our minds, whether we are intellectuals or not, are under constant attack by the two great enemies of truth: propaganda on the one hand and wishful thinking on the other. There is no chance of exercising responsible and objective judgement. There is no access to truth, so people either doubt everything they read and hear, or nourish themselves with rumours, hearsay, false hopes. This is poor meat for an active mind. As a result (a compensation?), people have become event-addicted. Something has to be happening or to be about to happen all the time, because one cannot bear the void; the moment there is a lull, unmarked by any 'development', despondency pounces, life becomes intolerable. It is like walking on burning sand—you have to keep moving. So life is continually being lived at a false, forced pace.

What is left? Personal relationships, perhaps, the old panacea. But even these are undergoing radical changes. Real friendships are closer, deeper   →

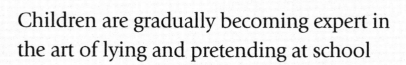

Children are gradually becoming expert in the art of lying and pretending at school

→ than ever before, because they have become a vital need: 'we must love each other or die'. But at the same time, unbridgeable gaps have opened up between people and families of opposing views. There can be no common ground, for this is not merely a political disagreement that can be settled by civilized discussion. The very fact that friendship can succumb under such conditions proves what a wide area of our life the dictatorship affects. If it affected but a portion of it, it could be easily sealed off and friendship could flourish undisturbed. But the moment there is disagreement on this one vital subject, the whole edifice collapses, the whole function of friendship becomes meaningless. There is no longer anything to say—literally. Contact is cut off like a switch, sometimes against friends' own will. One is forced into intolerance, ruthlessness, inflexibility. Forgiveness and understanding have become dangerous luxuries.

What I am trying to say is that one has to be pretty abnormal to remain impervious to all this. No matter how much of a conformist one is, no matter how self-centered or even how hard-pressed by practical considerations, there must come a time when one's awareness and one's concern extend beyond the strictly personal and take in the general, the public predicament. There is nothing more demoralizing than to be bound to a public body, an administration, a government with which one can never for a moment identify, which is the exact opposite of everything one believes in. One cannot live side by side with Philistinism, chauvinism, bigotry, blatant hypocrisy, crass ignorance, injustice, violence and brutality and not be affected by them, even if one manages—only just—to keep them out of one's own life. The private and the public course are not parallel, they inevitably touch and

We hate the present; we fear the future; we stand still, locked in a perpetual rejection

mingle. When they are not allowed to touch, there is total civic alienation. There are no means of expressing dissent, or of taking action towards changing what is wrong. The extent of this alienation is also due to the all pervasiveness of the regime's spirit. If a political party one disagreed with were to govern the country, there would still remain some persons in public positions whom one could respect and rely upon, there would still remain some newspapers one could read, there would still remain some independent organizations and institutions. But under this regime there is no relief; no exception: the regime has penetrated every single aspect of public life. One must take one's daily dose of lying, hypocrisy and distortion in the press, or not read the papers at all—which one often does for a spell, only to go back to them again soon, in the hope of extracting, from between the lines, some particle of truth, some omen, some symptom. The radio is a thing one listens to cringing, when one must listen to it, or a thing one pounces upon to switch off the moment it abandons the neutrality of music for the far from neutral, to put it mildly, news bulletins. In the street one keeps one's eyes lowered to avoid the slogans and posters, the screaming nationalism of which it is impossible to grow accustomed to. National holidays have become occasions for locking oneself up in one's house, shutting out the clockwork show outside.

This dissociation from everything public, from everything that has to do with the state, becomes in the end a terrible malady. It causes debilitation

and suffocation; we need windows to our house, no matter how comfortable it may be; we need to look out, and here there is nothing to look out upon. There is the feeling that we can invest nothing of ourselves—neither our work, nor our intelligence, nor our imagination, nor our enthusiasm, nor our children—in the world that surrounds us. We hate the present; we fear the future; we stand still, locked in a perpetual rejection. Many people, unable to bear this mutilation, leave the country, many more will leave if the situation remains unchanged. Those who remain, I suppose, have still not reached the ultimate point of dissociation. Possibly they can still sense the real Greece under the Greece of the colonels. But it needs a tremendous act of faith to hold on through all those solid layers of hate, shame and fear. I often think of the waste—the enormous vital energy, the talent, the courage, the virtue that is being expended every day in this harsh and thankless struggle, when it could have been put to such better use to make this country a place where the colonels would be an impossibility.

A sad and ugly picture, on the whole. Perhaps nothing more than that— nothing more than the picture presented by many countries in the world today. But suffering is not lessened by the fact that it is not exceptional. It is not its uniqueness, but the frequency of its occurrence that should impress us. ✖

Article from issue 1, volume 1, 1972

51(01):57/60|DOI:10.1177/03064220221084531

The practice of destroying allegedly 'offensive' literature did not die out with Adolf Hitler and the Nazis, enthusiastic burners of books. It continues to this day and, alarmingly, is on the rise, notably in the USA

1972-1981

Two letters

Kurt Vonnegut's novel Slaughterhouse Five was consigned to the flames in a school furnace in North Dakota and books written by him were regularly thrown out of school libraries

VONNEGUT'S WROTE TO the chairman of the school board in Drake, North Dakota, published below, alongside Vonnegut's exchange with Felix Kuznetsov, a Soviet Writers Union official, over the persecution of writers in the USSR.

'You have insulted me'
My novel Slaughterhouse-Five was actually burned in a furnace by a school janitor in Drake, North Dakota, on instructions from the school committee there, and the school board made public statements about the unwholesomeness of the book. Even by the standards of Queen Victoria, the only offensive line in the entire novel is this: 'Get out of the road, you dumb motherfucker.' This is spoken by an American antitank gunner to an unarmed American chaplain's assistant during the Battle of the Bulge in Europe in December 1944, the largest single defeat of American arms (the Confederacy excluded) in history. The chaplain's assistant had attracted enemy fire.

So on 16 November, 1973, I wrote as follows to Charles McCarthy of Drake, North Dakota:

Dear Mr McCarthy: I am writing to you in your capacity as chairman of the Drake School Board. I am among those American writers whose books have been destroyed in the now famous furnace of your school.

Certain members of your community have suggested that my work is evil. This is extraordinarily insulting to me. The news from Drake indicates to me that books and writers are very unreal to you people.

I am writing this letter to let you know how real I am. I want you to know, too, that my publisher and I have done absolutely nothing to exploit the disgusting news from Drake. We are not clapping each other on the back, crowing about all the books we will sell because of the news. We have declined to go on television, have written no fiery letters to editorial pages, have granted no lengthy interviews. We are angered - and sickened and saddened. And no copies of this letter have been sent to anybody else. You now hold the only copy in your hands. It is a strictly private letter from me to the people of Drake, who have done so much to damage my reputation in the eyes of their children and then in the eyes of the world. Do you have the courage and ordinary decency to show this letter to the people, or will it, too, be consigned to the fires of your furnace?

I gather from what I read in the papers and hear on television that you imagine me, and some other writers, too, as being sort of ratlike people who enjoy making money from poisoning the minds of young people. I am in fact a large, strong person, fifty-one years old, who did a lot of farm work as a boy, who is good with tools. I have raised six children, three my own and three adopted. They have all turned out well. Two of them are farmers. I am a combat infantry veteran from World War II, and hold a Purple Heart. I have earned whatever I own by hard work. I have never been arrested or sued for anything. I am so much trusted with young people and by young people that I have served on the faculties of the University of Iowa, Harvard, and the City College of New York. Every year I receive at least a dozen invitations to be commencement speaker at colleges and high schools. My books are probably more widely used in schools than those of any other living American fiction writer.

If you were to bother to read my books, to behave as educated persons would, you would learn that they are not sexy, and do not argue in favour of wildness of any kind. They beg that people be kinder and more responsible than they often are. It is true that some of the characters speak coarsely. That is because people speak coarsely ➔

→ in real life. Especially soldiers and hardworking men speak coarsely, and even our most sheltered children know that. And we all know, too, that those words really don't damate children much. They, didn't damage us when we were young. It was evil deeds and lying that hurt us.

After I have said all this, I am sure you are still ready to respond, in effect, 'Yes, yes—but it still remains our right and our responsibility to decide what books our children are going to be made to read in our community.' This is surely so. But it is also true that if you exercise that right and fulfil that responsibility in an ignorant, harsh, un-American manner, then people are entitled to call you bad citizens and fools. Even your own children are entitled to call you that.

I read in the newspaper that your community is mystified by the outcry from all over the country about what you have done. Well, you have discovered that Drake is a part of American civilisation, and your fellow Americans can't stand it that you have behaved in such an uncivilised way. Perhaps you will learn from that that books are sacred to free men for very good reasons, and that wars have been fought against nations which hate books and burn them. If you are an American, you must allow all ideas to circulate freely in your community, not merely your own. If you and your board are now determined to show that you in fact have wisdom and maturity when you exercise your powers over the education of your young, then you should acknowledge that it was a rotten lesson you taught young people in a free society when you denounced and then burned books — books you hadn't even read. You should also resolve to expose your children to all sorts of opinions and information, in order that they will be better equipped

RIGHT: Book burning continues in the USA today. This scene from New Mexico 2001 sees copies of Harry Potter on the fire

to make decisions and to survive.

Again: you have insulted me, and I am a good citizen, and I am very real.

That was seven years ago. There has so far been no reply. At this very moment, as I write in New York City, Slaughterhouse-Five has been banned from school libraries not fifty miles from here. A legal battle begun several years ago rages on. The school board in question has found lawyers eager to attack the First Amendment tooth and nail. There is never a shortage anywhere of lawyers eager to attack the First Amendment, as though it were nothing more than a clause in a lease from a crooked slumlord.

'We continue to care'

I spoke at Gatsby's house in the afternoon of 16 September 1979. When I got back to my own house in New York City, I wrote a letter to a friend in the Soviet Union, Felix Kuznetsov, a distinguished critic and teacher, and an officer in the Union of Writers of the USSR in Moscow ... Felix Kuznetsov and I had become friends during the previous summer — at an ecumenical meeting in New York City, sponsored

by the Charles F. Kettering Foundation, of American and Soviet literary persons, about ten to a side. The American delegation was headed by Norman Cousins, and included myself and Edward Albee and Arthur Miller and William Styron and John Updike. All of us had been published in the Soviet Union. I am almost entirely in print over there — with the exception of Mother Night and Jailbird. Few, if any, of the Soviet delegates had had anything published here, and so their work was unknown to us.

We Americans were told by the Soviets that we should be embarrassed that their country published so much of our work, and that we published so little of theirs. Our reply was that we would work to get more of them published over here, but that we felt, too, that the USSR could easily have put together a delegation whose works were admired and published here — and that we could easily have put together a delegation so unfamiliar to them that its members could have been sewer commissioners from Fresno, as far as anybody in the Soviet Union knew.

Felix Kuznetsov and I got along very well, at any rate, I had him over to my house, and we sat in my garden out back and talked away the better part of an afternoon.

But then, after everybody went home, there was some trouble in the Soviet Union about the publication of an outlaw magazine called Metropol. Most of Metropol's writers and editors were young, impatient with the strictures placed on their writings by old poops. Nothing in Metropol, incidentally, was nearly as offensive as calling a chaplain's assistant a 'dumb motherfucker'. But the Metropol people were denounced, and the magazine was suppressed, and ways were discussed for making life harder for anyone associated with it.

So Albee and Styron and Updike and I sent a cable to the Writers' Union, saying that we thought it was wrong to penalise writers for what they wrote, no matter what they wrote. Felix Kuznetsov made an official reply on behalf of the union, giving the sense of a large meeting in which distinguished writer after distinguished writer testified that those who wrote for Metropol weren't really writers, that they were pornographers and other sorts of disturbers of the peace, and so on. He asked that his reply be published in The New York Times, and it was published there. Why not?

And I privately wrote to Kuznetsov as follows:

Dear Professor Kuznetsov — dear Felix — I thank you for your prompt and frank and thoughtful letter of 20 August, and for the supplementary materials which accompanied it. I apologise for not replying in your own beautiful language, and I wish that we both might have employed from the first a more conversational tone in our discussion of the Metropol affair. I will try to recapture the amiable, brotherly mood of our long talk in my garden here about a year ago.

You speak of us in your letter as 'American authors'. We do not feel especially American in this instance, since we spoke only for ourselves without consulting with any American institution whatsoever. We are simply 'authors' in this case, expressing loyalty to the great and vulnerable family of writers throughout the world. You and all other members of the Union of Writers surely have the same family feelings. Those of us who sent the cable are so far from being organised that I have no idea what sorts of replies the others may be making to you.

As you must know, your response to our cable was printed recently in The New York Times, and perhaps elsewhere. The controversy has attracted little attention. It is a matter of interest, seemingly, only to other writers. Nobody cares much about writers but writers. And, if it weren't for a few of us like the signers of the cable, I wonder if there would be anybody to care about writers — no matter how much trouble they were in. Should we, too, stop caring?

Well — I understand that our cultures are so different that we can never agree about freedom of expression. It is natural that we should disagree, and perhaps even commendable. What you may not know about our own culture is that writers such as those who signed the cable are routinely attacked by fellow citizens as being pornographers or corrupters of children and celebrators of violence and persons of no talent and so on. In my own case, such charges are brought against my works in court several times a year, usually by parents who, for religious or political reasons, do not want their children to read what I have to say. The parents, incidentally, often find their charges supported by the lowest courts. The charges so far have been invariably overthrown in higher courts, those closer to the soul of the Constitution of the United States. Please convey the contents of this letter to my brothers and sisters in the Writers' Union, as we conveyed your letter to The New York Times. This letter is specifically for you, to do with as you please. I am not sending carbon copies to anyone. It has not even been read by my wife.

That homely detail, if brought to the attention of the Writers' Union, might help its members to understand what I do not think is at all well understood now. That we are not nationalists, taking part in some cold-war enterprise. We simply care deeply about how things are going for writers here, there, and everywhere. Even when they are declared nonwriters, as we have been, we continue to care.

Kuznetsov gave me a prompt and likewise private answer. It was gracious and humane. I could assume that we were still friends. He said nothing against his union or his government. Neither did he say anything to discourage me from feeling that writers everywhere, good and bad, were all first cousins — first cousins, at least.

And all the argle-bargling that goes on between educated persons in the United States and the Soviet Union is so touching and comical, really, as long as it does not lead to war. It draws its energy, in my opinion, from a desperate wish on both sides that each other's utopias should work much better than they do. We want to tinker with theirs, to make it work much better than it does — so that people there, for example, can say whatever they please without fear of punishment. They want to tinker with ours, so that everybody here who wants a job can have one, and so that we don't have to tolerate the sales of fist-fucking films and snuff films and so on. ✖

Extracted from Palm Sunday by Kurt Vonnegut, published by Vintage on 18th June 1981 at £7.95 Copyright © Kurt Vonnegut

This article appeared in volume 10, issue 6

51(01):61/63|DOI:10.1177/03064220221085930

1 9 8 2 | 1 9 9 1

Winning friends, making enemies, influencing people

PHILIP SPENDER, who was at Index from the start, saw it turn from a new publication into one informing policy in South Africa in the 1980s

CAME TO INDEX on Censorship in 1972 to sell copies of the magazine into bookshops just as the first issue came out. When George Theiner became editor in 1982, I became assistant editor.

There was always too much copy and not enough money, and people frowned at our low circulation figures.

Soon we had specialists for central and eastern Europe, Africa, Asia, Latin America, the USSR and the Middle East. They questioned whether there were too many pages about Theiner's country – Czechoslovakia – and not enough about their own regions.

The magazine flourished, with 10 issues a year and the content spread around the world via newspapers and dissident networks. Local supporters organised conferences and created anthologies on stage and radio. While the number of individual subscribers seemed low, many of them were journalists, writers and academics, and what they read informed their work.

"I believe that the influence of Index on Censorship goes much further than you can see here in London," wrote Jacobo Timerman, one of Argentina's most distinguished newspaper journalists, in Index in 1982.

"I was surprised that the editor and publisher of a very important newspaper in the city of Bahia Blanca ... was impressed and worried for the first time when Index published a short item saying that his newspaper, La Nueva Provincia, is an anti-Semitic newspaper."

Friends at the Weekly Mail in South Africa told us: "When officials of the department of home affairs briefed their minister, Stoffel Botha, for his meeting with the Weekly Mail editors in May, his reading list was topped by a small London-based magazine called Index on Censorship."

Elliott Abrams, assistant secretary of state for human rights and humanitarian affairs in the US administration under president Ronald Reagan, complained of a "pattern of Anti-American bias" in Index's coverage of Latin America. Theiner responded in 1985 in an article called "How objective are we?", explaining why Index had a duty to provide a platform for views from all sides, with anti-American views as legitimate as any others.

"It is an inescapable fact that the policies adopted by the US in Central and South America for many decades – with their stubborn support of brutal dictatorships such as those of Batista, Somoza, Stroessner and Pinochet – have resulted in much anti-American feeling in that part of the world. It is then inevitable that some contributors to Index give vent to sentiments that can only be described as anti-American – but that is hardly a reason to condemn Index for its 'anti-Americanism'."

Several people made a great impression on me during my time at Index. Anthony Thomas made a TV drama-documentary entitled Death of a Princess about the public beheading of a young Saudi woman in 1978, which the Saudis tried to suppress, claiming it was "anti-Islamic".

He knew the Arab world well and after research found the Saudi version of events to be untrue.

"Then I discovered something else," he said. "Although the story had been repressed in the Middle East – people were not allowed to comment on it – she had already become a mythical figure and everybody talked about her passionately. I felt that people were not so much talking about her, but about themselves. She had a catalytic influence." →

People were not so much talking about her, but about themselves. The princess had a catalytic influence

→ We learned from him what the execution of this princess meant in different communities and understood better some of the currents of thought swirling in the Middle East – insights unobtainable from newspaper reports.

Naji al-Ali, one of the Arab world's most popular cartoonists, was another person providing nuance from the Middle East. He was interviewed by Index in 1984.

"My job, I felt, was to speak up for those people, my people, who are in camps in Egypt, in Algeria, the simple Arabs all over the region who have very few outlets for their points of view," he said.

Born in Palestine, he was exiled to Lebanon. He fled from Lebanon to Kuwait, then fled Kuwait and ended up in London. All the while his cartoons circulated in the Middle East, ridiculing political leaders. "I also draw rich Palestinians who scream all day about the land and about sacrifices when in fact they are more interested in their financial deals and private gains," he said. He was assassinated in London in July 1987 by an unknown assailant. His cartoons survive; I saw one on a wall near Jaffa.

The most famous Czech dissident during the 1980s was Václav Havel, whose work started appearing in Index in 1976. His play Temptation, translated by Theiner and published in Index in 1986, appeared alongside Havel's reflections on the genesis of the play, its background, and his anxieties lest it be somehow destroyed by the authorities before completion. This was also the nightmare of Vasily Grossman, who submitted his greatest work,

He was assassinated in London in 1987 by an unknown assailant. His cartoons survive

Life and Fate, to a literary journal, who referred it to the KGB, who confiscated it. Grossman "felt he had been strangled". Robert Chandler introduced an excerpt of it in Index in 1982 – the first time anything from the novel had appeared in English.

Most of the writers in Index were almost unknown outside their countries. To present them was to open up new worlds. Miriam Tlali, for example, was a published writer during the apartheid era in South Africa. In Index in 1984 she explained the obstacles facing black writers like herself – the extraordinary range of restrictions imposed by apartheid laws – and how difficult it was to discover and read contemporary black writers.

New forms of censorship crop up and old ones persist. An exceptional collaboration with The Independent newspaper took place

in 1988. The broadsheet, as it was then, devoted two full pages to questioning the state of liberty in the UK, drawing its content from Index 8/1988.

Two focal points of that exercise resonate today – threats to the independence of the BBC and the curtailment of public protest.

Much of the credit for Index in the 1980s goes to Theiner, who was assistant editor from 1973 to 1982 and editor from 1982 to 1988. To appreciate why, read his obituary in Index in 1988.

Mark Bonham-Carter, then chairman, wrote: "He was the best of companions and the most loyal servant of our cause." ✖

Philip Spender worked at Index from 1972 until 1996. He was assistant editor and then managing editor between 1982 and 1989

51(01):65/66|DOI:10.1177/03064220221084440

RIGHT: Activists paint signs for a march against the Communist regime in Czechoslovakia in 1989. The country was a key focus for Index in the 1980s

Under the helm of George Theiner, Index published some of the most remarkable work from his native Czechoslovakia, including original plays from Václav Havel, documenting the country's metamorphosis from the straitjacket of Communism, through to the Velvet Revolution and independence

1982-1991

The nurse and the poet

KAREL KYNCL's article on the poet Ivan Blatny, Czechoslovakia's first non-person, is an extraordinary story of hope, resilience and the unusual, winding paths of fate

WHEN SHE WAS at school, Frances Meacham liked literature, but as for poetry, she actually hated it. And yet she was fated, in later life, after saving two stage plays for a small European nation, to unearth a rich poetic source which, without her, would doubtless have remained hidden from us, forever silted over by human folly and malice.

'A small nation' obviously means that this nation does not speak English. And that brings me to yet another paradox: the only language Miss Meacham really knows is her own.

Love, however, requires no knowledge of foreign languages. And it was love which first aroused her interest in Czechoslovakia. This was after the war, when the young nurse worked there in various hospitals for a year and a half and fell in love with a young Czech professor.

Everything seemed rosy but then the big history took over. In February 1948 the Communists usurped power in Czechoslovakia by means of an overnight bloodless coup, and the secret police began to take an interest in the young English nursing sister. Its agents would turn up in the early hours of the morning, asking many questions: What was she doing in Czechoslovakia? Was she perhaps a spy? And, since she claims she isn't, would she care to assist the police in their responsible work? After all, she had all these Czech friends, what were they saying about the new regime? Did they perhaps want her to put them in touch with someone in the West?

Miss Meacham did not intend to assist the Communist police by word or deed, and so she decided to return home. In her handbag she carried away the text of two plays which Olga Scheinpflugová, a famous Czech actress and author, and widow of the great Czech writer Karel Capek, had entrusted to her. Plays which otherwise would doubtless have ended up in a furnace or on the shelves of some police archive.

Apart from the plays, Frances Meacham also managed, with the help of others, to smuggle out her young professor, who, like so many of his fellow-countrymen, had come to the conclusion that he could not live under the Communists.

But alas, their love affair did not have a happy ending: the anti-Communist professor was to prove a disappointment. While it was true that he opposed Communism, he turned out to be in favour of Fascism, and Miss Meacham then as now considered the one to be as bad as the other, seeing very little difference between the two -isms; and so she and the professor parted company.

As the years passed, the young nurse gradually became, as she puts it, today's 'reluctant spinster'. A description that says quite a lot about her sense of humour, her capacity for self-irony, and her remarkable mental equilibrium.

Her experience would have been sufficient for most people to make them despise everything that had to do with Czechoslovakia. Miss Meacham, obviously, isn't 'most people'. 'It's such a wonderful country, where I got to know so many marvellous people', she says. 'How could I ever forget it?'

To this day she corresponds with some of those old friends, and in →

 ## What was she doing in Czechoslovakia?
Was she perhaps a spy?

LEFT: Ivan Blatny in **1948**

CREDIT: A. Cook/Express/Getty Images

→ particular with a former patient of hers, who towards the end of the war gave birth in an English hospital, with Miss Meacham's assistance. Eight years ago she visited her in Czechoslovakia. During that visit she took part in a conversation which, while seemingly banal, was to have important consequences for Czech literature. No, for European literature.

'Where in England do you live, Miss Meacham?' a man asked her, thus beginning the Czech version of the favourite British conversational gambit about the weather. 'In a small town near Ipswich,' Miss Meacham replied.

'Did you say Ipswich? Why, I have a friend there — in a hospital.'

'Really?' said Miss Meacham, struck by the coincidence. 'I work in an Ipswich hospital.'

'Oh, but my friend isn't in an ordinary hospital. He has been in a mental institution there for the past 30 years.'

'You mean St Clement's?'

'That's right, St Clement's. He is a Czech poet by the name of Ivan Blatny.'

To hate poetry — or at least to take no interest in it —is one thing. The tragic fate of a human being is something else. Miss Frances Meacham was deeply moved as she listened to the life story of a Central European child of our time.

Ivan Blatny was born the year after the First World War ended; as a young man he experienced the Nazi occupation of his country and the Second World War; when that was over he took a deep breath and was ready to enjoy life — but then breathing became difficult and life not very enjoyable following the Communist coup of 1948. He happened to be in Britain at the time, as a member of a delegation of Czech writers, and he decided to stay here. Speaking on the BBC, he gave the following reason for his decision: culture in Czechoslovakia was in the doldrums, the country's poets were forced to write optimistic rubbish, the Party interfered in both the artist's life and in his work. This was all true, though perhaps only partially so. In the thirty years that followed, interference in art and culture was only a marginal activity of the Czechoslovak Communist Party: its hammer fell, in one way or another, on every one of Czechoslovakia's fifteen million inhabitants, its sickle mowing down countless lives. Yet, even if Ivan Blatny could have foreseen all this in the first few months of 1948, he would most probably still have given the same reason for his decision to emigrate: the Party's assault on Czech literature. For poetry had become the one and only aim of his life, and without it he felt he could not exist. Throughout the next thirty-eight years, right until today, he has really only existed through his poetry... but let's not anticipate.

In his second collection of verse the then 23-year-old Blatny expressed his existential feelings as follows:
This life full of unpleasantness
Lost keys quarrels dealings with officials
This rainy life with its procession of postmen bringing subpoenas
This was written during the greatest war in the history of mankind. When the war finished, our poet was conscious of feelings of great relief and wide new horizons spanned by a rainbow. His fourth collection (if we omit his two children's books), published in 1947 when Blatny was 28, had the title Searching for the Present. He was never to find it; the present, instead, found and trapped Ivan Blatny.

In his native Czechoslovakia, where more than anywhere else people

Ivan Blatny became the first such 'non-person' in Czechoslovakia

tend to seek their national identity in literature, he was celebrated as an unrivalled candidate for one of the top places among the country's younger poets. When he announced his decision to stay in Britain, there followed a storm of abuse, carefully orchestrated by the new 'leading force' in the country, the Communist Party of Czechoslovakia. 'Blatny's action is one of political, poetic and human baseness... the suicide of one whom, until recently, we referred to as a Czech poet,' a group of Prague writers said in their statement. 'As soon as he stepped on foreign soil Ivan Blatny died forever for Czech literature.'

The Party's journalists wrote, and said, the same — only slightly less grammatically: 'traitor', 'scoundrel', 'Judas', 'renegade', 'villain'. Amidst the noise generated by the Czech media it might easily have escaped notice that the 'crime' the poet had committed was simply that he had refused to return to a country in which he, in all conscience, found he could not live.

Complete silence followed the loud racket of the media. Orwell's novel, Nineteen Eighty-Four, had only just been published, but many of his 'non-persons' had been eking out a meagre existence in the Soviet Union for some years. Ivan Blatny became the first such 'non-person' in Czechoslovakia. His books vanished from the shelves of public libraries, his name was erased from the pages of literary journals and from the country's literary history, no one mentioned him any more. He ceased to exist.

The excommunication and the Old Testament-like curses which befell

him had a dire influence on Blatny's later life. One is almost tempted to say it was a kind of Communist voodoo. Deprived of his roots, spat upon and reviled, he found himself unable to adapt to life in a foreign country. Moreover, the silence which settled upon him once the initial rage had exhausted itself was like the premonition of an evil fate: perhaps they would abduct him and take him back to Prague, imprison him, kill him? Sensitivity and a vivid imagination — these essential qualities in a poet, now turned against him, and there was no one to help and take care of this helpless young man. Less than two years after his arrival in Britain Ivan Blatny was in a mental institution.

Frances Meacham listened to this story and was moved by it, but she did not let it rest there. Shortly after her return home she made her way to St Clement's hospital in Ipswich to see inmate Blatny.

Her colleagues at St Clements did not disguise their scepticism. 'He won't talk to you. He hardly communicates with anybody, just sits and stares into space. Or at the screen of a switched-off TV set.' It seemed as if Ivan Blatny was irrevocably lost to this world. Not only did he not wish to speak to anyone, an unexpected visit was to him a disturbance of the unchanging, grey routine of his days and revived in his subconscious the very horrors which had, all those years ago, sent him to the institution. His life was an unending, monotonous round of days and nights, interrupted only by the drinking of tea, the swallowing of pills, and a few hazy memories. Anything that broke ➜

Miss Meacham's garage is without a doubt the most literary edifice of its kind

→ this monotony seemed to him like a threat, it spelled danger and doom.

Fortunately, Frances Meacham possessed not only compassion but also the experience of many years working as a nurse, and the patience and gentleness without which she could not have carried on her profession. Several visits to St Clement's, and inmate Blatny began to be Ivan Blatny again, an individual human being ready to believe that this woman, who was the first person in many years to show any interest in him, actually meant him no harm. In the end he confided to her that he had once, a long time ago, done some writing in the mental hospital; and even now he occasionally jotted something down, in the loo, after the lights had gone out in the dormitories and the other patients had fallen asleep. But the male nurses usually threw his stuff out the next day. And why not — what good was it anyway?

Right at the bottom of the drawer which contained all his worldly goods there lay a folder full of his scribblings, sheets of paper which had somehow escaped the attention of the nurses. Of course she would take them and look after them for him. Why not?

Frances Meacham took the manuscript home and put it in a box. Next time she visited the hospital, she brought Blatny a supply of fresh paper. 'This man used to be a famous poet,' she told the management committee of St Clement's. 'Don't throw away what he writes. And how about giving him a typewriter?'

She photocopied the manuscript and sent it to a Czech emigre publishing house in Toronto which is run by one of Czechoslovakia's greatest novelists, Josef Skvorecky. He, too, is a 'non-person' in present-day Czechoslovakia, and he too was a victim of Orwell's 'memory-hole'. 'I thought Ivan Blatny died years ago,' he wrote back to Miss Meacham. 'The poems you sent me are marvellous. Please send me everything he has written.'

And thus, 31 years after the publication of Blatny's Searching for the Present, another collection of his verse, Old Abodes, came out in Canada. Not as a curio, but mature poetry full of an inner strength which can take its place with some of the very best that has been written in Europe in the second half of this century. An exacting critic has praised the volume as 'one of the finest in modern Czech poetry, a fascinating revelation, one might say a miracle'.

Out of the depths of non-memory there emerged a great poet — or, I should say, was discovered, thanks to an English nurse who couldn't stand poetry when she was at school.

At the other end of the corridor in St Clement's Mental Home at Ipswich there appeared a small, thin, hunched figure, obviously clad in his Sunday best. In his hand he held some 50 sheets of paper covered with handwriting, which he handed to Frances Meacham. She will take them home, put them in plastic bags to keep them from getting damp, and store them, together with the other thousands of pages of Blatny's manuscripts, in her garage.

Miss Meacham's garage is without a doubt the most literary edifice of its kind anywhere in Britain.

I leaf through Ivan Blatny's output over the last fortnight: a kind of diary of a Surrealist poet, commenting on daily events, based on Apollinaire's free association of ideas, the melody of words, snatches of conversation and the sounds of the world outside his windows. Most of the verses are in Czech — a crystal-clear Czech, quite incredible when one realises where and how the poet has spent more than half his life. Here and there, however, a word, sentence or verse appears in English, French, or German. And paradoxically, this too is in the best of Czech poetic traditions: in the Middle Ages what was called 'macaroni' poetry enjoyed great popularity in Bohemia — it consisted of a mixture of Latin and Czech or Czech and German.

The forefinger of Blatny's right hand is so yellow with nicotine it's almost black. A carton of cigarettes is hardly the most appropriate present for a poet, but Blatny is obviously very pleased to have it. His pocket money doesn't go too far, and cigarettes and the fortunes of Ipswich Town Football Club are practically the only two follies he can afford. 'Well, sometimes I also kiss a lady's hand, but I don't get any further than that,' he says, smiling, as if he had made a terrible joke. But it is a joke that sends chills down your spine.

And then the 66-year-old poet, who has spent the last 35 years in mental hospitals, engages in a tussle with Miss Meacham over how many cigarettes he is to take back to his room with him. Sixty, they finally compromise. The rest will be looked after by Frances, who will deal them out to him in small doses.

'You see,' Ivan Blatny explains, 'some patients steal things from you. Mainly cigarettes and sweets. And then there is one chap here who's fascinated by clean white paper, just like me. Whenever he can he pinches my sheets and scribbles all over them. Just like me.'

Another smile. Another example of black humour.

'What about the nurses? Do they still throw out your manuscripts?'

'No, not very often. But even if they do, it doesn't matter... I can always write some more. But maybe you shouldn't mention this when you write your piece, it might look as if I'm complaining, and I'm not, really. I'm happy here.'

'But wouldn't you perhaps be happier somewhere else? Let's say somewhere where you would have a view of the sea from your window?'

A startled glance.

'No, no, certainly not! They sometimes say I don't belong here in St Clement's and that they'll send me to Clacton-on-Sea. That would be terrible... Here we have high ceilings, the park, lots of space...'

The space of the 'lunatic asylum' — to give the institution its common name — in which Blatny has now spent the larger part of his life has to him become a true 'asylum', having shed its derogative adjective. But it has to be this particular asylum of St Clement's in Ipswich. Any change is terrible, menacing.

'You know, I'm still not a British citizen,' says Blatny. 'If they were to deport me, do you think I'd end up in jail?' He looks at me anxiously — the old nightmare looms.

'Nonsense. Nobody would dare deport you.'

'Let's hope so...'

He does not say that only a few years ago it wasn't nonsense. That he was then in real danger of being deported because ignorant people had actually considered shipping this sick man back to his country of origin. Luckily, they soon dropped the idea — but the anxiety remains: 'Really, don't write about those verses they threw out. They don't matter.'

'What does matter?'

'Poetry. Life as such. Being able to get over one's depression. Never to have to be sad.'

'Do you succeed?'

'Not always. Today I do. It's marvellous that you have come. Today, I'm in seventeenth heaven.'

'Seventeenth? You have them numbered, do you? And which is the highest?'

'There isn't any, no maximum,' says Ivan Blatny. 'That converges to the infinite.' He thinks for a while, then adds: 'I love life.' Another pause. 'I love life. And I realise that I couldn't commit suicide. You need 20 tablets of Luminal for a mortal dose, but even if I could obtain them, I don't expect they'd work. And to jump from a high building? What if I were to break my bones and live?' Another pause. 'I love life. If one day I stop loving it, I'd like to get euthanasia...' The longest pause of all, then a sudden smile: 'For the time being I intend to live according to Shaw's Back to Methuselah — a long, long life.'

I give Blatny a long essay about him and his poetry which circulates in *samizdat* in his native country. The old poet shows his excitement: 'So they haven't forgotten me... If as you say they keep retyping my stuff like that, they must like me. After all, no one forces them to do it... I'll read it tonight, after lights out. I'll take it with me to the loo, it's quiet there.' He stops speaking suddenly. 'It's embarrassing, isn't it, that I should be so happy about it. Makes me look like a megalomaniac, don't you think?'

'No, I don't.'

'In any case,' he continues, smiling, 'don't Christians say Love your neighbour as yourself? Surely that means that self-love is the highest form of love.'

The photographer holds out his lightmeter to measure the intensity of light in the darkened room. Blatny looks at the instrument and reads its trademark out loud: 'LUNASIX.' Then he says:

'Light-meter LUNASIX should only be used in the light of the lune ...'

The germ of a new poem? In the lunatic asylum?

The 66-year-old poet, who has succeeded at a terrible cost in becoming a total poet, a walking and breathing organ of poetry, returns to his asylum to write more of his unending life's poem. A damaged violin that has not lost its fantastic sound.

His oeuvre today appears in Czech — both in *samizdat* at home and in printed form abroad. Some of his work has been published in German, and some has been broadcast in Norwegian on Norwegian television. Perhaps British readers, too, will in time discover Ivan Blatny. If not, they will be that much the poorer.

A fine source of poetry somewhat reminiscent of the inner monologue of James Joyce springs up in St Clement's Hospital in Ipswich. Joyce, too, was an emigre, living outside his own country. Unlike Blatny he did not have (nor need) Nurse Frances Meacham, who did not care for poetry. ✖

Karel Kyncl was a Czech writer and an editor at Index. This article was from issue 15, volume 3, 1986

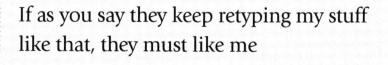

If as you say they keep retyping my stuff like that, they must like me

51(01):67/71|DOI:10.1177/03064220221084533

The 1970s and 80s saw battles rage between left wing and right wing governments, and guerrilla forces, across Latin America. Free speech was a casualty, but there was a not-so-secret way of subverting the system

1982-1991

Tuning in to revolution

As conflict gripped Central America, the power of communication between those fighting for survival was strengthened by the most basic of modern technologies – the radio. JANE MCINTOSH reported on its importance

LATE AT NIGHT in the Guatemalan mountains around Lake Atitlan, a tiny, medium-wave transistor radio picks up 'Radio Sandino' from Nicaragua. There's a news programme discussing the private business sector and the anti-revolutionary activities of some of its members. Listening to the occasional machine-gun fire from the Guatemalan army troops outside, patrolling the Atitlan area, it's as if the news is coming from a different planet. The power and importance of radio stations in Central America's revolution becomes crystal clear.

Throughout Latin America, the distance, the mountainous and difficult terrain, make communications by land difficult. Few people are able to afford television in rural areas, and as the majority of the populations are illiterate, written information is of little use. The ruling military and right-wing governments which predominate in the region have learnt this lesson well and radio stations are their primary means for transmitting the information they wish the people to hear.

But the relatively cheap, simple and mobile technology of radio transmission and reception has made it the most appropriate means for popular and revolutionary groups to transmit their information – between themselves and

to the civilian populations. Central America, and particularly Guatemala, El Salvador and Nicaragua, provide good examples of the new uses being found for old technology.

It is significant that Radio Sandino was the strongest station to be picked up around Lake Atitlan, for it was the Guatemalan people living there who first demonstrated some of the potential for local and community radio. But that was before Nicaragua's revolution and before Guatemala had been turned into a war zone.

In 1964 in Guatemala there was one radio receiver for every twenty people while the six major daily newspapers produced in the capital were only circulating 2.3 copies for every 100 people. Five years later there were over 90 privately and commercially owned radio stations. The majority of them were inaccessible and run for profit through advertisements. Like the controlled press, they showed little inclination to provide any dissenting voice to government press handouts in reporting events.

But radio stations in rural areas – the majority set up by Catholic church groups in the 1960s – began to involve local people. With social, and particularly educational, provision virtually non-existent in rural areas,

radios were seen as the best means to reach people in isolated areas. Throughout the 1970s, as peasant organisation grew around demands for land and an end to government military repression, the locally influenced or controlled radio stations took their place as community information services.

In February 1976 came the earthquake which killed 20,000 — mainly poor and Indian people living in ramshackle houses. This was about the same number as those killed through government repression over the previous ten years. As reconstruction began, the communities had to look to themselves for the organisation and help to rebuild their lives. Aid agencies which had come in with funds for the earthquake disaster stayed to support longer-term development projects — and some communities found themselves able to extend or begin new services by radio for surrounding areas.

Education by radio

Lake Atitlan is one of the most beautiful parts of Guatemala and became a prime centre for tourist development in the 1970s. The lakeside communities of about 50,000 mainly Tzutiyil and Cakchikel speaking Indians found themselves pushed off their small farming plots onto even worse lands around the lake. Already poor, the tourist influx disrupted their lives and conditions worsened. Malnutrition is widespread and health services minimal. 73% of men and 90% of women are illiterate and only a third of the children ever go to school.

The radio station was set up in Santiago de Atitlan in 1968 by local priests. As time went by it became an independent association made up of local community people. It was the only radio station in the country to be owned and run by Indian peoples although Maya Quiche Indians make up 60% of the total 7.5 million people in Guatemala.

The basic aims of the radio were those of a school; to promote adult education through literacy courses and programmes designed to improve living conditions, health and agricultural production. From classes given over the radio it became more of a community information centre announcing where teachers in the area would give classes. After 1976 and with the growth of peasant demands throughout the country, the radio took its part in local community demands.

But as a tourist centre, Atitlan had to remain free of disruption or dissent, as the visitors might otherwise take their much needed foreign exchange elsewhere. As peaceful, persistent demands from the peasants began to turn into guerrilla warfare against the military regime, so repression intensified. At the end of 1980, 18 truck-loads of troops took over Santiago de Atitlan. The director of the Voice of Atitlan radio station was killed by security forces and the station's equipment taken away or destroyed.

Today, the rural population in the western highlands has to be as alert and mobile as the guerrillas themselves to escape army massacre. Systems of lookouts warn villagers against

ABOVE: A reconstruction of Radio Venceremos, at the Museo de la Palabra y Imagen, San Salvador

imminent attack while Radio Sandino reminds them what it can be like 'after the revolution'.

Reporting the other side

Radio Venceremos, the official radio station for the Farabundi Marti Liberation Front (FMLN) in El Salvador, first broadcast on 10 January 1981. It combines the role of radio for military use, reports of guerrilla actions, local propaganda and, increasingly, as a means for sending out its side of the story to the international news media.

With propaganda so much a part of the war in El Salvador, local press, radio and TV reports are strictly censored by the government. The Catholic radio station 'Panamerican Voice' was shut down and the liberal newspapers La Cronica del Pueblo and El Independiente closed. Assassinations and imprisonment of journalists are (as in Guatemala) a favoured means of extending press censorship.

Venceremos, like Radio Sandino before it in Nicaragua, is intended to break the silence from the guerrillas and counter the misinformation sent to the national news agencies. Today, its short-wave transmissions reach not just Central America and the Caribbean but the USA and Europe as well. The BBC monitoring service listens in and Venceremos has begun to be cited as a source by news agencies and press alike.

Clearly aware of the international media's ability to affect its progress in what (through US support for the junta) was becoming an international war, Venceremos began to counter US attempts to claim Soviet and Cuban involvement in the civil war. Through on-the-spot reports, reports of guerrilla actions and interviews with victims of government repression, the other side of the guerrilla war began to be heard.

In January this year a team from Venceremos went into Mozote in Morazan province shortly after army troops had left the village devastated. →

➔ Interviews with the survivors were enough to tell the story:

'At the moment we are looking at a peasant who has the jacket of one of his sons. He continues to look hopelessly for his children, trying to recognise them among the mutilated bodies.'

In June this year, the FMLN shot down a helicopter and captured Colonel Castillo, the Deputy Minister of Defence, who was on board. The incident became an exchange between the army and Radio Venceremos which exemplifies the power the station has.

Initially the army completely denied the radio report that the helicopter had been shot down. Then it admitted the helicopter had suffered a mechanical failure and crashed in Morazan province and presumed the passengers, including the Colonel, to be dead. Venceremos went on the air to announce that the Deputy Minister was in guerrilla hands, which the army denied, saying only that he had 'disappeared and not been recovered'. As the army was unable to find and reach the wreck of the helicopter, Venceremos asked the Red Cross to collect the bodies of those killed in the crash and to evacuate 43 soldiers, captured when the guerrillas seized Perquin, a town in the same province.

The army continued to deny Venceremos reports until the Colonel, the fourth highest officer in the Salvadorean army, was interviewed on the radio and admitted his capture by the guerrillas, albeit with a qualification, 'in El Salvador we are not fighting a conventional war and I simply regard myself as a prisoner' not a prisoner of war. He added, 'I hope that an international organisation such as the Red Cross will try to rescue me'.

The radio transmissions from the guerrillas had not just managed to get the events straight in military terms but reported their military achievement in capturing a high-ranking officer. The reports reached Reuters and European newspapers within days.

Before Venceremos, news of the war had to be brought out of the country and sent in communiques from the individual organisations in the guerrilla Front. But now this single voice speaking for the guerrillas is beginning to be taken seriously and is, at least, an alternative source to the military government itself, as well as providing information to the civilian population.

Transformation

In revolutionary Nicaragua, the Sandinistas' Radio Sandino was transformed during the reorganisation of the news media which had previously been dominated by the Somoza dictatorship. Two new newspapers have been set up, Barricada, the official Sandinista daily, and Nuevo Diario, an independent but pro Sandinista paper. La Prensa, the traditional opposition paper to the Somoza dictatorship, a mere shadow of its former self, is now right wing, rarely missing a chance to condemn the government.

Radio Sandino is the equivalent to Barricada on the air waves. After the civil war in 1979 it provided services such as helping to locate lost families and friends. Since then it has been of key importance involving Nicaraguans who live in isolated areas in the new social programmes and keeping them up to date with the trials and tribulations of the revolution.

But just as the popular movements have recognised the importance of community radio, so the hemispheric giants reflect its power at the other end of the scale. The US Voice of America, the BBC World Service and Radio Moscow all beam their own signals towards the transistors of Central America. The Reagan Administration has asked Congress for US$10 million to build a radio station in Miami which will tell the Cubans what is really happening on their island — from the US point of view. But at the end of June, Congress was up in arms when the New York Times reported that four 80-metre-high radio antennas had been built near Florida for the government's Radio Marti. Some members of Congress are concerned about the damaging effect propaganda transmissions could have on the already cold US relations with Cuba.

The relatively cheap and accessible technology of radio is of key importance for people whose poverty, illiteracy, isolation and exploitation exclude them from other channels. As the sound of gunfire continues to resound throughout Central America, so the power of communication between the peoples fighting for survival can be strengthened by the most basic of modern technologies. Transmitting from one to another, celebrating victories and consoling in defeat, the rest of the world can now listen in to revolutionary radios in Central America. ✖

Jane McIntosh is a freelance journalist who specialises in Central America. This article appeared in 1982, volume 11, issue 5

51(01):72/74|DOI:10.1177/03064220221084530

 The other side of the guerrilla war began to be heard

'Extremely important
and profoundly disturbing'
ARCHBISHOP DESMOND TUTU

Do
Not
Disturb

'A withering assault on the
murderous Rwandan regime
of Paul Kagame – very driven,
very impassioned'
JOHN LE CARRÉ

'An extremely important and
profoundly disturbing book'
ARCHBISHOP
DESMOND TUTU

The Story of
a Political Murder
and an African
Regime Gone Bad

MICHELA WRONG

'A withering assault on the murderous regime of Kagame,
and a melancholy love song to the last dreams
of the African Great Lakes'
JOHN LE CARRÉ

It has been called the year that made the modern world. 1989 saw walls, real and metaphorical, come down across Eastern Europe, while China's crushing of students in Tiananmen saw a more assertive global power

1982-1991

'Animal can't dash me human rights'

Fela Kuti, the godfather of Afrobeat, was a thorn in the side of Nigerian politicians in the 1970s and 80s. He talked to **JANE BRYCE** for Index in 1989

THE NIGERIAN MUSICIAN, Fela Anikulapo-Kuti, has been jailed twice for his outspoken attacks on government corruption and police repression, most recently for almost a year in 1986. Since his release, he has continued to speak and sing about the injustice and oppression he sees in his own country. In an atmosphere of increasing intimidation, which has even affected Nigeria's notoriously fearless and frank press, Fela has come to be seen as a rallying point for the disaffected masses and university students. Songs such as 'Beasts of No Nation', with its refrain, 'Animal can't dash me human rights', have not endeared him to the military regime of President Babangida, which used the human rights issue as a justification for seizing power in 1985.

Babangida's Structural Adjustment Policy, and the consequent economic slump and rampant inflation, have brought ordinary people to the point of desperation. Countrywide riots erupted in May; shortly before, a concert by Fela due to be held for a student audience of 20,000 in his hometown of Abeokuta was forcibly aborted by police. In London recently, Fela explained the background in the following interview with Jane Bryce.

People are starving terribly in Nigeria. My country has become a 'settlement', a refugee camp. Anybody in any kind of authority, such as the army or police, uses the word 'settle' for bribery. If you're in any kind of trouble, you 'settle' it, before they let you go. When Babangida came to England to see Margaret Thatcher, Nigerians said he came to 'settle'.

Conditions for ordinary people, Fela said, are as bad as in South Africa. Nigeria has its own form of apartheid.

We have a law called 'Wandering'. The police start arresting people from 5pm onwards, even if they have an address and a job. Police stations have become banks; the Commissioner is the bank manager. They lock you up for weeks or months or even years without charge. Many people die in jail.

In this context, according to Fela, some kind of protest was inevitable, and he even called a press conference to warn the President. When the uprising came, therefore, it was not spontaneous.

It was like putting a match to gas. People wanted to resist the acute oppression that is happening in my country. The first little riot was in Lagos State University. At this time, the Chinese protests had started [in Tiananmen Square], but it was still peaceful. The Nigerian government came out with a statement to the effect that Nigerian students should copy the Chinese students, that they are civilised there, that they don't use violence. Everything has since blown up in everybody's faces, but I was so mad at the time. I felt that every time something happens in Africa, these motherfuckers come to quote some country we know nothing about. We don't want to know about China, we want to know about Africa.

Some time before this, in April, the government had received information about student meetings at which a protest was being planned. Fela's concert was scheduled for 8 April in Asero Stadium in Abeokuta. But →

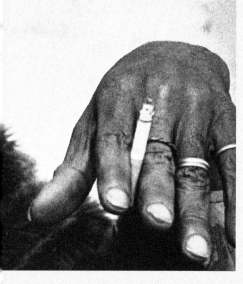

LEFT: Fela Kuti strikes a pose during an interview before a concert with his band Egypt 80 at the Hamburg Fabrik in 1992

Every time something happens in Africa, these motherfuckers come to quote some country we know nothing about. We don't want to know about China, we want to know about Africa

Police surrounded the stadium and threatened to shoot anyone who went near it. It was a very big operation. That's what the government does in order to scare people

→ *before the concert over 1,000 fully armed police descended on the town in 'Operation Silence Fela'.*

When we arrived in my bus at the outskirts of Abeokuta, we saw this barrage of police cars and armoured vehicles, 15-20 of them in a line, blowing sirens, coming slowly towards us. I said to my band, 'We're not going to play tonight'. Police surrounded the stadium and threatened to shoot anyone who went near it. It was a very big operation. That's what the government does in order to scare people.

That was to have been my first student gig since I left jail. Many students came from all over the country for the show. The authorities felt that if Fela got there and started to talk about the elections, the Debt-Equity Swap, the things I always talk about, to 20,000 students, it would definitely cause unrest. So they stopped me from playing.

Fela does not see this incident in isolation, but as part of a general repressive tendency which includes the banning of the Academic Staff Union of Universities, the National Association of Nigerian Students, and the break-up of the Nigerian Labour Congress, along with the harassment of individuals: on 17 June the social critic and educationalist Tai Solarin, and elderly union leader Michael Imoudu, were arrested and interrogated, and the radical lawyer, Gani Fawehinmi, is still in detention.

I know the mentality of my people. We talk and laugh. But I knew that

we were really suffering. The students may have motivated people, but everyone joined in. It was a popular uprising. The theme was, 'Babangida must go'. Half the country rose up, starting in Ibadan, then Lagos, Aba, Enugu and Benin.

Official figures in Nigeria are notoriously unreliable, and there have been conflicting accounts of the numbers shot by police in the course of quelling the protests.

The police claimed 10 people died in Lagos, but the papers reported that 50 bodies were found in one mortuary alone. I heard another report that there were 123 dead in Lagos. The authorities admitted to 7 in Benin, though people have told me the figure was over 100. A friend in Benin said that, in her house alone, 3 old women were shot in the legs. If 123 died in Lagos in 2 days, consider that the Benin uprising went on for 4 days, and think how many must have been shot.

I am now convinced that the Nigerian government has no moral right to condemn the Botha regime for violating the rights of our brothers and sisters in South Africa. For instance, in both South Africa and Nigeria, progressive organisations are proscribed; law-abiding citizens are detained without trial; police attack and kill innocent people at night, destroy their homes and rape the women; patriots are labelled 'radicals and political extremists', or 'anarchists and terrorists'; trade unionists are jailed for life...

Nigeria is currently preparing to return to civilian rule in 1992, but Fela will not be participating in the elections. He sees his role as speaking out against what he sees happening in Nigeria:

The world needs information about Nigeria. They don't know that it is Africans' blood that the leaders are using to rule. There is not enough to eat in Nigeria, there are no medicines, everything is expensive. Margaret Thatcher said that the Nigerian economy is buoyant. Not only did she say it in England, she said it in Nigeria too. I challenged her in Nigeria on the grounds that she has no right to comment on our economic situation because she doesn't live here. You cannot come to Nigeria and tell Nigerians that our economy is buoyant. She has no political mandate. But then Babangida says she is the best leader in the world. Can you imagine how stupid he is?

What will he do on his return to Nigeria?

They want to scare me off coming home, but nothing they can do will keep me out of my country. I must go home. I've been through prison before, practising for the future. I learnt how to get bored. That's all they can do to me. There's no way they can prevent me from going back. ✖

Jane Bryce is a writer and academic specialising in African and Caribbean literature. This article was published in volume 18, issue 9, 1989

51(01):76/78|DOI:10.1177/03064220221084534

Index does not concern itself only with the big battles. The pages of the magazine have always been filled with debate on thorny issues related to culture and society, debates both evergreen and of the moment

1982-1991

Why should music be censorable?

One of the greatest musicians of the 20th century, YEHUDI MENUHIN, writes about his desire to ban "muzak"

COULD CIRCLE THE thorny centre of the argument, but I shall plunge into the brambles. There is a case to be made for restricting certain types of musical activity — as there is for regulating other potent human drives.

(a) In an ideal world it should be possible to protect people from 'music' injurious to the ear, soul and sensibility.

(b) Such music, or muzak, is the deadening refrain piped into lifts, arcades, restaurants and aircraft to a captive audience who must be abused in this fashion without consultation.

(c) I would dearly like to see (and hear) some system for regulating these unwelcome broadcasts by restricting the financial gain of those operators who exploit both music and the hapless consumers of their product.

Why can there not be zones of silence prescribed, as now exist near hospitals, where one is free of man-made, mechanical, recorded or amplified noise, or those degenerate soundwaves which pass for music?

Today we regulate drugs, food, films — and think it right to do so. Why can there not exist similar proscriptions on the infliction of *ersatz* music, which is no less open to abuse?

There are of course certain types of real music which are censored — and this is in itself a token of its power. This has been recognised by governments and philosophers since the time of Plato. Music in some regimes has charms only when it conforms to the propaganda of the day; in these regimes it is not art but power which is music to the ears. I remember in Russia in 1945 hearing an oratorio, for that is what it was, in praise of Lenin. Again, in China, until recently, music and musicians suffered considerably under the Gang of Four.

Commercial interests and tyrants:

ABOVE: Yehudi Menuhin, left, rehearsing at the Royal Albert Hall in London in 1962

both attempt the censorship of music, the former by harnessing its potency for financial gain, the latter for the consolidation of their own power. ✖

Yehudi Menuhin was a violinist and conductor who spent the majority of his career in Britain. This article appeared in volume 12, issue 1, 1983

51(01):79/79|DOI:10.1177/03064220221084544

1 9 9 2 | 2 0 0 1

1992-2001

The snake sheds its skin

JUDITH VIDAL-HALL
edited Index in the years immediately after the fall of the USSR. Despite hope, a new world order did not give way to new freedoms

"MAY YOU LIVE in interesting times," goes the old Chinese proverb. More a threat than a promise, it was the first phrase that came to mind when I was asked to talk about my years as editor of Index, from 1992 until 2007.

It was a time of global reconfiguration with the fall of the Berlin Wall, the end of the Soviet Union and the reunification of eastern and western Europe. For Index, too, it was – in the words of its founder, Stephen Spender, in the first issue of our newly designed version in 1994 – a time of "renewal" as it "moved into an entirely different world" from that which existed when, in response to the request of Pavel Litvinov in Moscow in 1968, the first issue of the magazine was published in 1972.

With hindsight, our first issue of the "new" magazine seemed like a fitting celebration of its 21st anniversary the year before.

But it was not an easy transition. "Go home," our main funder in the USA told us. "Thank you so much for all you have done, but the Cold War is over and your job successfully completed. We shall be ceasing your funding. Use what remains to close down in an orderly manner…"

How wrong they were. Index was never a weapon in the Cold War but was, from its start, "dedicated to the diffusion of worldwide knowledge of censorship wherever this happened – not only in that part of the world dominated by the Soviet Union but all over the world, wherever there was censorship". For instance, 1989 – the year The Wall came down in Europe – was a year that saw other walls remain firmly established around the world. It was the year that exposed China's brutal attack on the protesters in Tiananmen

ABOVE: A Roma band rehearse before a wedding performance in Zrenjanin, Serbia, in 2015. From the 1990s, Index featured many voices of, and stories from, Gypsies, travellers and Roma people

Square, where one of their demands was for freedom of speech and the press; there was still an apartheid regime in South Africa; and the oppressive regime of the colonels in Greece was still going strong.

At Index, our first task under the leadership of new CEO Ursula Owen was to secure funding and, once that was completed, to go for a totally new-look magazine. While we remained true to the original brief, the greater use of photographs, a new section we called Babel that gave prominence to voices in their own words   →

We were hit by a second world-changing event that affected the global configuration: 9/11

→ (not usually heard in the media generally) and country files and special issues gave more attention to less visited places and aspects of censorship that, until then, had been largely ignored.

We devoted entire issues to censorship in film and photography, in music and poetry, and in the arts generally, including one that still stands out: the silencing of humour in performance and cartoons. We brought attention to subjects on which there was still, at the time, great reticence: gay culture, the importance of protecting privacy if free expression was to survive, and the long-silenced voices of the Roma, Gypsies and travellers, a much-abused and persecuted minority within the European Union.

My last issue as editor focused on a topic now in the media limelight but which in 2007 was

New keywords were "terrorism" and "Islamophobia", and to this day they remain the focus of conflict

still a near-taboo subject: slavery.

Just short of a decade after I joined Index, we were hit by a second world-changing event that affected the global configuration: 9/11. The new keywords were "terrorism" and "Islamophobia", and to this day they remain the focus of conflict and the silencing of voices.

If I try to sum up how my time at Index served the magazine, it would be to claim that we expanded the conventional understanding of censorship – from being a man with a big stick or a prison cell to hand, to encompassing the silence that

continues to be the worst enemy of free expression.

The Berlin Wall fell in 1989. A decade later I wrote that the "Wall of Silence had expanded its reach to encompass the world". The implications of the vastly expanded freedom of expression potentially unleashed by technology – and the new opportunities it facilitated for the manipulation and distortion of this – were left to my successors. ✖

Judith Vidal-Hall was editor and director at Index from 1992 to 2007

51(01):81/82

DOI:10.1177/03064220221084580

ABOVE: Human rights protesters practising Falun Gong meditation in London's Whitehall during then Chinese President Jiang Zemin's visit to the UK in October 1999

Joy in the West at the end of the Soviet Union evaporated when war erupted in former Yugoslavia. The pages of Index filled with stories of genocide, as well as questions about the nature of the reporter in such circumstances

1992-2001

Close-up of death

SLAVENKA DRAKULIC recounted watching a newsreel in Sarajevo in the immediate aftermath of an explosion in which a two-year-old girl was killed. In this moving article, she wondered whether the principle of "never again" had fed into a growing audience appetite for atrocity without stopping the slaughter

THEY SAY THAT a little girl, AM, was killed while eating a Ramadan-pie. It seems that it happened like this: it was morning at the end of February, bright and chilly. You ask yourself how that woman, her mother, made the pie in Sarajevo, 10 months after the beginning of the war? What flour did she use, what oil, what did she fill it with? She must have baked it the night before — but then again, how? There is no electricity, or there is, but only sometimes. Or did she do it on an open fire? But there is no wood: all the trees in the city have been cut long ago... In any case, still half asleep, the two-and-a-half-year-old girl had been sitting at the table, eating breakfast. At that moment, she heard the sound of shelling. Maybe she was frightened by it, so she ran to her mother—but maybe not. The sound of shelling is normal around here. No, she couldn't have heard that sound, they say that those who get hit have no time to hear anything, they have no time to get frightened at all. A shell went through the roof of their house and landed in the kitchen. The girl fell to the floor. It all happened with lightning speed and she was dead before her parents or her grandfather had time to understand what was happening. By the time her

father took her in his hands and looked for help, it was all over. Then — then a TV camera arrives on the scene. Judging by certain details this happened perhaps only one or two hours after the shelling. We see the small kitchen already without the little girl, the floor is covered with brick and plaster debris, scattered shoes, her little boots. The TV camera zooms in on the roof, on the hole left by a shell, as sky and cold descend into the kitchen through it. The father is sitting with his arms on the table, crying. The camera shoots a close-up of his blue eyes and his tears — in fact it looks as if he is crying on camera — so that we, the television spectators, can be sure that his tears are real, that he really cried, the little one's father. He has on a white pullover made of a rough peasant's wool. You do not usually sit in your kitchen dressed warmly like that, but what do we know about the kind of cold that he is suffering from at this moment?

From his eyes, the camera moves to that pullover so that we can see a

red stain on it, left where he held his girl when he picked her up from the floor — when it was already too late. The blood is not dry yet, the stain is bright red, it looks fresh. I know that raw, handspun wool that his pullover was made with. I can feel it under my fingers. It takes forever to dry, soaked blood stays wet a long time... Looking at this blood is nauseating. Still the camera returns to it several times. This is unnecessary, but you have no defence from those kinds of pictures — and there is no one to tell how useless it is.

Now we are in the hospital, this is the first time we see the mother, too. The reporter's voice explains that she has been wounded in her stomach. Then he (or was it she?) says something absolutely too much, too much in the moment of despair of the woman whose child has just died. The voice says that the young woman probably will not be able to have any more children. She lies on a kind of stretcher, covering her face with her hands. She sobs, her voice comes out as if   →

Looking at this blood is nauseating. Still the camera returns to it several times

CREDIT: Johnny Saunderson/Alamy

→ broken in pieces. The father comes in, in his white pullover with the red stain, and embraces her. It is clear that they meet there for the first time after the little one's death, in a hospital room. On camera — for the first time. The mother lets out something, in some other setting you could probably call it a cry, a howl. But now it is only a sound of emptiness; with that sound the woman tells her husband she has just lost everything. This is the end, this has to be the end. The camera can't go

any further than the inhuman suffering of the mother who has lost her child. Neither we, the television spectators, nor the people that we do not see who are standing behind camera—a reporter, a cameraman, a soundman — can stand all this any longer. This has to stop, I repeat to myself while the camera rolls on. I don't believe my eyes, but that's how it is: now we are looking at a white sheet with red spots. We have already forbidden this, we recognise that same sign. Red on white,

that's the sign of her death. My God, how very bright her blood is, I think, while my whole being cries: enough, enough, enough. I don't want the camera to enter under that cover hiding her small body. But someone's hand surpasses my thoughts and lifts the white sheet. Her face, we see her face. Her small deformed face, no longer human, framed by untidy tufts of her black hair. Her half-closed eyes. We see a close-up of death. Then cut. The funeral. People talking, an off-screen

Something has crept into us, the signs of our own dying

ABOVE: The war in Sarajevo was well documented by the media. Here the BBC reports from Sarajavo the day after shells were fired killing 15 and wounding hundreds, 1993

filmed only a couple of hours after they have lost their child, and that the whole tragedy has happened on camera. The only thing we have not witnessed is the moment of death of the two-and-a-halfyear-old AM. (A take from outside, when the shell hits the roof. Then, from inside, a scene where the girl falls from her chair, in slow motion, as if she's flying. A piece of pie drops from her hand and rolls on the ground. That's it! The reporter is pleased.) Well, why not? By now, we too, the public, are mature enough to stand it, all in the name of documentation, which we obviously believe in. That is the only thing we have not seen on our TV screens so far.

We have already seen beheaded corpses being eaten by pigs and dogs. Eyes gouged out, scattered bodily parts that do not belong to anyone, anything. Skeletons and half-rotten skulls, children without legs, babies killed by sniper fire. A 12-year-old rape victim talking about it on camera.

Day after day. Death in Bosnia has been more and more well-documented. In 10 months, Sarajevo has been hit by 800,000 shells. In the city, 80,000 kids are imprisoned — that makes it the biggest children's prison in the world. Five thousand of them were killed or simply died. The rest await hunger and long death, slow death. Fifty years ago this is how Jews suffered. Now it's the Muslims' turn. Do you remember Auschwitz? Really, does anyone remember Anne Frank? Oh yes, we do remember it all and, because of that memory, we have the idea that everything has to be carefully documented, so that shameful history can never be repeated. And yet, here

they are. Generations have learned about concentration camps at school, about factories of death; generations whose parents swear that it could never happen again — at least not in Europe —precisely because of the living memory of the recent past. They are fighting this war. What, then, has all that documentation changed? And what is being changed now, by the conscious, precise bookkeeping of death that is happening in our lives, in our living rooms, while we watch transmissions of the dying in Sarajevo? The little girl's death is only one horror out of many, each of which prepares us for something even worse.

The biggest change has happened within ourselves, the audience, spectators, public. We have started to believe in our role in this casting: that it is possible to play the public. As if the war is theatre. Slowly, and without our noticing it, something has crept into us, a kind of hardness, an inability to see the truth — the signs of our own dying, the close-up of the girl's dead face was one scene too much. Because it was senseless. The feeling that for the first time it is possible to watch war from so near in its most macabre details, makes sense only if, because of that, something can change for the better. But nothing changes. Therefore, this kind of documentation is turning into a perversion, into a pornography of dying. ✖

Slavenka Drakulic is a Croatian journalist and writer, whose works have been translated into many languages. This article first appeared in volume 22, issue 7, July 1992

51(01):83/85|DOI:10.1177/03064220221084441

voice, the father, the grandfather, a little coffin in the shallow, frozen ground. The report is finished. It has lasted a total of three minutes...

A moment later, we become aware that the TV broadcast that we have just seen is the tragedy of one family

As civil war continued in the Balkans, misinformation spread and a feeling took hold that the world didn't care enough because most victims were Muslim. Salman Rushdie, a regular contributor to Index, tackled the subject

1992-2001

Bosnia on my mind

I have never been to Sarajevo, but I feel that I belong to it. There is a Sarajevo of the mind, an imagined Sarajevo whose ruination and torment exiles us all, wrote SALMAN RUSHDIE in 1994

T IS, IN spite of some signs that things may be improving, still impossibly hard to make any sort of statement at all about the situation in Bosnia-Hercegovina. It is possible to read that it was the threat of air strikes that persuaded the Serbs to withdraw their heavy artillery from positions above and around Sarajevo, that it was the Russians who persuaded them, that in fact the Serbs relocated their tanks in civilian areas where air strikes against them would not be possible and from which they could attack Sarajevo just as easily as before, that the Russians and Greeks are backing Nato, that the Russians and Greeks, in defiance of Nato are ganging up with their Orthodox allies the Serbs to ensure the success of Serbian strategy, that now that the Bosnian Croats under Tudjman are willing to form a federation with the 'Muslims' this may provide the basis for a deal with the Bosnian Serbs to preserve some sort of unified state of Bosnia-Hercegovina, that the partition of Bosnia into three mini-states is inevitable and the 'Muslims' must be forced to accept it, that black is white and yes is no and down is up and stop is go and it remains only to join the demented old codgers in James Fentons Ballad of the Shrieking Man and sing:

Tramps are mad
And truth is mad
And so are trees and trunks and tracks.
The horror maps have played us true.
The horror moon that slits the clouds
The gun
The goon
The burly sacks
The purple waistcoats of the natterjacks
Have done their bit as you can see
To prise the madness from our sanity.

It will not do, however, this codger-fashion despair. It will not do to decide, in the saloon bars of our hearts, that they have hated each other for millennia over there, they have been wanting to slaughter each other for centuries, and now the goblins are out of the bottle, the warlords are standing at their roadblocks, let them get on with it. Equally unsatisfactory is the cleaned-up, Newspeak version of the above, which says the Situation Is Complex and there are No Easy Answers and do we really want Our Boys to be embroiled forever in What Is, After All, A Civil War?

It will not do because there is still such a thing as truth, however much the war and the world's politicians may have shredded it. And that truth, for me, lies in the nature and meaning of the city of Sarajevo, where, as Susan Sontag has said, the twentieth century began, and where, with terrible symmetry, it is ending.

I have never been to Sarajevo, but I feel that I belong to it, in a way. I am proud to be an honorary member of the PEN club of ex-Yugoslavian writers, and I hope they will not think me presumptuous if I say that as a result of this newly-forged connection I, too, can claim to be, in some sense, an exile from Sarajevo, even though it is a city I do not know.

There is a Sarajevo of the mind, an imagined Sarajevo whose ruination and torment exiles us all. That Sarajevo represents something like an ideal; a city in which the values of pluralism, tolerance and coexistence have created a unique and resilient culture. In that Sarajevo there actually exists that secularist Islam for which so many

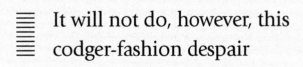
It will not do, however, this codger-fashion despair

people are fighting elsewhere in the world. The people of that Sarajevo do not define themselves by faith or tribe, but simply, and honourably, as citizens.

If that city is lost, then we are all its refugees. If the culture of Sarajevo dies, then we are all its orphans.

Sarajevo's truth (as opposed to the saloon-bar version) is that the different communities have not been hating each other since the dawn of time, but have been good neighbours, schoolfriends, work-mates and lovers; that in this city miscegenation and intermarriage have

been not the exception, but the norm. (And if they were bad neighbours, enemies at school, and rivals at work, and if their marriages failed, it was for the ordinary human reasons of personality and affinity, rather than the 'cleansing' evils of nationalism).

Sarajevo's truth (as opposed to the

ABOVE: Muslim prayer beads on top of the grave of a young man who died during the civil war

Newspeak version) is that the city has been the scene not of a civil war but of a war of aggression by the Serbs; that if the Serbs do once and for all →

 If the culture of Sarajevo dies, then we are all its orphans

A city, a people, does not have an unlimited supply of spirit

→ cease their bombardments, it will be because they have already seized 'their' quarter of the city, forcing a de facto partition on what should have remained united; and that the outside world seems bent on imposing on this hybrid city the 'logic', the 'reality', of ethnicity, and on giving the aggressor the spoils of war.

Sarajevo's truth is that its citizens, who reject definition by religion or confession, who wish to be simply Bosnians, have for their pains been labelled by the outside world as 'Muslims'. It is instructive to imagine how things might have gone in former Yugoslavia if the Bosnians had been Christians and the Serbs had been Muslims, even Muslims 'in name only'. Would Europe have supported a 'Serbian Muslim' carve-up of the defunct state? It's only a guess, but I guess that it would not. Which being true, it must also be true that the 'Muslim' tag is part of the reason for Europe's indifference to Sarajevo's fate.

I have not been to Sarajevo — I have wanted to, but it has thus far proved impossible to arrange — but I have in recent months met three of its many extraordinary citizens: Zdravko Grebo, of the radio station that is the city's voice and conscience, Radio Zid; Haris Pasovic, a man bursting with projects, the man who brought about last year's Sarajevo Film Festival — and what an achievement, to stage a festival of over a hundred movies in the midst of such a war!; and Kemal Kurspahic, editor of Sarajevo's battling newspaper Oslobodjenje. They taught me a further, simple truth: that to define the people of besieged Sarajevo simply as entities in need of basic supplies would be to visit upon them a second privation: by reducing them to mere statistical victimhood, it would deny them their personalities, their individuality, their idiosyncrasies — in short, their humanity. When UNPROFOR officers limit the number of personal letters that can be carried in or out of the city; when permission for artists to visit the city is refused, as Pasovic can attest it has been, and when Western government spokesmen avow that culture is a luxury in wartime, this denial of Sarajevo's humanity is precisely the crime they are committing.

Grebo, limping from a wound, overwhelmingly impressive in his gentle dignity — seems to embody Sarajevo's spirit; Pasovic, its determination to keep its culture alive. Kurspahic is more melancholy, and a recent essay by his Oslobodjenje colleague Zlatko Dizdarevic expresses the city's present mood. "Sarajevo no longer believes anyone ... Sarajevo has seen everything there is to see till now, and it has felt the worst there is to feel upon its own skin. The results are obvious. Until six or seven months ago, every true Sarajevan needed at least an hour to walk from the Holiday Inn to the cathedral. You had to stop and say hello to so many people, to ask after everyone. Now that same distance takes just 15 minutes because no one stops. No one has anything left to ask anyone." He tells of a boy whose father was killed, and who now says, "Last night I dreamt about my father. I dreamt about him on purpose." "Somebody will one day have to watch out", Dizdarevic warns, "for boys from Sarajevo who dream about their murdered fathers on purpose."

A city, a people, does not have an unlimited supply of spirit, not even this city, this people. Will the secular 'Muslims' of today become vengeful fundamentalists of tomorrow, dreaming on purpose of the dead? So far, by all accounts, hard-line Islamism has made amazingly small strides in the city, but that's just so far. Will Sarajevo be saved? Sarajevo scarcely believes it will. But the fact remains: that the fight for the survival of the unique culture of Sarajevo is a fight for what matters most to us about our own.

I have just seen a strange short film in which a man driving down the sniper-infested streets of Sarajevo repeats, over and over, like a mantra, my name. Salman Rushdie, Salman Rushdie, Salman Rushdie; Salman Rushdie; Salman Rushdie, Salman Rushdie; Salman Rushdie, Salman Rushdie; Salman Rushdie, Salman Rushdie. Is he chanting it to remind him of his danger, or as a kind of spell to keep him safe? I hope it is the latter, and it is in that spirit of sympathetic magic that I have begun to murmur, under my breath, the name of this unknown city of which I declare myself to be an imaginary citizen:

Sarajevo, Sarajevo, Sarajevo,
Sarajevo,
Sarajevo, Sarajevo,
Sarajevo, Sarajevo, Sarajevo,
Sarajevo, Sarajevo,
Sarajevo ✖

Salman Rushdie is a multi-award-winning author, essayist and academic. This article originally appeared in volume 23, issue 1, May 1994

51(01):86/88|DOI:10.1177/03064220221084442

When the 90s drew to a close, the world was still coming to terms with the bloody events that had defined the decade. Index's network of on-the-ground correspondents came across stories rarely found elsewhere

1992-2001

Laughing in Rwanda

FRANÇOIS VINSOT reported on the first time he heard people laugh in Rwanda after the genocide – and why in this instance it was the tonic everyone needed

SIX YEARS AFTER the genocide, in a street in Kigali, a young girl was huddled on the ground yelling gibberish, throwing dust at passers-by. A crowd gathered and an indignant shopkeeper moved the sick girl out of the way, which only made her yell even louder. A woman passing by relieved the tension by laughing and a few others followed suit. Everybody continued on their way, leaving this bothersome person to whatever her fate might be. I couldn't see the funny side: all I saw was her pain, but then, it was not my story. I suppose I must have missed the point.

I've heard lots of stories told by Rwandans, stories that were horrible, bizarre, often tragic, but I don't remember ever hearing a funny story, nor of any Rwandan comedian.

And then, one evening, the people of Kigali were invited to a show put together by artists from all over Africa. It was devoted to the idea of remembrance and the duty to maintain a written record, and it was, of course, focused on the genocide. Not, on the face of it, the sort of thing to make you split your sides. The text was a montage of testimony by survivors and, from the outset, the audience found it harrowing. It was one of those official functions where it's as important to be

seen as it is to watch the show, and it managed to take everyone by surprise.

There were some very explicit scenes of fake violence and accounts of atrocities so minutely detailed that they sounded like messages from beyond the grave. All this was interspersed with pounding musical improvisations, spotlights cutting through the darkness like machineguns, and presented in a monotone by an old man who seemed to carry the weight of the world on his shoulders. This continued until a character emerged from the audience and interrupted him. He was an imposing, wide-eyed giant of a man who seemed to creep along like a leopard and swallow up all the available space. To begin with, he spoke like a raving madman, and there were one or two laughs from the audience, then a few more. He stopped dead, stared into the audience, trying to see who it was that had laughed. Then he burst into uncontrollable laughter. It was not the laughter of communication but it carried more significance than any cry; so much so that the other actors gathered round him, waiting to see what he might have to say. The man seemed to grow calmer for a moment. Then he hoisted himself on to a table and said: "We are all Rwandans on the outside, but they're different

outsides, and because we're all coming from all these outsides, we've forgotten where the inside is and we're all going crazy. For example, on the roads, we don't know which side to drive on anymore! Those who come from Uganda play it careful and keep to the left, those coming from Burundi play it safe and keep to the right. That kind of madness is really dangerous, yet it would be so simple if everybody were just to drive in the middle of the road!"

Almost without noticing it, many Rwandans had just heard their first funny story for a long time and they burst into laughter and applause and waved their arms about for joy. The actor continued to act the part of a fool but his words became serious, tragic once more. It was no good, though: the minute he opened his mouth the crowd would laugh and shout things out to him. It had taken a first-class actor from Cote d'Ivoire to dare, after all this time, to make the Rwandans laugh. That laughter still echoes in my memory like some painful surprise. ✖

François Vinsot was a former Africa correspondent for the BBC. This article was in Volume 29, Issue 6, November 2000

51(01):89/89|DOI:10.1177/03064220221084511

2 0 0 2 | 2 0 1 1

2002-2011

The fatwa made publishers lose their nerve

Former editor **JO GLANVILLE** reflects on how insulting Islam became a recurring subject for Index. In this essay, she shows how some issues are not black-and-white and demonstrates why it's our duty to continue to debate and to challenge

N 2008 I edited an issue of Index on Censorship marking the 20th anniversary of The Satanic Verses' publication. It included an essay by Peter Mayer, chief executive of Penguin when the book was published. He had never written about it before, so this was a bit of a coup.

No publisher today would give the go-ahead to a novel that took imaginative liberties with Islam. In an essay in the same issue, the writer Kenan Malik, then a trustee of Index, identified the trend of censorship since Salman Rushdie's novel was published as evidence that "the fatwa has effectively been internalised". We have all succumbed to our own inner censor without any prompting from an ayatollah. It has since become routine for publishers to revise or drop books on any subject, never mind Islam, that are perceived to cause offence. Even an inoffensive book whose author has

been accused of outraging public morality in his or her professional life may run the risk of getting pulped. Where once publishers were in the vanguard of the fight against censorship and pushing the boundaries they are now part of a culture of self-censorship.

"It is this idea of speech as intrinsically good that has been transformed," wrote Malik in Index. "Today, in liberal eyes, free speech is as likely to be seen as a threat to liberty as its shield." His observation, after more than a decade, remains utterly contemporary.

The Satanic Verses marked the watershed. A religious leader calling for the murder of a writer (as well as everyone involved with the publication) was of course shocking. But the number of British voices that supported censorship at the time, and abandoned Rushdie, was also astonishing. John le Carré wrote: "Nobody has a God-given

right to insult a great religion and be published with impunity." Roald Dahl called Rushdie "a dangerous opportunist". The Archbishop of Canterbury urged the BBC to drop a programme about the novel.

Mayer's essay for Index remains a rousing reminder of what a commitment to freedom of expression looks like:

"At ad hoc, in-house discussions and at formal board meetings, we chose to frame the argument as one not only respecting the central importance of free speech, but transcending the case of this one book. The fate of the book affected the future of free inquiry, without which there would be no publishing as we knew it, but also, by extension, no civil society as we knew it."

Mayer himself faced death threats, blood-stained warnings through his letterbox and his own child was threatened.

A year later, I interviewed the Danish academic Jytte Klausen for Index about her book The Cartoons that Shook the World, which was the first scholarly examination of the Danish cartoons controversy. The Danish newspaper Jyllands Posten published caricatures of the Prophet Mohammed in 2005. Klausen argued in the book that the protests and violence that followed the cartoons' publication took place in regions that were already hotspots: the cartoons were a pretext and not the cause of conflict. Klausen's plan had been to include a facsimile of the cartoons as they were originally published around the margins of an editorial. Her publisher, Yale University Press, ultimately decided not to include the cartoons in the book for fear of the violence that might follow. Christopher Hitchens described Yale's decision as "the latest and perhaps the worst   →

No publisher today would give the go-ahead to a novel that took imaginative liberties with Islam

→ episode in the steady surrender to religious extremism". I wanted to include the cartoons alongside Klausen's interview as a stand against censorship. The board of Index was consulted by the chief executive and did not give me permission to publish them.

Jonathan Dimbleby , then chair of the board,went public with the reasons for the decision, alongside Malik's dissenting view. Dimbleby pointed out that the home of a publisher had been firebombed the previous year for publishing the novel The Jewel of Medina, which had been criticised for its portrayal of Islam. The board was concerned for the safety of Index on Censorship's staff and for the organisations that shared a

The home of a publisher had been firebombed the previous year for publishing the novel

building with it. Malik criticised the decision as an act of "pre-emptive" censorship: "Index is not only helping strengthen the culture of censorship, it is also weakening its authority to challenge that culture."

The threat is still real. In 2020, the French schoolteacher Samuel Paty was murdered after showing his schoolchildren caricatures published by the satirical newspaper Charlie Hebdo, whose staff were murdered in an horrific attack in 2015. The urge

to censor, meanwhile, has become entrenched. Fourteen years after the Index anniversary issue on The Satanic Verses, the decision not to publish in the name of protecting minorities and not causing offence is no longer surprising. Resisting that trend remains one of the biggest tests. ✖

Jo Glanville was editor-in-chief at Index between 2006 and 2012

51(01):91/92|DOI:10.1177/03064220221084552

ABOVE: Writer Salman Rushdie is interviewed by the BBC's David Frost in the aftermath of the fatwa, which continues to impact some publishing decisions to this day

The new century saw a bolder Russia under the increasingly repressive Vladimir Putin. Journalists were targeted –
but one brave woman stood out: the internationally acclaimed war reporter murdered for her sins in 2006

2002-2011

Standing alone

Russian journalist **ANNA POLITKOVSKAYA** was a lone voice reporting on Chechnya, which
even now remains near-impossible to cover. She described the war on the ground

JUST BEFORE MY last trip to Chechnya in mid-September my colleagues at Novaya Gazeta began to receive threats and were told to pass on the message that I shouldn't go to Chechnya any more. If I did, my life would be in danger. As always, our paper has its "own people" on the general staff and the ministry of defence — people who broadly share our views. We spoke to people at the ministry but, despite their advice, I did go back to Chechnya, only to find myself blockaded in the capital, Grozny. The city was sealed off after a series of strange events. Controls were so tight you couldn't even move between different districts within the city, let alone make your way out of Grozny on foot. On that day, 17 September, a helicopter carrying a commission headed by Major-General Anatoly Pozdnyakov from the general staff in Moscow was shot down directly over the city. He was engaged in work quite unprecedented for a soldier in Chechnya.

Only an hour before the helicopter was shot down, he told me the task of his commission was to gather data on crimes committed by the military, analyse their findings, put them in some order and submit the information for the president's consideration. Nothing

of the kind had been done before. Their helicopter was shot down almost exactly over the city centre. All the members of the commission perished and, since they were already on their way to Khankala airbase to take a plane back to Moscow, so did all the material they had collected. That part of the story was published by Novaya Gazeta. Before the 19 September issue was sent to the printers, our chief editor Dmitry Muratov was summoned to the ministry of defence (or so I understand) and asked to explain how on earth such allegations could be made. He gave them an answer, after which the pressure really began. There should be no publication, he was told. Nevertheless, he decided to go ahead, publishing a very truncated version of what I had written.

At that point, the same people at the ministry who had claimed our report was false now conceded it was true. But they began to warn of new threats: they had learned that certain people had run out of patience with my articles. It was, in other words, the

same kind of conversation as before my last trip to Chechnya. Then we heard that a particular officer, a Lieutenant Larin, whom I had described in print as a war criminal, was sending letters to the newspaper and similar notes to the ministry. The deaths and torture of several people lie on his conscience and the evidence against him is incontrovertible. Soon there were warnings that I'd better stay at home. Meanwhile, the internal affairs ministry would track down and arrest this self-appointed military hitman, and deputy minister Vasilyev would himself take charge of the operation.

I was supposed to remain at our apartment and go nowhere. But they made no progress in finding Larin, and I began to realise that this was simply another way of forcing me to stop work. The newspaper decided I should leave the country until the editors were sure I could again live a normal life and resume my work.

The paper was forced to omit from my story the sort of detail that is vital to the credibility of an article like →

They had learned that certain people had run out of patience with my articles

→ this, which suggested the military themselves had downed the helicopter. All my subsequent difficulties began with those details. If these details surface, the ministry of defence warned our chief editor, that's the end for you...

In fact, since I was moving around the city at the time, I can personally testify to what happened, as can others who were there with me. And these were no ordinary citizens: among them were Chechen policemen and Grozny Energy Company employees who, like me, were trapped inside the city. FSB [former KGB] General Platonov was also there. Currently, he is a deputy to Anatoly Chubais, chief executive of United Energy Systems, a key Kremlin player throughout the 1990s and a hawk on Chechnya. All these saw and knew exactly what I know. Platonov is not only Chubais's deputy but remains

BELOW: A rally in Pushkin Square, Moscow, in 2008, on the second anniversary of the murder of Anna Politkovskaya

a deputy to FSB director Patrushev (in early 2001, the 'antiterrorist operation' in Chechnya was transferred from the military command of the Combined Forces Group to the FSB and its director Patrushev in Moscow placed in overall charge). No one else saw and knew as much about what happened as Platonov — he couldn't help but see it. Not one person was allowed into the city centre after 9am that morning. And yet a helicopter was downed there.

Different branches of the military are split over future policy in Chechnya. There are good reasons why the recent public statements of defence ministry spokesmen all repeat the same phrases: 'We deny the possibility of negotiations'; 'It's out of the question'; 'We are just doing our job.' Indeed they are: their 'sweep and cleanse' operations have become even more brutal. Let us suppose that those representing certain other branches of the military on the ground in Chechnya are pursuing a rather different policy. That is where you should seek the

reason for the deaths of all the commission members. I'm just a small cog in that machine — someone who happened to be in the thick of events when no other journalists were around.

Those who want to continue fighting seem to have the upper hand; they represent the more powerful section within the so-called CFG, the Combined Forces Group. To avoid repetition of the disastrous lack of coordination between ministries of defence and internal affairs and the FSB during the first Chechen conflict in 1994—96, overall command of army, police and other paramilitary and special units (CFG) in the present war was given to the military. Although the FSB supposedly now exercise overall control of the 'anti-terrorist operation', the military are too strong for them. On the fateful day the helicopter was downed and the commission perished, not even servicemen and officers were permitted to enter the central, cordoned-off area of Grozny. Only defence ministry officials were allowed

through. Even FSB and ministry of justice people were kept out; that was extraordinary. No one was permitted to enter the area where the helicopter was about to fall: representatives of other military bodies and organisations, even ranking officers, had no right to go there.

I don't think we should expect too much from the defence ministry, nor from President Putin [in the light of the US-led campaign in Afghanistan]. He has received carte blanche to take the measures and employ the forces he considers necessary in Chechnya. I'm thinking of Prime Minister Blair's recent activities and words spoken by Chancellor Schroeder when Putin was visiting Germany. As you know, it was then said that Europe should re-examine its stance on Chechnya.

Their position was already pretty feeble and bore no relation to the real state of affairs in Chechnya and the abuse of human rights there. If, however, they are going to alter their position, then it's clear what will happen. In practical terms they'll support Putin. Whatever he does will be fine by them. I think he's been working steadily and persistently towards that end for some time. And I'm sure he'll make good use of it now. Not for the first time in the present war, there's been a battle to see whose nerve is stronger. Putin held back [over the West's 'anti-terrorist operation'] for some while: we shan't support the Northern Alliance in Afghanistan, he said, but we'll offer them back-up. Then he agreed to supply them with arms and, evidently, advisers. In exchange he received a free hand in Chechnya. That's the way things are likely to go, I'm afraid.

I can't say when it will happen, but whatever happens there will be a more intensive 'liquidation of Chechen partisans'. As always in Russia,

People in my country have no protection from this lawless regime

however, it all depends on the methods to be used. What will the 'liquidation of Chechen bandits' amount to this time? Will they herd everyone else into concentration camps or hold repeated sweep operations in all the population centres in Chechnya?

I can't answer for Chechen President Maskhadov, but will offer a brief analysis of his actions. In my view, he is doing nothing whatsoever. He has retreated into his shell and is thinking, to the exclusion of all else, about his own immediate future — he's forgotten the Chechen nation. Just as the federal authorities in Moscow have abandoned the Chechens, so now have the other side. The nation has to fend for itself, with no leadership or protection. It survives as best it can. If people need to take revenge for their tortured and murdered relatives, they will. If they need to say nothing, they'll keep their mouths shut. In such circumstances, which are the equivalent of a civil war, and under continuing pressure from the federal forces, no one today can say whom the Chechen nation would vote for if elections were held. No one now has any idea whom they'd elect and in that respect everyone has committed the same enormous mistake.

Maskhadov has obviously been driven into a corner. But the struggle for independence has become an obsession with him: he will hear of nothing else. I don't really understand what use independence will be to him, when he, Shamil Basayev and his immediate bodyguard are all that's left. The first duty of a president is to fight for the well-being of his nation.

I have my own president and it makes no difference that I personally did not vote for Putin. He remains the most important figure in the Russian state. And I'd like him to enable me, and everyone else, to live a normal life. I'm referring to the laws that should govern our existence. I find myself in a situation, however, where no one gives a damn how I survive. I'm cut off from my family. I don't know what will happen in the future to my two children. It is not law that rules Russia today. There's no person and no organisation to which you can turn and be certain that the laws have any force.

I have no thoughts about my future. And that's the worst of all. I just want everything to change so I can go back and live in Moscow again. I can't imagine spending any length of time here. Or in any other place, for that matter. I must do all in my power to return to Moscow. But I have no idea when that will be. If people in my country have no protection from this lawless regime, that means I survive here while others are dying. Over the last year I've been in that position too often. People who were my witnesses and informants in Chechnya have died for that reason, and that reason alone, as soon as I left their homes. If it again proves the case, then how can I go on living abroad while others are dying in my place? ✖

Anna Politkovskaya was a US-born Russian journalist, writer, and human rights activist. This article appeared in Index Volume 31, issue 1, 2002

51(01):93/95|DOI:10.1177/03064220221084546

CREDIT: Oleg Kozyrev/PA

The 11 September terrorist attacks changed the global landscape. The pages of Index filled up with profiles of prisoners in Guatanamo Bay, reports from Iraq and Afghanistan and commentary on the "war on terror"

2002-2011

Fortress America

In the wake of 9/11, US Border Patrol ramped up security and surveillance of those entering and leaving the country. RUBÉN MARTÍNEZ reported powerfully from the US-Mexican border

LAST SUMMER I stood on the banks of the Rio Grande in Big National Park, Texas, and for a few moments I had trouble reconciling the fact that for some 1,000 miles the river — known to Mexicans as the Rio Bravo, the raging river — forms what is perhaps the most contested border in the world today.

It was August, and it was hot, yet there were no hordes of migrants gathered on the Mexican side readying to ford the slow, knee-deep waters (at many other points along the river, the waters can be deep and the current can be powerful enough to drag you under). Neither was there a phalanx of US Border Patrol agents waiting on this side. There was no evidence of the battery of surveillance equipment omnipresent at popular illegal crossings near San Diego, Tucson or El Paso — video cameras and seismic sensors, helicopters and unmanned 'drone' aircraft (the same kind currently being used in Iraq and Afghanistan).

Indeed, there wasn't a fence, not even an obelisk announcing my side

as American or the other Mexican. There was only the gentle rush of the river, the summer sun sparkling on the wavelets, and all around me — in the canyon cut by millions of river-years, in the stratified heights of the Sierra del Carmen, in the very sand I stood upon — the geological evidence that the land was here long before we or the border were, and would be here long after this very human frontier is lost to time.

In the midst of my reverie, two teenagers and an adult man appeared on the opposite bank. They called out a greeting to which I responded. The boys jumped into the river and came across to my side, clambering up on to the rocks above the waterline. They had now officially and illegally entered the United States of America. I took a quick look behind me; still no Border Patrol in sight.

The crew introduced themselves as denizens of Boquillas del Carmen, a modest town on the Mexican side, within plain view of the American shore. The older of the boys fished a plastic ziplock baggie out of his

pocket. Inside was a stamped letter bearing an American address — a relative living on this side. He asked me the favour of dropping it off at the post office a mile down the road. If he attempted to do so himself, he explained, he might indeed be apprehended as an 'illegal alien'.

Now the younger of the boys piped up and said that tomorrow was his birthday and would I do him the favour of buying some chocolate frosting at the general store (next to the post office)? I told him I would, and I did, though later I wondered how many 'birthdays' he'd had recently.

The father of the boys never completely crossed the river, preferring to sit on a rock about 25 feet from shore. He told me that things hadn't always been this way. Gringos and Mexicans had moved back and forth at will, he said, dating back to 1848, when the Treaty of Guadalupe Hidalgo designated the river the boundary between the United States and Mexico. In the wake of 9/11, the Border Patrol had suddenly clamped down on this

 There wasn't a fence, not even an obelisk announcing my side as American or the other Mexican

little 'informal' crossing. Presumably, Al-Qaida was about to smuggle dirty bombs across the Rio Grande.

Dragging this region into the post-9/11 national security state devastated the livelihoods of residents in Boquillas. For decades, the town had subsisted largely on the trickle of American tourists ferried over on canoes and hosted at a couple of modest bars. Likewise, Mexicans had shopped and worked across the river in the US.

Before departing, the boys asked if I wanted to cross over to their side

for a visit. I looked at the river, at the village rising from the sand on the opposite bank and at my new friends. And I realised that for the first time in my life, I was seeing the line between the US and Mexico the way Mexicans generally see it. If I crossed the river, I'd become an illegal American in Mexico. And if I returned to the US at the same spot, I'd be an illegal American in America.

It is one of the great regrets of my life that I didn't cross. Quixotic or not, I should have jumped across that river

ABOVE: A rider crosses the border near Boquillas del Carmen, Mexico, in 2017

– because in the end, that's what it is, a river, and rivers are meant to be crossed like mountains are to be climbed.

Afterwards, I began to think that this is precisely the real problem at the US—Mexico line today: that we, Americans, don't cross over and see the border as the citizens of the developing world see it, those who live in the global realm, a world without borders. Americans do get around, of course ➔

The proposal was lambasted by advocates of immigrants' rights as institutionalised exploitation

→ — but as tourists, as consumers of the 'other'. From the migrant point of view, borders are permeable rather than solid, moving rather than fixed, politically expedient rather than morally imperative.

In America, we speak of migrants as 'illegals' because they have broken the letter of immigration law. But from the migrant point of view, US immigration policy seems to be breaking the laws of nature — or at least of globalisation. For fiscal year 2004, the federal government has budgeted over US$9 billion for border protection. Credible politicians talk of building a wall along the entire southern frontier, the Great Wall of America.

And yet, to date not a single suspected terrorist has been apprehended trying to make illegal entry on the US—Mexico line. (Most national security experts agree that the much more likely scenario is for terrorists to attempt entry along the largely unguarded Canadian border; as for the 9/11 hijackers, all entered legally on tourist or student visas.)

The most concrete result of a decade's worth of restrictive immigration policy is not a more 'secure' nation but the death of thousands of undocumented immigrants. Several walls – none of which runs for more than 20 miles – have been raised at the most heavily trafficked illicit crossings but they haven't stopped or even stemmed the flow. Like water following the path of least resistance, the smugglers push their human cargo around the walls and thus into much more isolated and hazardous desert terrain. Every year

since the first wall was built (at San Diego in 1994), the number of migrant deaths at the line has increased.

This year, by all accounts, will see a massive increase in migrant crossings, apprehensions and deaths. At the beginning of the year, President George W Bush proposed a 'guest worker' programme. The proposal was lambasted by advocates of immigrants' rights as institutionalised exploitation (there would be no guarantee of citizenship after a worker's 'contract' expired, no mechanism for family reunification, and the reform would only target immigrants in the lowest wage brackets), but for many other observers — in particular the migrants themselves — Bush had taken a step, however tentative, in the right direction; and many who'd been waiting for just such a signal decided it was the right time to cross over.

Unfortunately for the migrants, the Bush plan is more of a symbolic election-year stunt — apparently an appeal to those Latino citizens in the US (many of whom once crossed illegally themselves) who hold the proverbial 'swing vote' power in several key states. It is highly unlikely that there will be a vote on Bush's plan, or on the Democratic Party's more liberal alternatives, this year.

But the toll is already obvious on the border. Some 84 migrants have perished on the Arizona stretch of the border since last October, a rate triple that of the previous 12 months. On average, one migrant a day perishes on the US—Mexico line; in the last decade, well over 3,000 migrants have died attempting entry.

I have written about the border for going on 20 years now, and while I admit I probably indulged rhetorical excess back in the 1980s when I compared the situation here to the old divide between East and West Berlin, today the comparison is rather more precise. With billions of dollars' worth of technology, the presence of some 10,000 Border Patrol agents — in addition to Customs, Drug Enforcement Agency and other federal officers — we are finally achieving in deed what restrictionist politicians have envisioned with their rhetoric: Fortress America.

The problem for the wall-builders is that the migrants continue to cross anyway. The Border Patrol tallied some 1,400 detentions in south-eastern Arizona on a single day last month. The general rale of thumb has long been that for each migrant detained, another gets through.

A long hot summer is predicted for the drought-stricken American Southwest. A new record number of deaths will be set. The politicians will try to proclaim success in 'sealing the border'. But the migrants by their very numbers — those who die, those apprehended and turned away, those that make it into the interior — will tell us otherwise. ✖

Rubén Martínez is an award-winning writer, teacher and performer. He is the author of, among other titles, The New Americans and Crossing Over: A Mexican Family on the Migrant Trail. This article appeared in issue 33, volume 3, 2004

51(01):96/98|DOI:10.1177/03064220221084549

Cartoonists are the canary in the coalmine. Throughout its half-century, Index has given them space, particularly those persecuted and forced to flee their homelands. And there has always been room, too, for extraordinary British artists such as Martin Rowson, whose work from 2009 graces this page

2002-2011

51(01):99/99|DOI:10.1177/03064220221084548

....

China's global power status was cemented in the 2000s. Hopes that its new wealth would equate to more freedom for the people rapidly vanished. Instead, as the decade advanced, the reverse happened

.... **2002-2011** ....

Conspiracy of silence

Artist AI WEIWEI's critical commentary and campaigning have led to him being arrested, imprisoned and assaulted. In 2009, Index published a blogpost that the Chinese government did not want people to read

AST MAY, THE celebrated Chinese artist Ai Weiwei reported that his blog had suddenly been closed down. He had just posted details about plain-clothes policemen following him and intimidating his family and associates. Even his mother had been interrogated.

Following the devastating earthquake in Sichuan last year, Ai Weiwei had begun a campaign investigating why so many schools had collapsed. He researched and published on his blog the names of 4,000 schoolchildren who died in the disaster.

In August, he travelled to Chengdu in Sichuan to support the activist Tan Zuoren, who had been accused of 'undermining the authority of the state' after calling for an investigation into the collapse of school buildings in the earthquake. On 12 August at 3am, about 30 armed police stormed the hotel where Ai Weiwei was staying. He was assaulted and then arrested along with ten of his volunteers to prevent them from attending Tan Zuoren's trial.

In September, while preparing for a show in Munich, Ai Weiwei was admitted to hospital and underwent brain surgery for a haematoma – the condition was believed to be the delayed physical effects of the incident in Chengdu. Ai Weiwei's installation 'Remembering', commemorating the deaths of the Sichuan schoolchildren, opened at the Haus der Kunst gallery in Munich in October.

We're delighted to publish one of Ai Weiwei's censored blogs, below. It was first published on 16 May.

How could we have degenerated to this?

They are arrogant enough to believe that stolen authority could change the facts or alter the will of others. At the same time they are fragile enough to believe that one dissenting voice could bring down their mighty force.

This is because they don't believe that when the public truly has the power to cast their own vote, that their disreputable names will be written upon any of the ballots.

They have already lost hope in themselves, and they don't want the voice of the people to be heard; but they don't allow the people to hear this or know that people who think like them might exist.

You can think it, but you can't speak it. No one else knows what you're thinking; when the pain and despair belong exclusively to you, it cannot be a threat. Of course, you'd be best off without the ability for independent thought, only then will there be greater safety, more harmony.

If you cannot improve on your own reality, then you can only rely on destroying the reality of others to maintain balance. If we never knew about Sanlu milk powder, never heard of Weng'an [where riots followed alleged cover-up of girl's death in 2008], Gansu [where protests took place in 2008], Tibet or Beichuan [a town that lost half its population in the earthquake], of course we would be much more peaceful. Supposing we didn't understand the world, it would seem much smaller. If we didn't know the earth was round, we would abandon all hope on the road. We don't understand our rights, and thus believe in saviours, believe that all death was meant to be, believe that we should be grateful for life, that central television is not base and indecent, and that none of this is evil. If we did know, we would be able to imagine the world could be another way, or that being an evil-doer is not inevitably a prerequisite to power.

Imagine if you knew nothing of the outside world, the rest of the world would take shape as whatever others were willing to tell you. They are selling you out, and you don't feel the sting, maybe you're even helping them count the money they sold you out for. Your ignorance and your

silence are the price you pay for the security of your lifestyle, it becomes an important reason why you exist, it is the price of maintaining the status quo in your republic, the grand, benevolent mother.

But if you cannot see or hear, you know absolutely nothing. Even if you know, you are unable to speak out – speak out and you'll disappear. It doesn't matter if you are suffering, joyous, melancholy, without an imagination, without sympathy, without the desire or potential to change, you are an outstanding example of a modern slave. You won't inquire into the nature of this world, but isn't that just what you need? You are able to eat and drink, bear sons and daughters, abide by the

law and pay taxes. You are supporting a horde of people who regard you as part of a flatulent mass of citizens, people whose main job is to squander your wealth through corruption, while keeping it all a dark secret and misleading you in order to sustain your misfortune. Your misfortune becomes the good luck of others; this issue is a little complicated, it's probably best if you didn't know about it.

Neither the people nor the working class can exist without individual voices or the free exchange of information, and when there can be no common interests for humanity, you have no existence.

Authentic societal transformation can never be achieved in such a

ABOVE: Chinese artist Ai Weiwei with his work Sunflower Seeds, which was displayed at the Tate Modern in London, 2010

place, as the first step in social transformation is to regain the power of freedom of expression.

A society lacking in freedom of expression is dark and you can't see its bottom; the blackest places begin to look as if they are bright. ✖

Ai Weiwei is a Chinese artist, documentarian and activist. This article was translated by Lee Ambrozy. It was published in volume 38, issue 4, 2009. © Ai Weiwei

51(01):100/101|DOI:10.1177/03064220221084545

2 0 1 2 | 2 0 2 1

To better days

RACHAEL JOLLEY reflects on the hope that kept the light burning in times of darkness during her seven years as editor of Index

ABOVE: A demonstration of the Mothers of the Plaza de Mayo in Buenos Aires in 2013. To this day, people are still trying to find out what happened to their relatives who disappeared in Argentina in the 1970s

"WHAT DOES NOT change over the decades is the desire of those in power to limit information which might be unsuitable to their needs." These were the words of Argentinian-Scottish journalist Andrew Graham-Yooll in 2015, reflecting on his years reporting from Argentina in the pages of Index on Censorship.

The faces of the powerful have changed since he wrote that, but their desire never will. Look around you. Consult the history books. There are plenty of lessons there.

Graham-Yooll reported from Buenos Aires in the 1970s. Despite getting badly beaten up, he kept working and smuggled documents out to Index and the Telegraph to tell the world what terrifying things were happening there. He kept a list of the disappeared – something that official forces tried desperately to stop anyone knowing. He went on to become editor at Index and, decades later, his legacy is still with us.

The struggle continues today for the families of those murdered men and women. They are still trying to find out what happened to their sons and daughters and to the children that were taken away from them. Now DNA tests are helping those grandparents find them.

After Graham-Yooll died in 2019, playwright Ariel Dorfman – another friend of Index – wrote to me about him: "For a man on such a serious mission, of such vast courage, always so close to horror and death and sorrow, Andrew

was vitality itself, with a wonderful smile and sense of humour."

Looking back on my seven years at the helm of Index, I saw that same seriousness and dark humour in other contributors who kept on reporting even when their lives were under threat.

The struggle to get important words out of prison has been part of Index's work since its first issue and this continued during my editorship. We published poems written by Nazanin Zaghari-Ratcliffe, the Iranian-British citizen who was arrested and imprisoned in 2015 before boarding a plane in Tehran. These were smuggled out of jail alongside poems from her inmate, Golrokh Ebrahimi Iraee.

Zaghari-Ratcliffe's husband, Richard, told me later how important it felt to Nazanin at the time that her work was being published professionally.

In 2019, the magazine was able to interview imprisoned Turkish journalist Ahmet Altan and publish an extract of his forthcoming book in English for the first time. He let us know why it mattered. "Tell readers that their existence gives thousands of people in prison like me the strength to go on," he said.

It's impossible to forget the day we heard of the murder of staff at the French magazine Charlie Hebdo. Index had to react to this attack on freedom of expression just over 200 miles away. We contacted reporters and editors all over the world, from Dublin to Brazil to Johannesburg, that day

and they all wanted to join Index in making statements about the essential role of the freedom of the media and the need to protect it.

In the next issue, we ran a special section with essays from Dorfman, playwright David Edgar, TV writer Arthur Matthews and journalists Richard Sambrook, Raymond Louw and Hannah Leung. These important pieces were later turned into a book.

In the week that I write this, in early 2022, a defender of human rights has been killed in Mexico – Verónica Guerrero, a lawyer who led local opposition to an unauthorised rubbish dump in Tonalá, Jalisco. And we are starting to read of more murders – of at least 20 human rights defenders and four journalists in Latin America in January 2022.

The threats are not going away. They are local and global. Some journalists I commissioned just a few years ago would now not dare to write under their own names. Writers disappear or are frightened into stopping their work, but the brave and the determined don't stop hoping for better days. ✖

Rachael Jolley was editor-in-chief at Index from 2013 until 2020

DOI:10.1177/03064220221084571

On the 400th anniversary of the death of Shakespeare, we devoted an issue to the resounding influence of the Bard and how his plays have been used around the world to sneak past censors and take on the authorities

2012-2021

Plays, protests and the censor's pencil

Shakespeare was no stranger to censorship from the Elizabethan and Jacobean police states. Actor and writer **SIMON CALLOW** charted how the Bard's plays amused monarchs and dictators but also prompted their anger

WHEN I WAS at drama school in the early 1970s, there was a middle-aged Iranian on the directors' course called Rokneddin. He'd been ejected from the Shah's Iran for staging subversive productions. Rokneddin was no political firebrand: he had simply tried to put on Shakespeare's history plays, which, like all plays in which a king died, were banned in Iran under the Pahlavi dynasty. The plays reminded people all too vividly that the divine right of kings had severe limits.

After the revolution Rokneddin went back, and tried to ply his trade again: this time he disappeared into prison, never to be seen again. At the time the Shah's proscription was seen as the act of an exotic tyrant. That is not to say the English monarchy has always celebrated Shakespeare's entire canon. During the period of George III's madness in 18th-century Britain, King Lear was banished from the stage because the parallels were too obvious.

Shakespeare has had this unique symbolic significance for a long time. From the end of the 17th century, initially in England, and then increasingly in translation across

Europe, his stock began its inexorable rise, until he was acclaimed across the whole of the Western world, to a degree never before or since equalled by any other writer. His work was a mirror in which people of widely diverse cultures could see themselves – in Scandinavia, in the Middle East, in Spain and the Americas.

He was fervently admired in France, despite his barbaric non-conformism to the laws of classical drama. In Germany and Russia, he was clasped to those nations' bosoms, claimed by them as, respectively, German and Russian. Shakespeare's perceived universality – which expanded in the 19th and 20th centuries to include Africa, India, China and Japan – inevitably meant that his work would be recruited to embody the positions of various political and philosophical groupings. And with this came, equally

inevitably, censorship and suppression.

Not that Shakespeare was a stranger to censorship in his own time, living and working as he did in, first, the Elizabethan, then the Jacobean, police state where people's actions and their very thoughts were under constant surveillance. The theatre in which he worked was heavily patrolled by the Master of the Revels, who was charged not only with providing entertainment for the monarch, but with averting controversy, particularly in the sphere of foreign relations. Sometimes this meant deleting matters offensive to allies, sometimes it meant suppressing criticism – or perceived criticism – of the crown, sometimes, more rarely, it meant eliminating morally or sexually offensive material. The theatre was a minefield of significance for dramatists and their companies. Even a simple dig at German and Spanish dress

> During George III's madness in 18th-century Britain, King Lear was banished from the stage

had to be cut from Much Ado About Nothing because of contemporary diplomatic sensitivities. But the reach of the censor went well beyond the explicit. The characters and narratives in Shakespeare's plays were perceived symbolically, as commentaries on current events.

In 1601 Shakespeare and his company, the Lord Chamberlain's Men, ran into danger on this account: the Earl of Essex and his supporter, the Earl of Southampton, Shakespeare's patron and possibly his lover, were planning a rebellion against the ageing Queen. They decided that it would help to rally support if Shakespeare's old play about a wayward despot, King Richard II, were to be revived. Comparisons between Richard and Elizabeth were common – even the Queen knew about them.

"I am Richard II, know ye not that?" she said to the keeper of records. "This tragedy," she continued, raging against the players' apparent impunity, "was played 40 times in open streets and houses." For the 1601 revival, the company really went out on a limb, adding the famous scene, possibly specially commissioned for the occasion, in which the king abdicates and is deposed. For their pains, the actors, including Shakespeare, found themselves arraigned by the Privy Council. Any one of them, including Shakespeare, could have been imprisoned for life, like Southampton, or, like Essex, beheaded. In the end they got off on the shaky plea that they were just doing their job. The rebellion, of course, had failed abjectly. Had the rebellion succeeded, it might have been a different matter.

After Shakespeare's death, his plays were subjected to a different, internal, sort of censorship: on moral grounds, or those of taste. Happy endings were imposed, filth extirpated, difficult

ABOVE: Actors from Shakespeare's Globe in London stage Hamlet for dozens of refugees and migrants in Calais in 2016

characters, like the fool in Lear, excised. But by the end of the 19th century, theatrical reformers had begun to establish the wildly controversial idea that Shakespeare might have known what he was doing. Almost immediately after this revelation directors began to use the plays to make points about the modern world. Especially in the wake of World War I, the martial dimension of the plays was subjected to intense scrutiny, and Shakespeare's patriotism was rarely taken at face value, until World War II, when, in Olivier's famous film, Henry V again became a rallying cry. But

post-war productions have once again used the plays as a retort in which to examine our present preoccupations: Peter Brook's bleak absurdist King Lear, for example; Peter Hall's grimly realistic The Wars of the Roses; Jonathan Miller's Alzheimer's-stricken King Lear. Devastating truths have been confronted, but subversion has rarely been attempted.

Elsewhere, however, the plays have been keenly probed for political →

→ endorsement, or denounced for its absence. In 1941, Joseph Stalin banned Hamlet. The historian Arthur Mendel wrote: "The very idea of showing on the stage a thoughtful, reflective hero who took nothing on faith, who intently scrutinized the life around him in an effort to discover for himself, without outside 'prompting,' the reasons for its defects, separating truth from falsehood, the very idea seemed almost 'criminal'." Having Hamlet suppressed must have been a nasty shock for Russians: at least since the times of novelist and short story writer Ivan Turgenev, the Danish Prince had been identified with the Russian soul. Ten years earlier, Adolf Hitler, had claimed the play as quintessentially Aryan, and described Nazi Germany as resembling Elizabethan England, in its youthfulness and vitality (unlike the allegedly decadent and moribund British Empire). In his Germany, Hamlet was reimagined as a proto-German warrior. Only weeks after Hitler took power in 1933 an official

The play's the thing

KATHLEEN E. MCLUSKIE looks at how Shakespeare managed to steer clear of conflicts with the censors

IN THE EARLIEST texts of Richard II, the scene in which the king is formally stripped of his crown does not appear. It might be assumed that it was excised from the text because of the political anxiety about Elizabeth's succession and this view gains support from the story that Shakespeare's company was invited – against their better judgement – to perform the play on the eve of the Earl of Essex's attempted coup. Members of Shakespeare's company were questioned about that performance but no harm came to them: they were just doing their job and the play was an old one that had been performed before. Within days of Essex's trial, they were playing at court again and the deposition scene was printed in the 1608 text, as well as in the Folio of Shakespeare's collected works.

It is impossible to tell whether the "deposition scene" had been performed all along and simply cut from the text by a nervous publisher; whether the Master of the Revels, whose job it was to protect the court from offence and the playwrights from official disapproval, had insisted it be cut; or indeed, whether Shakespeare had second thoughts about the emotional development of the play and wrote one of his most poetically powerful confrontations for the new edition.

We certainly have one very powerful example of Shakespeare's ability to work with the censor to try to keep a good play on the stage. In the unique censored copy of the play Sir Thomas More, amid the muddle of different contributors to the play and passages marked for cutting,

there is a passage by Shakespeare written to rework a censored scene in which Londoners stage an anti-immigration riot. Master of the Revels Edmund Tilney had clearly instructed the authors to "leave out the insurrection" and, to cover the missing material, Shakespeare provided a poetic plea from Sir Thomas More to the rebels. The speech asked them to imagine "the wretched strangers/Their babies at their backs with their poor luggage/ plodding to the ports and coasts for transportation". His speech insisted that disorder only endorsed further disorder where "men like ravenous fishes/Would feed on one another".

The case that Shakespeare makes here and elsewhere against violent disorder may not tell us about his personal view of the regulation and censorship of drama in Elizabethan England. In the absence of other evidence, we might conclude that he was content to write the plays and manage the company with little sense of how important his works would later be for the causes of freedom.

The familiar modern pattern of censorship – in which writers and artists bravely find ways to express subversive opinions in the face of dangerous reprisals from the state or religious authorities – cannot really be applied to the ramshackle system of regulation and control of theatre that existed in Shakespeare's time. Formally, there existed a variety of proscriptions – against writing English history, or dealing with religion, or representing a living monarch – but they were ignored by many

playwrights, including Shakespeare.

From time to time, of course, the authorities of crown and church responded with vicious and summary brutality – pamphleteer John Stubbs lost his hand, writer William Prynne lost his ears and the dramatist Ben Jonson was thrown in jail over his controversial play Isle of Dogs. But far more often during the Shakespearian period, from the 1580s to the 1620s, fierce threats to close the theatres once and for all or to call writers to be questioned by the Privy Council of the royal court dwindled into inaction: the offended nobleman was mollified, the period of political anxiety passed on; the delicate balance of support and control, on which courtly entertainment and a growing print and theatre industry depended, remained in place.

On the whole, and unlike some other dramatists, Shakespeare kept clear of controversy. There is scant evidence that his plays caused any official disquiet and concern is only identifiable through odd inconsistencies in the texts of his plays.

The censors cared about sedition, treason, religious and political dissent, but plays were censored more for insulting particular individuals, not so much for big ideas. Shakespeare's talent was to deal with big ideas in the context of human dilemmas that allows them to be applied to contemporary politics.

Kathleen E. McLuskie is emeritus professor of Shakespeare Studies at the University of Birmingham

party publication appeared titled Shakespeare – A Germanic Writer.

As the Nazi newspaper Der Stürmer asserted: "If the courtier Laertes is drawn to Paris and the humanist Horatio seems more Roman than Danish, it is surely no accident that Hamlet's alma mater should be Wittenberg." A leading magazine of the time interpreted Hamlet's being denied his inheritance as a prefiguring of the Treaty of Versailles, and compared Gertrude's behaviour to that of Weimar's spineless politicians. When Britain declared war on Germany, Shakespeare was exempt from the ban on foreign playwrights because he was considered a German, even classic, author. In 1937, a production of Richard III was staged with a club-footed Richard, unmistakably modelled on Joseph Goebbels. Soldiers were attired in Nazi uniforms, and the ghosts who haunt Richard the night before Bosworth Field were openly compared to Hitler's victims in the Night of the Long Knives.

The comedies remained very popular. The Merchant of Venice was broadcast shortly after Kristallnacht and then given a splendid stage production in Vienna in 1943 to celebrate the city's being officially rid of Jews. Werner Krauss as Shylock made the audience shudder, "with a crash and a weird train of shadows, something revoltingly alien and startlingly repulsive crawled across the stage."

It is a measure of the extraordinary potency of the plays that such different regimes feel obliged to remake Shakespeare in their own image, to force the plays to toe the party line. Shakespeare cannot be ignored, so he must be made to conform. But it is equally a tribute to Shakespeare's own lack of censoriousness that the transformation is so easily effected. As

In 1937, a production of Richard III was staged with a club-footed Richard, unmistakably modelled on Goebbels

with The Bible, you can prove almost anything from Shakespeare. His job was to capture life, not to judge it, and he succeeded triumphantly, but what must it have cost him? He endured enormous pressure from the censors, which seems to be reflected in a line from the great Sonnet 66 of which the first line is: "Tired with all these, for restful death I cry". In it, among the oppressions Shakespeare lists, he speaks in a great resonant line of: "art, made tongue-tied by authority".

All Shakespeare's working life the Master of the Revels, responsible for licensing every play performed in England, was Edmund Tilney. Early in Shakespeare's career, Tilney was involved in rewriting and censoring a highly contentious play. It was on the subject of Sir Thomas More, beheaded, of course, by Elizabeth's father, Henry VIII, and therefore a hot potato politically. We have one of the speeches it is believed that Shakespeare wrote for the play, the only surviving manuscript in his own hand. It is one of the finest things he ever wrote. More's plea on behalf of the migrants was written against a background of anti-immigrant riots in London. Its astonishing timeliness reminds one of why Shakespeare endures eternally, speaking to all of mankind. This is Thomas More's speech, first demanding order be restored:

*Grant them removed, and grant
that this your noise
Hath chid down all the majesty
of England*

*And then to the rioters
themselves:*

*Imagine that you see the
wretched strangers,
Their babies at their backs, with
their poor luggage
Plodding to the ports and coasts
for transportation,
And that you sit as kings in your
desires,
Authority quite silenced by your
brawl
And you in ruff of your opinions
clothed.
What had you got? I'll tell you:
you had taught
How insolence and strong hand
should prevail,
How order should be quelled,
and by this pattern
Not one of you should live an
agèd man,
For other ruffians, as their fancies
wrought
With selfsame hand, self reasons
and self right,
Would shark on you, and men
like ravenous fishes
Would feed on one another.*

The speech was never spoken, the play never heard: Tilney banned it. Art once again tongue-tied by authority. ✖

Simon Callow is an actor, director and writer. He played Mr Tilney in the film Shakespeare in Love. This article appeared in volume 45, issue 1, 2016

51(01):104/107

DOI:10.1177/03064220221084555

It is 2017 and Donald Trump, in his pomp as president, is raving at the the press for peddling 'fake news'.
Then, irony of ironies, the scion of a former Soviet dictator raises her concern about freedom in the USA

The enemies of those people

Nikita Khrushchev's great-granddaughter **NINA KHRUSHCHEVA** now lives in the USA. Here she talked
about growing up in the Soviet Union and her fears for the future role of the American press

EVERY REGIME FROM the Romans to the French during the 1789 revolution to the Nazis and to the Soviets has dubbed those who disagreed with their often-brutal ideology as the "enemy of the people". Journalists have habitually topped the "enemy" lists, censored, harassed, injured, even killed just for doing their job – speaking truth to power, challenging the narratives of the supremacy of the rulers. Democracies normally have known better. Even George W. Bush, not the most liberal of US presidents, recently said: "Power can be very addictive… and it's important for the media to call to account people who abuse their power, whether it be here or elsewhere."

Enter the flashy property tycoon Donald Trump and the USA has joined the not so savoury club of the non-democrats. In February, the newly minted US president tweeted, "The FAKE NEWS media (failing @nytimes, @NBCNews, @ABC, @CBS, @CNN) is not my enemy, it is the enemy of the American People!" Many shivered in disbelief: A verbal déjà vu of the Nazi propaganda minister Joseph Goebbels, who dubbed the Jews the "sworn enemy of the German people".

In May Trump's campaign committee produced a television ad lauding his first 100 days in office as an unprecedented "success" and labelling major television networks – CNN, MSNBC, ABC, CBS – and their correspondents as "fake news" for not reporting his "winning".

Once a Soviet citizen, I've been checking my surroundings. Am I living in cosmopolitan New York? Am I back in a homogeneous Moscow reading the Pravda headlines about the drummed-up victories of the communist state and the denunciations of the enemies who plot to take it down? In fact, when I was growing up in the 1970s, not even Pravda used such ominous language for Kremlin critics.

In the first half of the last century, the term *vragi naroda* – enemies of the people – applied to those who disagreed with the Bolshevik government on the issues ranging from the planned economy to atheism. They took their cue from the French revolutionaries of the 1790s whose Reign of Terror led to thousands being executed for "betraying" the newly founded First Republic.

Under Joseph Stalin being labelled an "enemy of the people" became even more dangerous because it resulted in immediate death or imprisonment in a labour camp. But after Nikita Khrushchev, my great-grandfather, denounced Stalin and his system of gulag camps in his 1956 speech to the Soviet Communist Party, the *vragi* formula fell out of use.

Trump, appearing less democratic than the Soviet autocrat Khrushchev, has found himself using the "enemies of the people" line, and joining the current pantheon of world rulers who share his anti-free-speech podium: Russia's Vladimir Putin, Turkey's Recep Erdogan and China's Xi Jinping.

Of course, in the USA journalists, including MSNBC's Andrea Mitchell and CNN's Wolf Blitzer, who Trump so blatantly labelled as "fake" in a recent commercial, can freely provide the real facts on the president's megalomaniacal narrative. Their lives are not in danger compared to those reporting from other places. And yet when Trump tweets or his ads attack the news, even if not as brutally as the Kremlin's Pravda once did, and with less deadly consequences, it can still amount to an attempt at

Many shivered in disbelief at Trump's verbal déjà vu of Joseph Goebbels dubbing the Jews the sworn enemy of the people

state censorship. Political fear, after all, is not only about personal experience or individual threats, it is a condition of society. Threats shouted from the top, even without physical harm, restrict public debate and public policy. They reinforce social and political inequalities and create an atmosphere of mistrust and animosity between political parties and social groups.

In democratic societies, the free press guarantees that the state's menacing language should never turn into menacing actions against its people, as happened with Stalin's gulags. With Trump, who has more in common with Putin and Xi than with Canada's Justin Trudeau or Germany's Angela Merkel, we can no longer be so certain. ✘

Nina Khrushcheva is a professor of international affairs at The New School in New York. She is the author of The Lost Khrushchev: A Journey into the Gulag of the Russian Mind

This article first appeared in Volume 46, issue 2, 2017

51(01):108/109

DOI:10.1177/03064220221085932

LEFT: Russian dolls of US president Donald Trump, UK prime minister Theresa May and Chinese president Xi Jinping in a souvenir shop in Moscow in 2018

CREDIT: Scott D'arcy/PA

An unwelcome feature of the 2010s was the re-emergence of the so-called strongmen leaders. All over the world a rejuvenated type of masculine leadership saw the silencing of journalists, women and minorities

2012-2021

'We're not scared of these things'

MIRIAM GRACE A GO, news editor of the Philippine website Rappler, described how the newsroom kept going despite attacks from President Duterte – and asked CEO Maria Ressa for her thoughts

MY CHAT CHANNEL with the reporters was particularly frenzied one Tuesday morning back in February. We had played out this scenario before in our conversations — what if, one day, the palace gets so pissed off with us that they stop Pia at the gates? Or boot her out of the press office? — and now it was happening.

Pia Ranada, our reporter covering Philippine President Rodrigo Duterte, was live on Facebook and Twitter documenting how a presidential guard wouldn't let her into Malacañang, the presidential compound, where she had regularly gone since this administration began. There had been an order, but the guard couldn't say from whom.

After 20 minutes, Ranada was allowed into the building where the press office was. She was in for a long day, though. It was the president himself who had ordered the ban, the

head of the internal house affairs told Ranada. In fact, she'd been banned from all the buildings in the compound, including the press office. A bit later, it was announced that the ban would cover even our chief executive officer and executive editor, Maria Ressa.

Ranada told me later that she was scared. Her hands were shaking while taking the video. But she was also angry and wanted answers. "I didn't want them to get away with what they were doing," she said.

What happened that day was the culmination of nearly two years of intensified attacks on Rappler, our news website. Those attacks had gone on practically since Duterte had taken office.

Such a twist of fate.

On 9 May 2016, the night of the election, Duterte granted his first interview to Rappler. By October 2016, however, Rappler had gathered solid

data to show that his administration was engaging in systematic disinformation, carrying out "social media campaigns meant to shape public opinion, tear down reputations and cripple traditional media institutions", Ressa said as an introduction to a three-part series on the weaponisation of the internet.

A deluge of nasty, personal attacks flooded into her Facebook accounts, inboxes and Twitter. Ressa, the person in the newsroom who most preferred to engage even obvious trolls (a lot of times against our advice), didn't take long to realise that she was talking to people who didn't intend to listen or understand.

"They were just trying to bash me into silence," she said, looking back.

It was ugly. "Maria, you are waste of sperm! Your mother should have swallowed you!"; "Me to the RP Government: Make sure Maria Ressa gets publicly raped to death when Martial law expands to Luzon. It would bring joy in my heart."

The Facebook accounts of some staff, editors and regular contributors were stalked by trolls. Photos of their families were stolen and posted with

Photos of their families were stolen and posted with messages wishing they were murdered and raped

messages wishing they were murdered and raped. There was one time when a proclaimed Duterte supporter got a photo of our office building on Google Maps and posted it, telling other diehard supporters of the president that this was where they should go in order to harm Rappler employees.

"The whole thing was shocking because we'd never lived through anything like that before," Ressa told me. Yet, she asked, which self-respecting journalist wouldn't have written about it? "The data was all there. It was clear. The reason they attacked us was because we were right. In retrospect, it was extremely important for us to have done that story; otherwise, more Filipinos would have been misled."

"What made it difficult was," Ressa realised after the backlash, she was a journalist who "also ran a company."

And, indeed, the government stepped up its attacks and went after the company itself. In Duterte's State of the Nation address in July 2017, he accused Rappler of being foreign-owned. By insisting in subsequent speeches that we were "funded by the CIA" and "fully American-owned", he was laying down the argument that we were violating the constitution, which requires media companies to be

ABOVE: Maria Ressa, Rappler's CEO and executive editor, accepts her Nobel Peace Prize (shared with Russian journalist Dmitry Muratov) in Oslo in December last year. Ressa has been the victim of a campaign of intimidation since Rodrigo Duterte came to power in 2016

wholly owned by Filipinos. By January this year, the Securities and Exchange Commission ordered the company's licence to operate to be revoked (we're still here because we appealed the decision in court). We have also had a cyber libel case filed against us.

"The charges are ludicrous," said Ressa, "but they are complex enough that people can get lost."

Snide remarks designed to make →

What it didn't realise was that, by targeting Rappler, it had roused a bigger enemy

→ the public doubt Rappler's credibility are loosely made by government officials. During their daily coverage, our reporters have to parry cabinet officials who stop them at press conferences with "Rappler? Haven't you shut down?".

At events attended by the president, organisers must check their lists of journalists coming and strike off any Rappler reporters. In April, one of our reporters, who insisted on covering the National Games in a city more than 400km from Manila, was booted out of a press conference and told by education officials to listen instead to the loudspeakers installed outside.

Lately, state auditors have been releasing reports on individual agencies. Rappler, like many other news outlets, reported on the findings about questionable contracts, misused funds and unexplained releases. Yet, every time, Duterte's officials would issue a statement singling out Rappler and calling our report "fake news" instead of trying to clear their names of mishandling taxpayers' money. Daily, our journalists receive messages calling them paid hacks who deserve to lose their jobs and get jailed, raped or murdered.

Yet, even in these times, we continue to produce exclusives, getting documents from agencies, inside stories from cabinet officials and briefings from those who remain professional and non-partisan in government. And when reporters worry about losing access to officials, I share with them my principle from when I myself was a reporter: there will always be one other person who knows the information, one other source of those same documents, one other expert who knows an issue like the back of his hand. The administration may think that it can slow us down with these distractions – yes, the cases are distractions – but what it didn't realise was that, by targeting Rappler, it had roused a bigger enemy. #StandWithRappler has quickly given way to #DefendPressFreedom. Media organisations, here and abroad, have banded together to guard more aggressively against what they see as a creeping attempt to silence dissent here. Campus organisations, even those in schools, and civil-society groups have started organising forums on media literacy and press freedom, requesting to hear from Rappler and other journalists who have experienced the battle with lies and disinformation firsthand.

Something else the administration didn't realise was that when a reporter is freed from physically following Duterte around and sitting through, sometimes, three speeches a day, she has time to work on more substantial stories that scrutinise the government.

When we say it's business as usual at Rappler, we mean it. Sure, we have additional security, both physically and digitally, and there are contingency plans in place, but it's the same newsroom where you find people working practically 24/7. Some days, we're crowded at the office when almost everybody has decided to hold meetings at the same time. Some days, someone could bring a skateboard and glide through the newsroom without knocking anybody down because three-quarters of our 100-or-so workforce have decided to work from home.

The reporters jog at night in the park just outside the office. Sometimes I cook for them. Sometimes I remind them to get a day off and recharge.

In between the banter, though, we also ask each other: Why are we holding the line? Why do we keep moving the line? There's a spirit that Rapplers see and reinforce in each other, Ressa points out, that says: "We're not scared of these things."

I had shared with the team how the testing (I don't want to call it a "crisis") of Rappler had made me draw confidence from the fifth verse of the 23rd Psalm: "You prepare a feast for me in the presence of my enemies. You anoint my head with oil." I think it has encouraged some of them, too.

So when, amid the attacks on us, international recognitions come, one fellow manager would say, "So this is the feast?" I would tell her, "Brace yourself, it's just the appetiser."

And when government agents came to our office to serve notices of investigations and subpoenas, some staff would say, "For clarification, is this still part of Psalm 23?" And they would be told, "This is the 'walking through the valley of the shadow of death' part." And guess what? We are able to laugh and then focus on our work again.

"The mission of journalism has never been needed as much as it is today," Ressa likes to say. "That's why Rapplers have come back day after day with the best hard-hitting stories they can find. We're stubborn." ✖

Miriam Grace A Go is an award-winning journalist and head of news at Rappler. From volume 47, issue 2, 2018

51(01):110/112

DOI:10.1177/03064220221084558

Publishing work by political prisoners – most recently letters from dissidents targeted by the Lukashenka regime in Belarus – has been a prominent feature of the magazine from the start

2012-2021

Windows on the world

British-Iranian charity worker **NAZANIN ZAGHARI-RATCLIFFE** and writer and activist **GOLROKH EBRAHIMI IRAEE** both found power through poetry in Evin prison, Tehran. This is an introduction to the women and, overleaf, are the poems we published

NAZANIN ZAGHARI-RATCLIFFE COULD be facing her third Christmas away from her family. She was arrested on 3 April 2016 by Iran's Revolutionary Guard at the airport in Tehran when returning to London from visiting her family. She was with her daughter, Gabriella, who was then 21-months old. No reasons were given at the time of her arrest.

She writes from prison about her experiences and thoughts via her poetry, published overleaf, and describes how the writing makes her feel.

"It is hard to write about freedom when you have so little of it in your life. It is hard to describe how it feels to be tied by force to one place. But it is the hope of being free that keeps me going, the hope of gaining freedom back one day," she said.

"I realise now how I took freedom for granted. It is important to cherish freedom today, as you never know what tomorrow brings. The road ahead is bumpy and bendy, scary and still unclear.

"But I could not have come this far without the love and support of those outside – those I know who are out there, and those I don't – who are following my story and sharing it with shock.

"Talking about freedom when surrounded by brick walls feels tough, but we all share the same sky. One day we will all be under the same blue sky, singing our freedom songs."

In August 2018, Zaghari-Ratcliffe was released for three days from Evin prison, in Tehran, where she is now. Evin is notorious for housing Iran's political prisoners.

Following a secret trial in August 2016, she was sentenced to five years in prison on unspecified charges relating to national security. She spent eight-and-a-half months in solitary confinement before she was transferred to the women's political wing.

In October 2017, she was informed of three new charges and told that she could face an additional 16 years in prison. Her family was required to provide bail money to prevent her from being returned to solitary confinement. The court date was later postponed in the wake of then UK foreign secretary Boris Johnson's visit to the country, and in May 2018 it was reopened.

Also in the prison is Golrokh Ebrahimi Iraee, a writer and political activist who is serving a six-year sentence for charges related to an unpublished story she wrote criticising the practice of stoning in Iran.

In September 2014, government forces searched the home of Iraee and her husband, Arash Sadeghi, in Tehran, where they found the unpublished story. They arrested them both. Sadeghi was taken to Evin, while Iraee went to a secret location for three days before going to Evin, where she was interrogated for 17 days. During this time, she had to listen to the guards beat her husband in the next cell.

Iraee was sentenced to six years in 2016 and had her stories and poems confiscated on her first night in prison.

On her poetry, Iraee said: "It is bitter writing about a generation that, four decades ago, had the same hopes that I have today who were hanged, burned, abused and tortured in prison. But it is a reality – to hold on to the image of those men and women, with their pain and suffering, with a song on their lips and aim in their heart, who →

 Talking about freedom when surrounded by brick walls feels tough, but we all share the same sky

→ looked for freedom and justice. The songs of those who endured the most shocking violence without knowing how or why.

"Today I am writing for them from here, from where they once sang the song of freedom. It means that their beliefs are still alive. Alive in me, alive in all of us here, and kept alive by those who hear our words in a faraway land and keep them in your thoughts and hearts.

"I also hope that the day will come when the scale of justice in our song

....

BELOW: Richard Ratcliffe, the husband of Nazanin Zaghari-Ratcliffe, outside the Foreign Office in London last October during his second hunger strike in two years in protest at Britain's lack of meaningful action to free his wife from incarceration in Iran

It is bitter writing about a generation that, four decades ago, were hanged, burned, abused and tortured in prison

will reach enough people's ears that those responsible for such pain will be held to account."

Iraee was released from prison on 3 January 2017 after a 71-day hunger strike by her husband and a campaign on Twitter, but shortly after returned to prison.

In January 2018, she faced additional charges. She was subsequently transferred to Shahr-e-Rey prison, a former industrial chicken

farm on the outskirts of Tehran, after she refused to go to court.

In early February, Iraee began a hunger strike which seriously damaged her health and in early April she was transferred to hospital in a critical condition. She is now back in the women's political wing in Evin. For now.

Poems written in prison by Zaghari-Ratcliffe and Iraee are published here for the first time. ✖

For Our Parents

By **NAZANIN ZAGHARI-RATCLIFFE**

I am sitting in a corner
Reviewing my dreams
And ploughing through my memories .
I think about my mum, who
Every time I touch Gabriella's hair
Or kiss the back of her neck
Her eyes fill up with tears
I think of her safe hands, full of love,
And her longing look.

I think of my Dad
Whose hair has gone completely grey
Tired of walking up and down in the corridors
Of the courts
And the hope at the end of his eyes
That yet again reminds me
That these days will pass, however hard

I think of your mum
That nothing would make her happier
Than seeing and embracing her granddaughter
After 19 months
To bring a smile on her lips and her pale face
And give her energy on her tired body
Flattened from illness

I think of your dad
Who turned 68 this month without us
His silence is full of words for me
I think of freedom, of return
Of that glorious moment of rolling into
your arms
The arms I have longed for the past 500 days
I think of my orchids and African violets
Have they bloomed without me?
It is true that the world in its great hugeness
Sometimes gets so small
As small as the eye in the needle
And unreachable like a dream

And I still
Am sitting in my corner
Reviewing my dreams
And ploughing through my memories

Autumn Light

By **NAZANIN ZAGHARI-RATCLIFFE**

The diagonal light falling on my bed
Tells me that there is another autumn
on the way
Without you
A child turned three
Without us
The bars of the prison grew around us
So unjustly and fearlessly
And we left our dreams behind them
We walked on the stairs that led to captivity
Our night time stories remained unfinished
And lost in the silence of the night
Nothing is the same here
And without you even fennel tea loses its odour

Standing Straight

By **GOLROKH EBRAHIMI IRAEE**

Standing
Mountains
Firm but quiet
While people of the city
Full of uproar
Crawl on their knees
From here to there

It is not that they are restless – No
But whoever is shorter
Is safer
From constant bullets   →

→

And their whispers
Are not reported
To the ears of the city
By the wind.
It is the one who is standing
Against the grim vultures
Of the city
Standing straight
Holding in the square
Of the city for a while
Where an unknown grave
Repeats their name with a tremble

And it is the one
Who puts their hand on their knee
Aiming to stand up
In front of the grim vultures of the city
The vultures who
Dress like policemen
And pull the trigger without asking
Your name

The Lips of the Wind

By GOLROKH EBRAHIMI IRAEE

I've left your hands
Beyond borders
Beyond time

Now I turn into wind
Over these mud bricks
Piled on each other
These cement bricks
That fill up the sky of the city
That city that has swallowed me

I turn into an arrow
On Arash's bow
To pass through the darkness
Of night, whistling
To the sun

I turn into a flag
In the hands
Of Kaveh, fluttering
In front of the eyes
Of the people of the city
Who haven't even asked
In whispers
What is the story of
This wall
Standing up in front of them

I turn into a poem
On the lips of the wind
And pass through
This inevitable boundary
Over the dreams
And becomes real

Until the cups of our tea
Which are emptied next
To each other
To fill the loneliness of our afternoons
Until they won't be gloomy anymore
And no longer will we be
Without each other

Counting Up, Counting Down

By GOLROKH EBRAHIMI IRAEE

One, two, three
I have counted the bricks in this wall
I have counted
Your notches
On the walls of the cell
That has devoured me

And now it has been years
That I am counting that man
Who is a thousand bodies

In a shower of bullets
With his eyes closed
And hands tied up with a rope
And feet in chains

I have counted that woman
Who is a thousand women
Hanging from a gallows tree
Whose feet stayed still
When the wind
Swirled in her dress

I counted
Those virgin girls
Who had the freedom song
On their red lips
With their plaited hair
When just before execution
They turned to cry to the east of time
To the impudence of an action
Which planned to
Prevent them belonging to heaven

I've counted
The children of those rolled in blood
Lamenting in distress
Over unknown graves

I've counted
Every second of this
Open-ended, beginning
This dawnless night
This sewage
This decline
And this reaction

This wall fills up
With trembling notches
Which picture
The firmness of
A generation of pain
The entangled notches
Are an alphabet
That write the screams

Of the sewn lips

Until then
That sun passes by
Without distress
Over my city, Tehran
That as of many years ago
Has slept counting its own blood
And yet to wake up.

Sign up for updates on Zaghari-Ratcliffe's story here: https://www.change.org/p/free-nazanin-ratcliffe. For information on the Center for the Defenders of Human Rights, which aids women inside Evin, visit http://www.humanrights-ir.org

This article first appeared in volume 47, issue 3, 2018

51(01)113/117|DOI:10.1177/03064220221084564

FEATURES

"The vicious circle of suppression-anger-and-distrust
eventually will turn Hong Kong into a prison, a cage,
like Xinjiang. World, cry for Hong Kong people"

HONG KONG MEDIA MOGUL JIMMY LAI'S LETTERS WRITTEN FROM HIS PRISON CELL | BEIJING'S FEARLESS FOE WITH GOD ON HIS SIDE P119

Beijing's fearless foe with God on his side

Billionaire publisher **JIMMY LAI** could have fled to safety but chose to stay in Hong Kong to fight for freedom – and went to jail for his sins. We introduce him here. Overleaf, we publish a sheaf of his letters from prison

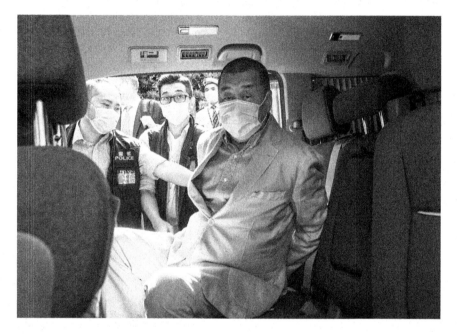

JIMMY LAI CHI-YING, Hong Kong's 74-year-old self-made billionaire, is a dissident. His cause is freedom. For championing this cause, he has been jailed since December 2020. One of the crimes he was found guilty of was lighting a candle in public to commemorate the 1989 Tiananmen Square massacre, when thousands were slaughtered. His real sin, however, was publishing Apple Daily, Hong Kong's lone voice for freedom. This voice was smothered in June 2021 with the jailing of its senior journalists.

Lai could have remained free – he has homes in Paris, London, Kyoto and Taipei – but chose to stay in solidarity with the Hong Kong democrats being prosecuted. The UK abandoned Hong Kong in 1997 on China's promise that

ABOVE: Jimmy Lai is handcuffed by police after being arrested in his apartment in August 2020 for allegedly breaching Hong Kong's draconian National Security Law

its seven million-plus people would have "a high degree of autonomy" with "Hong Kong people ruling Hong Kong".

However, the democrats' demand for China to honour this pledge was rebuffed from the start and dealt a final blow in 2020 when Beijing imposed direct rule by promulgating a vague

and sweeping National Security Law along with an electoral system modelled on Iran's that allows only handpicked candidates. Virtually all democrat leaders have since been jailed.

Lai was born in Guangzhou. He escaped communist rule at the age of 12 by stealing his way into Hong Kong, hidden in the bottom of a small fishing boat. By the time he was in his 20s, he had risen from a child labourer to owning his own business.

He started Giordano, an international clothing retailer. Along the way he learned English – initially by reading the dictionary while living in the factory where he worked – and took to the brand of free-market economics espoused by Friedrich Hayek and Milton Friedman. He credited his success to the freedom he enjoyed in British Hong Kong. He vows to fight for this freedom so others may have the same opportunities.

Like most Hong Kong people, Lai's political awakening came in the spring of 1989 when a democratic movement led by students erupted in Tiananmen Square in Beijing. He was sympathetic to their aspirations and lent them support by raising money through his Giordano stores.

After communist tanks mowed down demonstrators on 4 June 1989, he dedicated himself to upholding their torch of democracy by going into publishing in Hong Kong, where the press remained free.

He first launched Next, a weekly magazine, in 1990, and then Apple Daily on the eve of Hong Kong's transition to Chinese rule. With their bold and fiercely independent editorial stance, both publications enjoyed wide readership and were successfully "cloned" in →

 His political awakening came in 1989 when the student-led democratic movement erupted in Beijing

As Apple Daily printed its final edition, thousands of people waited through the night

→ Taiwan. As the communists tightened their grip on Hong Kong, Lai was first forced to sell his controlling interest in Giordano and then his publications were subjected to orchestrated advertising boycotts. Though financial losses piled up, Lai did not waver. Readers' loyalty remained to the end: when Apple Daily printed its last edition of one million copies on 24 June 2021, thousands of people waited in the middle of the night for it to roll off the press.

Lai is now represented by the London-based lawyer Caoilfhionn Gallagher QC. She has called Lai "a man of courage and integrity" and vowed to "pursue all available legal remedies to vindicate Mr. Lai's rights".

Lai's wife Teresa is a devout Catholic. He himself converted to Catholicism when Hong Kong came under Chinese rule. China's communists, often godless, are known to be ruthless, but in this couple they may have met their match. Because of his faith, Lai does not seek temporal salvation. He quoted the 15th-century German priest Thomas à Kempis in a letter to a friend from prison: "If thou willingly bear the Cross, it will bear thee, and will bring thee to the end which thou seekest, even where there shall be the end of suffering; though it shall not be here." ✖

BELOW: Jimmy Lai attends a candlelight vigil to mark the 31st anniversary of the crackdown of pro-democracy protests at Beijing's Tiananmen Square in 1989

51(01):119/123|DOI:10.1177/03064220221084512

CREDIT: Tyrone Siu/Reuters/Alamy

'I don't want my life to be a lie'

JIMMY LAI has been in jail since December 2020. He has told friends and associates from his cell that he does not want to turn his "life into a lie" and willingly pays the price for upholding "truth, justice, and goodness". He said he bears this price gladly and sees it as God's grace in disguise. Here are excerpts from some of his prison letters

'The muted anger of the Hong Kong people is not going away'

Apple Daily published its last edition of one million copies on 24 June 2021. This was how he reacted to it from prison. While deploring what he called "this barbaric suppression", he was weighed down with guilt that his staff were incarcerated on his account and wished he could share "the pain of the cross" they bear. He vowed to find a spiritual way to help them.

THE FORCED CLOSURE of Apple Daily Hong Kong showed clearly what [a] shipwreck life in Hong Kong has become for them. The damage done [by] the Hong Kong government and Beijing's legitimacy long term is much greater [than] the temporary benefit of quieting down the voice of freedom of speech.

Yes, this barbaric suppression intimidation works. Hong Kong people are all quieted down. But the muted anger they have is not going away. Even those emigrating will have it forever. Many people are emigrating or planning to.

This Apple Daily shutdown only aggravates it, making it certain to people that the hopelessness of Hong Kong is irreversible. The more barbaric [the] treatment of Hong Kong people, [the] greater is their anger, and power of their potential resistance; [the] greater is the distrust of Beijing, of Hong Kong, [the] stricter is their rule to control.

The vicious circle of suppression-anger-and-distrust eventually will turn Hong Kong into a prison, a cage, like Xinjiang. World, cry for Hong Kong people.

Pastor Lee came to visit... Told me he had visited Cheung Kim Hung, our CEO, and Lo Wai Kong, our Chief Editor. They are both being remanded. Cheung, being a devout Christian, is doing fine. But Lo, who has no faith, is miserable.

What I can do to help him? Send him a Bible? But Bible is no faith, not panacea. Maybe I should ask Cardinal Zen to visit him to see what we can do for him.

It would be disingenuous to say that by creating Apple Daily I have put him in this situation. But I do have a guilty feeling and want to share his price of his cross, which is weighing too heavily on him. There must be something I can do to help. I will not cease until I find a way.

"If we suffer courageously, quietly, unselfishly, peacefully, the things [that] wreck our outer being perfect us within, and make us. And as [we] have seen, more truly ourselves."

'There is always a price to pay when you put truth, justice and goodness ahead of your own wellbeing'

Lai wrote in July 2021 to console his hotel staff in Canada for their suffering during the pandemic

and held out the hope that soon he could share "the coming prosperity" with them. He also updated them on his life in prison, telling them not to worry about him, though when they "pass by a church, do go in and pray for me".

Dear Bob,
If you are worry[ing] about me, please don't. I am keeping myself busy reading the scriptures, →

→ gospels, theology and books of the saints and their lives … Life is peaceful and edifying… There is always a price to pay when you put truth, justice, and goodness ahead of your own comfort, safety and physical wellbeing, or your life becomes a lie. I choose truth instead of a lie and pay the price. Luckily God has made this price a grace in disguise. I am so grateful.

So, don't worry about me. However, when you pass by a church, do go in [and] pray for me. Believers and non-believers, the sun shines on you the same. So the Lord will listen to you the same. Thank you! Hope to see you soon,
Cheers,
Jimmy.

'I am changed… I can't see myself going back to business again'

Lai wrote to a friend, James, in September 2021, saying that, by clinging to Christ, his life in prison "is full" and spiritually "at peace". However, he was worried about his wife, Teresa, whom he said was weighed down by grief.

James,

I am doing fine, keeping myself busy, studying gospels, scriptures, theology and books on the saints and lives and prayers, touching the fringe of Christ's cloak to live, so to speak. Life is full and at peace. I am learning and changed a lot. Can't see myself going back to business again. All have to depend on others.

I do worry about my wife Teresa. She has lost a lot of weight under the grief of my situation. Lucky she has God [to] abide [with] her. May God bless you all.
Cheers,
Uncle Jimmy

'But with her prayers, she will slug it through'

In October 2021, Lai wrote to a business associate about his happiness when his family visited him. He urged him to "keep writing".

I am doing fine here. Happy to see Teresa, Claire, Tim and Ian and my brother… Teresa looks weak and weighed down by grief. But with her prayers, she will slug it through.

I am keeping myself busy here. Spiritual study, drawing and trying to improve my English writing skill. Take care!

So sweet of you to write me. Please keep writing. May God be with you all! Cheers, Uncle Jimmy

'If thou willingly bear the Cross, it will bring thee [that] which thou seekest…'

In a November 2021 letter to a friend, Lai copied the following quote from the 15th-century German priest Thomas à Kempis, author of The Imitation of Christ.

"If thou willingly bear the Cross, it will bear thee, and will bring thee to the end which thou seekest, even where there shall be the end of suffering; though it shall not be here.

"If thou bear it unwillingly, thou makest a burden for thyself and greatly increaseth thy load, and yet thou must bear it."

'Lord, remember those who shed their blood in Tiananmen Square'

Lai was sentenced 13 months in jail for attending the vigil in Victoria Park, Hong Kong, on 4 June 2020 that marked the 31st anniversary of the Tiananmen Square massacre. He protested his innocence by reading the following statement in court before he was sentenced. He appealed to God to grant the young men and women who died in Tiananmen their redemption.

I did not join the 4 June vigil in Victoria Park. I lit a candle light in front of reporters to remind the world to commemorate and remember those brave young men and women who 31 years ago in Tiananmen Square put the truth, justice and goodness above their lives and died for them.

If [to] commemorate those who died because of injustice is a crime, then inflict on me that crime and let me suffer the punishment of the crime, so that I may share the burden and glory of those men and women who shed their blood on June 4th to proclaim truth, injustice and goodness.

Lord, remember those who shed their blood, but do not remember their cruelty. Remember the fruits those young men and women have borne because what they did and grant, Lord, that the fruits these young men and women have borne may be their redemption. May the power of love of the meek prevail over the power of destruction of the strong.

ABOVE: With his drawing in September 2021 of Jesus Christ on the cross, Lai wrote: "To have hope is to trust, to turn one's heart to God"

We should not be put up for sale

An app "auctioning" Muslim women brings to light growing misogyny and Islamophobia in India. **AISHWARYA JAGANI** spoke to two women who found themselves on it

ON 1 JANUARY 2022, scores of Indian women journalists, activists, artists and lawyers woke up to find themselves put up for sale on the internet. Bulli Bai, an app hosted on GitHub, listed hundreds of women, accompanied by often doctored photographs and captioned with the phrase "Your Bulli Bai Deal of the Day Is…" The women had a few things in common, but one stood out. They were all Muslim.

"It felt disgusting and pathetic. I felt awful that people can stoop to such lows just to satisfy their egos and political urges. It's dehumanising. Nobody should go through this. Nobody should be put on auction," Kashmiri Muslim journalist "J", who was on the list, told Index. She asked for her identity not to be revealed.

The list was clearly an attempt to sexualise, intimidate and humiliate the women, many of whom have spoken out about the increase in targeted harassment of Muslims in India now face. Some of them have been vocal critics of the policies of India's ruling party, the Bharatiya Janata Party (BJP).

The January incident came in the wake of a similar app that sprung up in July 2021 called Sulli Deals. The terms "*Bulli*" and "*Sulli*" are derogatory slurs used to refer to Muslim women.

Journalist Ayesha Minhaz told us she avoided social media the entire day, hoping to avoid seeing any of the names. "I think it was around midnight when one of my social media acquaintances reached out to me saying they saw my name on it," she said.

J, who had been taking a break from news and social media when the list came out, told us how taken aback she was when a fellow journalist called her to tell her about it.

More than 100 activists, journalists and politically vocal Muslim women were featured on the app, including Bollywood actor Shabana Azmi, journalists Ismat Ara and Mariya Salim, activist Sadaf Jafar and Indian-American entrepreneur Amina Kausar.

The continued persecution of Muslim women

Indian Muslims in the public eye have increasingly found themselves in danger of getting arrested, threatened with violence and effectively being censored since 2014 when anti-Muslim sentiments in India began to rise.

This persecution is often ignored or even encouraged by the right-wing government. In December 2021, Hindu supremacist leaders (many of whom had BJP connections) openly called for a genocide of Muslims at a three-day religious conclave in the state of Uttarakhand. Not long after, hundreds took an oath to make India a Hindu nation at a gathering by a Hindu supremacist organisation.

Muslim women are easy targets for the misogynistic right wing, and those on the list are among those who are routinely targeted and harassed online by extremist Hindu nationalists. The harassment is persistent and unrelenting.

"I had a nervous breakdown when the severity of the situation sank in. As a Muslim woman in India, I am not new to Islamophobia or anti-Muslim narratives and hate. But this was a new low," Mariya Salim, one of those on the GitHub list, wrote in an op-ed for The Wire.

"For the first time since I joined social media, I deactivated my Twitter account and cut all ties with the outside world. Messages of solidarity were pouring in from everywhere, but these were from the 'fringe' who care," she added. Minhaz told Index that although she had never been targeted in such an organised manner before, she was not new to trolling and sexually abusive messages.

"On Facebook, every other post about a new report [I post] has led to messages with pornographic videos or sexually abusive messages," she said.

"If the story had any criticism of any new developmental project or scheme, the comments would usually be of the nature of 'go to Pakistan' or the usual bigotry and Islamophobia, or propaganda messages and videos that were already proven to be fake. And these used to be from people I know, people I went to school or college with, people who had worked with me at some point."

Some of India's best known and award-winning journalists haven't been immune to this targeted abuse, either. Washington Post columnist Rana Ayyub, one of the country's highest profile journalists, has found herself the target of abuse multiple times. In 2018, a doctored pornographic video morphed to make it appear as though she was in it was circulated on the internet. Ayyub

The individuals most frequently targeted were women and Muslims

CREDIT: DB Pictures/Alamy

has also had multiple police reports filed against her for alleged wrongdoing.

In June 2020, Kashmiri photojournalist Masrat Zahra had terrorism charges filed against her for some Facebook posts she shared.

In January this year, The Wire published an investigation into Tek Fog, a sophisticated app allegedly used by the BJP to drive propaganda and generate automated abuse and targeted harassment against journalists, actors, comedians, activists and other social media influencers. The most frequently targeted individuals were women and Muslims, the report found.

Targeted for their identity, not their ideology

Although vocal critics of the ruling government and those with left-leaning political ideologies are targeted the most, this persistent harassment doesn't always spring from what Muslim women do or say. Often, simply being Muslim is enough.

"Even before the GitHub incident, the hatred and abusive comments [I received] weren't directed at the story's content alone," said Minhaz. "I once got trolled for a drought story."

Speculating on why she was targeted, Minhaz added: "Most Muslim women on the list were vocal against the ongoing persecution on their social media

accounts. I think that got me there, too."

In December 2019, after the BJP proposed a citizenship law discriminatory towards Indian Muslims, Muslim women became the face of the country-wide protests that followed. The Women of Shaheen Bagh spent more than 100 days and nights in Shaheen Bagh, a neighbourhood in South Delhi, as part of a peaceful sit-in protest.

Despite the many Indian Muslim women who have spoken out against the discrimination they face, and despite their strength, resilience and limitless stores of courage, the hate campaigns continue. "The targeting of Muslim women is not just a one-off thing; it is well ideated and deliberated," Saira Shah Salim, an activist and writer, wrote in an op-ed for India Today.

"This is not just an attack on Muslim women alone; it's an attack on a religious identity, a normalisation of the 'othering' and dehumanisation of Muslims."

Although no police action was taken in the Sulli Deals case, five people were arrested in January in connection with the Bulli Bai case.

A report by NDTV claimed that Neeraj Bishnoi, a 21-year old student who was arrested on 20 January for allegedly masterminding the whole campaign and creating the Bulli Bai app, displayed no remorse and had done what he thought was the "right thing".

ABOVE: Muslim women in Tanjore, Tamil Nadu, a state in India. Muslim women are increasingly under attack in the country

"I think the right-wing ecosystem has become more emboldened over the past few years. It's manifesting more often and in more violent forms, both online and offline," said Minhaz.

The lack of strong action by the authorities when Muslim women are harassed encourages radical right-wingers to continue targeting these women, often issuing violent and sexual threats.

J does not feel very positive about the arrests, and knows it won't change much.

"The only thing that helps is keeping in touch with people who are also going through this. We are sources of courage for each other," she said. Her parting words reflect the courage she and other women continue to hold on to, despite the intimidation and threats.

"The women on the list... they are people I take inspiration from. If I'm counted amongst these strong, powerful women who have stood up for the right things, then I must have done something right." ✖

Aishwarya Jagani is a freelance journalist based in India

51(01):124/125|DOI:10.1177/03064220221084510

Jennings

Our cartoonist on the current crop of libertarians who claim freedom as their motive, while harbouring authoritarian tendencies

51(01):126/127|DOI:10.1177/03064220221084509

BEN JENNINGS:
an award-winning
cartoonist for The
Guardian and The
Economist whose
work has been
exhibited around
the world

Amin's awful story is much more than popcorn for the eyes

The critically acclaimed animated film Flee tells the story of an Afghan family's flight into exile through the eyes of one man. Its director, Jonas Poher Rasmussen, talks to **JEMIMAH STEINFELD** about concerns over voyeurism and Denmark's current attitude towards migrants

HALFWAY THROUGH THE film Flee, the protagonist Amin is in a Finnish prison which houses refugees. Conditions are bleak. Then a TV crew turns up. They come, Amin says, they take pictures, and they leave, he assumes without much thought for those inside. Amin feels as though his suffering has been exploited.

I'm chatting to the film director, Jonas Poher Rasmussen, who is Danish, about that scene. There is no doubt that Amin's story is important and deserves to be told. It traces his family's exile from Afghanistan in the mid-90s and their treacherous, difficult journey to safety. It deals with sexuality - Amin is gay - and gives a voice to someone who might otherwise be nameless. But, at

> Anyone who works with stories about human rights abuses is all too aware of the immense responsibility in how they are told

the same time, it is a film, something to watch on a Saturday night in a cinema with popcorn. Anyone who works with stories concerning grave human rights abuses is all too aware of the immense responsibility in how they are told and when. Poher Rasmussen has thought about this too.

"There's the sequence with the cruise ship where, when it passes them [Amin and his family] by, tourists are taking photos and when he told me that story I felt I was one of those tourists," he says. "Because I am here in Denmark, I grew up in a very safe place and now I am telling his story. But the responsibility is really in how you tell it. If you spend the time and really go into depth and tell a nuanced portrait," he says.

Poher Rasmussen has done that. Flee is a triumph, a shattering story about identity and exile. It has already won some of the biggest awards and is now up for the best documentary, animation and international feature at the Oscars. Some of the film's strength is in its interesting cinematography – it blends illustration with real-life flashbacks and a soundtrack that, surprisingly, fizzes with nineties and noughties classics. But it's also because of the time taken over Amin's story. Poher Rasmussen, who has known Amin since his school days, says he spent as much as five years doing roughly 20 interviews with him. "It was a long, slow process," he said.

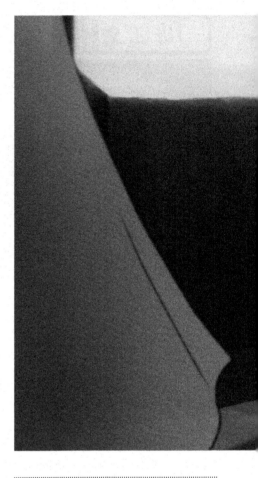

ABOVE: Amin and his mother in Kabul before they were forced to leave

Part of getting Amin to open up was an agreement that his identity would be kept secret.

"He really didn't want to be in the public eye," says Poher Rasmussen, explaining that Amin was keen to avoid meeting people in the street who had seen the film and who would ask him questions about some of the most difficult points in his life, as if that was acceptable small talk.

Poher Rasmussen got Amin to close his eyes when telling the story. The technique, which was used primarily to get Amin to remember events from years ago, creates a sense of closeness between interviewer and interviewee that feels more like a therapy session. Poher Rasmussen says that he wanted the film "to show how important it is to listen to stories and to

CREDIT: Final Cut For Real

share stories. Just the act of listening – how healing it is." He says that at "the core that's really what the film is about".

While the story takes place in the 90s and early 2000s, the film's timeliness to a 2022 audience cannot be ignored. This is not just because of the escalating crisis in Afghanistan; it's also because of a growth in anti-immigrant sentiment in Denmark. Last March Denmark became the first EU country to announce it would send Syrians back. The country's prime minister, Mette Frederiksen, has set a goal of "zero asylum-seekers".

Poher Rasmussen says Amin was welcomed when he arrived. "He was told that he was safe here and he was able to stay here. And that really enabled him to start building a life of his own." It's not the same today.

"The refugees who arrive now – if they're allowed to stay – are told that as soon as they can they will send them

back. That temporality doesn't give them anything to build on. It just creates this kind of limbo where you can't do anything and you won't be able to educate yourself, to work and become part of the community."

Poher Rasmussen says he wanted to bring "some nuance to the refugee story because a lot of time it is told in black and white and headlines and either you're for or you're against refugees".

He continues: "But no one is really for refugees, least of all refugees themselves ... being a refugee is not an identity, it's really a circumstance of life and hopefully people get through it and can start building a new life for themselves. Yes, Amin was a refugee and, yes, he fled from Afghanistan to Denmark but he's really so much more."

Poher Rasmussen says that until recently he was proud to be from Scandinavia broadly, and Denmark

 No one is really for refugees, least of all refugees themselves

specifically, because of a strong sense of trust in society. Today he's not so sure.

"We trust each other, we trust the government, we trust our friends, we trust our neighbours and we trusted Amin when he arrived. But I have a feeling this sense of trust is eroding somewhat. I really hope that what the film can show is how much value it is to show trust in someone." ✖

Jemimah Steinfeld is editor-in-chief at Index

51(01):128/129|DOI:10.1177/03064220221084565

Women defy gunmen in fight for justice

Six years after the murder of Mexican journalist Francisco Pacheco, his wife and daughter tell **TÉMORIS GRECKO** why they will not give up their cause

PRISCILLA PACHECO AND her mother Verónica Romero show up early in front of the Fiscalía General de la República, Mexico's attorney-general's office, a black high-rise building on a busy roundabout near Mexico City's downtown.

Usually, they attend a monthly meeting with the agent in charge of their case at the Special Prosecutor's Office for Crimes against Freedom of Expression (Feadle, in Spanish). But today, 24 September 2021, it's different. There's a new officer, the fourth one. His predecessors were dismissed for different reasons and, before they could take action, each needed to acquaint themselves with the facts.

"Give me three months so next time you come I'll have something new to show you," the women were told. So here they are.

Two gunmen had awaited journalist Francisco Pacheco in the dark, at dawn, as he returned home after dropping his daughter Priscilla at the bus station. It was in a narrow alley, on the mountain slopes, in an isolated part of town.

Five government entities are involved

in the crime's investigation; this doesn't seem to be enough. Priscilla and Verónica keep coming here because, nearly six years after the murder, on 25 April 2016, the prosecution has not presented the case before a judge. It has not even finished the preliminary inquiry. Possible witnesses and suspects have not been interviewed and the reconstruction of events has not happened.

"Every time we come it's a mental and physical setback for us," says Priscilla. "We'll give them a list of to-dos, missing procedures, work plans that they made but were never fulfilled." As they enter the building, Verónica says: "We are mentally prepared to be told 'He isn't there', that the agent is nowhere to be found."

The town of Taxco, in the southern state of Guerrero, is known for its pink stone churches standing out amid the pure white walls and red tile roofs of most houses, built by silver miners on steep cobbled streets on mountain slopes. Born here in 1966, Francisco Pacheco was a civil engineer who developed a passion for journalism and founded a weekly newspaper, El Foro de Taxco, in the late 1990s with Verónica and friends.

He took it seriously and the whole family became involved. At 10, eldest son Ali was conducting his first interviews. At 15, Priscilla saw a corpse on the roadside and Pacheco gave her a camera and told her to take pictures.

At 46, Pacheco became a student of communication sciences at Mexico's National Autonomous University. He went into daily coverage and

investigative journalism. His sarcastic opinion articles became a staple of Taxco's public life. Talking against the backdrop of the beautiful Santa Prisca church, local journalist Raymundo Ruiz says: "Politicians used to tease each other with his writings: 'Look, Pacheco said this about you'; 'Yeah, but he also said this about you'."

It seemed fun, but deep down it wasn't. Another colleague, Claudio Viveros, points out that "politicians are soft-skinned about humour: it drives them out of their minds".

There were ominous signs. After previewing critical stories on El Foro de Taxco's website, Salomón Majul, Taxco's mayor from 2012 until 2015, showed up with bodyguards to buy every copy before it went on sale. Pacheco gladly sold them and then reprinted the paper.

Majul was succeeded by his cousin, Omar Jalil Flores Majul, who excluded Pacheco from municipal office activities and press dispatches after he exposed the sorry state of police patrol while crime was at its highest recorded level in March 2016.

"Omar Jalil fails Taxco people" read the main headline on 3 April. The mayor said the city's budget was exhausted but Pacheco revealed the official figures of federal transfers to the local government. Then Pacheco exposed how the mayor was advertising himself, under the guise of a tourism promotion campaign paid with public money, on buses in Acapulco, the biggest urban centre in the state, which you would need to win if you ran for governor.

The story was published online on 24 April. Pacheco was murdered the next morning. The printed paper was never distributed.

Local prosecutors showed up first. But crimes against reporters are a   →

Priscilla was 16 when she heard the shots, ran out and found her father bleeding

RIGHT: On the Day of the Dead, on 1 November last year, Francisco Pacheco's portrait is one of the many on an altar to fallen journalists in Mexico City

→ federal matter, so Feadle came later followed by the Executive Commission for Attention to Victims, a presidential initiative. They all had the press take their pictures with the family, promising justice and support. Another government scheme, the Mechanism for the Protection of Journalists, told the Pachecos they would be under its wing.

But the Commission and the Mechanism quickly forgot about them. Two gunmen told Priscilla they had three days to leave Taxco or be executed. In a new city, they struggled to live on their low income and were subjected to more intimidation.

The fifth institution, the National Human Rights Commission, intervened in December 2017 to document the long string of failures of the other offices – particularly Feadle – and recommended corrective measures. That was more than four years ago.

Feadle was created in 2010 in response to the growing number of killings of journalists. Of the 94 murder cases it has agreed to investigate – it dismisses many cases – it has achieved only six sentences. Of the different causes driving violence against reporters, impunity is clearly the main one. In the six cases in which it has secured a sentence, success has been only limited: those in jail are the killers themselves but the masterminds never go to trial.

Another similarity is that, each time, Feadle acted only when it was under pressure. Julio César Colín of Article 19, which supported the Pachecos from 2017 to 2020, says fear, intimidation,

economic hardship and exhaustion force most relatives of victims to drop their struggles and forget. But in this case he "observed tenacity and determination in each member of the family to achieve truth and justice".

Ricardo Sánchez, the head of Feadle, has not responded to repeated requests from Index for an interview.

Now Priscilla and Verónica are coming out of the black building. They can hardly contain their tears. "These are cheap speeches, they didn't do anything in three months," says Priscilla. "They want me to trust, to have faith, patience … I've been patient for five years! They say 'It's a complicated case, there are perfect crimes'. What's here is corruption!"

But the Pachecos will not give up. They stage demonstrations, write articles, keep publishing El Foro de Taxco online and pressure the authorities. "We will carry on, in spite of the death threats," says Verónica.

"It's a debt of Mexican justice," adds Priscilla. "If we need to take this to international organisations, we will."

Her resolve shows every time.

Although she graduated as a copyright lawyer and is successful in that field, Priscilla's career has taken a new turn: last September, in a ceremony held online because of the pandemic, the Inter-American Human Rights Academy awarded her the title of Specialist in the Rights of Journalists.

"Do you swear to use the acquired knowledge and skills to protect freedom of expression?"

"Yes, I swear."

Months later, on 25 January this year, they come together, with a banner portraying Pacheco's picture, for another protest against the killing of journalists – this time three in two weeks.

Now 22, Priscilla was 16 when she heard the shots, ran out of their home and found her father bleeding. She shares a treasured memory: "I had a dream days after he died. He told me, 'You know what I thought the day they shot me? I thought of you'. What I best learned from him is determination in what I decide and what I do. Wherever I go, I will honour him." ✖

Témoris Grecko is a journalist and author based in Mexico City. His latest book is Killing the Story: Journalists Risking Their Lives to Uncover the Truth in Mexico (2020)

51(01):130/132|DOI:10.1177/03064220221085924

They say 'It's a complicated case, there are perfect crimes'. What's here is corruption!

CREDIT: Paola Macedo

Chaos censorship

Putin has put untruth and disinformation at the heart of
Russia's propaganda war says **JOHN SWEENEY** from Kyiv

SEMYON GUZMAN PUT down his ancient, cracked, no data mobile phone on the table of the Georgian restaurant in the centre of Kyiv and his face crumpled into one of his ironic trademark smiles: "I have a friend who used to be the head of our intelligence service. He saw this and said, good, we can't control these old ones."

True, that.

Now 75, Guzman is an old warrior from the disinformation wars from the time before yesterday. In 1971 he wrote a report on the abuse of Major General Petro Grigorenko, a Ukrainian veteran of the Great Patriotic War against the Nazis who took it into his head that the obscene privileges of the *nomenklatura* were against the principles of the Communist Party, as was the invasion of Czechoslovakia in 1968. Grigorenko was diagnosed as a paranoid delusionalist with cerebral arteriosclerosis, suffering from "an overestimation of his own personality reaching messianic proportions" and "reformist ideas".

Calling out this dark nonsense for what it was, Guzman went into battle, becoming the very first Soviet psychiatrist to condemn the state for deeming the sane mad. For this, he spent 10 years in the gulag, the first seven at the Perm penal colony in the Ural Mountains. No better a place than Kyiv right now to step back and consider that the disinformation war has always been with us. But now the new tech has been weaponised to sow chaos to billions in real time.

Leonid Brezhnev's war on truth was carried out by the liquid cosh and corrupt journalists writing bad prose in worse newspapers. There was no truth in Pravda and no news in Izvestia, but that was bleakly obvious. Vladimir Putin has revolutionised this old →

PICTURED: A woman holds a poster at the Brandenburg Gate in Berlin, Germany, in support of Ukraine's independence and sovereignty, February 2022

→ game, working with the toys of the new generation, running stories of the Ukrainians crucifying a boy in 2014, firing bots to stoke racial tension in the West as the UK voted on Brexit and the USA plumped for Donald Trump in 2016, and posting a video of a fake chemical weapon attack in the Donbas in February this year. This is censorship by chaos: pouring out so much disinformation that nobody knows what is what, that moral lines are blurred, people are confused, and so dark actors can carry on with impunity.

The "crucified boy" story was first aired on the state-owned Russia Channel One in 2014 during Putin's first, masked invasion of Ukraine's eastern oblasts, Donetsk and Luhansk. Channel One filmed eyewitness, Halyna Pyshnyak, reporting how Ukrainian soldiers had crucified a three-year-old boy. Television station RT ran a since-deleted online piece, proclaiming: "Kiev army now literally crucify babies in towns, forces mothers to watch".

The reaction of two opposition Russian politicians back then is striking. Boris Nemtsov said that it was an attempt to rally the naive to get behind war against Ukraine; Alexey Navalny

BELOW: Ukranian psychiatrist Semyon Guzman, who opposed the Soviet practice of sending dissidents to psychiatric hospitals, in Kyiv this February

Brezhnev's war on truth was carried out by the liquid cosh and corrupt journalists writing bad prose in worse newspapers

called Channel One Russia "nuts" for broadcasting the story. Nemtsov was later shot; Navalny, poisoned, now jailed.

Ukraine has issues, too, of course, but as a functioning democracy its society is far better placed to deal with fake news than Russia's. The British media can add to the chaos. In February Peter Hitchens in The Mail on Sunday noted that "Ukraine is, in fact, much like Russia in its corruption, political sleaze, oligarchs, dirty money and dodgy politics. It is not especially free and… there are quite a few Nazis."

The far-right fared so poorly at the last election that it did not pass the 5% threshold for election to parliament. Both the president and the prime minister are Jewish, and not at all Nazi. Their heels do not click. These are facts that Hitchens chose not to report because, perhaps, chaos makes better copy.

Looking further afield, Chinese media insistently report that, if there is such a place as Tibet everyone is happy there, and that the Uyghurs live model lives in their training camps. The acid test of that nonsense is that you could never

see a biography of the Dalai Lama in a Beijing book shop, but you could in Hong Kong. And now you can't.

Hitler, Stalin and Mao told big lies but the new tech has given dark actors like presidents Putin and Xi Jinping the ability to mess with our phones and tablets and laptops in a way that turbocharges confusion and chaos.

Grim as all of this is, it somehow feels less bleak than the year the poison hit its high tide, 2016. Thanks to the nerdy Sherlock Holmeses at Bellingcat and others, the Kremlin's fake news is getting called out very fast. There is more work to be done to label and correct the Chinese state's misinformation factories. But for now I suspect Semyon Guzman, a hero back in 1971 for standing up for the sane being locked up by the madmen in power, is also right to have a rubbish old phone. ✖

John Sweeney is an author and journalist who previously worked as a reporter for the Observer newspaper and the BBC

51(01):133/134|DOI:10.1177/03064220221085933

COMMENT

"Although the majority of citizens on the streets expressed their grievances peacefully, major news outlets ran stories that focused on the violence and destruction perpetrated by a minority"

EMILY COUCH ON THE BIASES THAT CREPT INTO REPORTING THE KAZAKHSTAN PROTESTS
| WE WALK A VERY THIN LINE WHEN WE REPORT 'US AND THEM' P138

In defence of the unreasonable

What was once thought of as unreasonable is now seen as common sense and vice versa.
ZIYAD MARAR looks at the reasons behind the need to be unreasonable

FOR YEARS NOW, the debate about free speech in academic settings has raged on. Concern is often expressed around the rise of a hyper-sensitive generation who demand trigger warnings, "no platforms" for those with offensive views and "safe spaces" which protect them against "micro-aggressions".

The chilling effect of these tendencies is, understandably, a cause for concern.

Universities should be enabling of debate and disagreement, of course. But this concern can have unintended consequences – especially when expressed by those with more power than the typical student.

Last year, the UK government decided to intervene with more legislative teeth and is providing for a free speech champion to sit on the board of the Office for Students. Their remit will be "to champion freedom of speech and academic freedom on campus, and responsibility for investigations of infringements of freedom of speech duties in higher education which may result in sanctions or individual redress via a new complaints scheme".

But which infringements will count? Commentators and legislators aspiring to objectivity, neutrality, reason and balance are prone to an illusion of

> ## It is easy to forget that the reason of one age was another age's unreason

transparency that is leaving something important out of the picture – they can forget to "check their privilege", as the woke might put it.

Dominant voices have long established the "reasonable-sounding" positions of their time on the grounds that they are rational, dispassionate and preserving common sense in the face of the irrational and unreasonable.

Thomas Jefferson's statement at the founding of the University of Virginia goes like this:

"This institution will be based on the illimitable freedom of the human mind. For here we are not afraid to follow truth wherever it may lead, nor to tolerate any error so long as reason is left free to combat it."

But it is easy to forget that the reason of one age was another age's unreason. And that the content of rational-seeming positions (including truths held to be self-evident to the slave-owning Jefferson) can change dramatically thanks to those who have struggled (usually unreasonably) against those who have more power.

To see tensions on campus in contrasting terms of enlightened versus unenlightened thinking is to take an ahistorical stance that obscures from view the political conflicts that have resulted in achieving the seemingly neutral ground on which we stand. And that process continues even now.

Power operates less visibly than those who have it would like to admit, which is why victors think like rational, neutral scientists and why victims have long memories, littered with grievances.

The irrational, the unreasonable and the uncomfortable are often the only weapons available to the

powerless. This is not to laud all unreasonable ideas, but it is to say we would do better to ask "who has the power?" before judging too quickly. Without this perspective in mind, we can drift towards a thinned out and misleading transparency with the ironic consequence that the free speech of those who oppose mainstream views, unreasonably, discourteously, can be seriously curbed. Meanwhile, as Jennifer Richeson, a social psychologist at Yale, has commented, a lot of what we are witnessing now is the "democratisation of discomfort". The elites are feeling as precarious as those who have long lived in the uncomfortable margins.

Students of today will be the opinion formers of the future. And some of what is derided as "political correctness gone mad" today will become common sense tomorrow. Not all of it, but some of it. As George Bernard Shaw very nearly said: "The reasonable *person* adapts *herself* to the world: the unreasonable person persists in trying to adapt the world to *herself*. Therefore, all progress depends on the unreasonable *person*."

Let's not forget that this italicised revision of Shaw's original owes much to generations of "unreasonable" women. Informed by Dale Spender's Man-Made Language they rejected the universal use of the word "he" as "non-PC" language in a way that "reasonable" people can now agree is mere common sense. ✖

Ziyad Marar FAcSS is president of global publishing at SAGE and author of The Happiness Paradox and Intimacy, and Judged: The Value of Being Misunderstood. He can be found @ZiyadMarar

51(01):136/137|DOI:10.1177/03064220221085928

We walk a very thin line when we report 'us and them'

Reverting to stereotypes when we talk about non-Western countries is lazy and feeds into the hands of dictators, says **EMILY COUCH**

WHEN PROTESTERS FILLED the streets of Kazakhstan in January, I tweeted about the Western media's failure to adequately engage local experts and accurately represent the complex dynamics of the unrest. The tweet envisaged a conversation between Western media and experts on the country, in which the former try to understand the events there but fail to because they can't move beyond an assumption of the country as both "mysterious" and "exotic". Although it was intended to be satirical, the tweet gained traction. It was born out of my increasing frustration with the way in which the Western media was reporting on these events. I am neither a Kazakhstan expert nor a "Central Asianist" but – as someone who has spent years both studying and working in the region that is often referred to as "Eurasia" – there was something deeply troubling about the way these events were being represented to a non-specialist Western audience.

Of course, no respected media outlet would use the term "exotic" outright, but exoticism – that is, the portrayal of something as "mysterious" or "dangerous" because it supposedly exists outside of Western norms – can pervade the perceptions and analyses of a place even if that particular word is absent. This distorted lens not only does a disservice to the citizens of these countries but also prevents us from truly understanding and engaging with the region in a meaningful way. It is commonplace to blame malign actors – namely, the Kremlin – for propagating misinformation or disinformation about the countries of the former Soviet Union. Western analysts, however, must also consider the role that they play in skewing perceptions of the region.

How exactly did exoticism manifest itself in the coverage of the January protests in Kazakhstan? Although the majority of citizens on the streets expressed their grievances peacefully, major news outlets ran stories that focused on the violence and destruction perpetrated by a minority, referring to the events as "riots". The BBC, for example, had an article headlined

Central Asia as a whole also suffers from a Western tendency to consider it as one homogenous block

It is clear that over-simplistic perceptions play into the hands of authoritarians

ABOVE: Kazakh soldiers guard a checkpoint after protests triggered by the increase in the cost of fuel in Almaty, Kazakhstan, in January this year

"Kazakhstan: Why are there riots and why are Russian troops there?" Le Monde wrote "Riots in Kazakhstan leave 225 dead". The use of the word "riots" rather than "protests" carries an implicit moral charge. "Protests" legitimises the expression of discontent, presenting it as orderly and confined to socially acceptable boundaries. "Riots", by contrast, shifts the focus away from the grievances of participants and implies chaos and illegitimacy.

Contrast this with the ongoing unrest in Belarus. Here, the focus has been on the peacefulness and dignity of the protesters in the face of the Lukashenka regime's cruelty. While it is true that

Belarus has not seen the seizing of key buildings and burning cars – images which have characterised the coverage of the unrest in Kazakhstan – the choice to focus on these images, and not on the many more which would illustrate that the majority of street actions were peaceful, is striking.

Central Asia as a whole also suffers from a Western tendency to consider it as one homogenous block. The habit of referring to the countries in this region as "the Stans" – the Orientalist connotations of which Diyora Shadijanova eloquently highlighted in a piece for The Calvert Journal – is a clear indication of this.

The rather embarrassing error of The New York Times in which an article referred to the non-existent country of "Kyrzbekistan" – as well as its, alas intentional, reference to Central Asia as "the moustache belt" – provide almost satirical examples of how Western discourse lumps these very different countries into one imaginative space.

Approaching the issue with an even wider lens, we can see that the problem of exoticism in Western perceptions affects the whole of what is often referred to as the "post-Soviet space". The term itself indicates that while the Iron Curtain may have vanished three decades ago, it remains an anchor for the Western imagination: on this side, there is us; on the other, them. The prevalence of the term "Putin's backyard" or – in policy circles – "Russia's sphere of influence" to refer to any country that was once a Soviet republic reinforces this notion that they are fundamentally different from the West by denying the assumption of autonomy and sovereignty accorded to countries such as the USA and France.

Take Ukraine for example. Since the Revolution of Dignity in 2013-14, Ukrainians have fought hard to show the world that they are part of Europe. Visit Kyiv and you will see almost as many EU flags as you would in Paris or Berlin. Yet, still, many Western

observers and policymakers struggle to take this conceptual step, continuing to perpetuate the Kremlin-backed narrative that Ukraine is an irreparably divided country shackled to its past.

As developments in Eurasia and eastern Europe once again dominate our headlines, it is vital that we have a broader conversation that examines the diversity within each of these countries – each has its own historically marginalised communities – and how internal Orientalist dynamics interact with those coming from the West. We should also unpack the racial dynamics implicit in conceptions of "the exotic", which were particularly evident in the media portrayal of the Kazakhstan protests. As these examples highlight, Western observers and policymakers have failed to treat these countries with the same degree of nuance and respect that we would expect for our own.

As someone who works in the human rights field, it is clear that over-simplistic perceptions play into the hands of authoritarians. The more we consider a society to be "mysterious", distant or fundamentally different from ours, the easier it is to think "that's just what happens over there". Only by moving away from this mindset can we make informed policy decisions that respect the agency of countries and citizens in this region and create meaningful networks of transnational solidarity. ✖

Emily Couch is a programme consultant for PEN America's Eurasia Programme

51(01):138/139|DOI:10.1177/03064220221084523

It's time to put down the detached watchdog

After years of working in Kurdistan, **FRÉDERIKE GEERDINK** questions whether Western newsrooms are failing in their duty to report accurately and really hold power to account

PICTURED: A Russian journalist covers the annual press conference of Vladimir Putin in 2019, displaying a T-shirt which does not hide his lack of partiality

WE NEED TO start a conversation about the "detached watchdog" in journalism. This is a role which journalists can assign to themselves and it has been hampering the rise of journalists from marginalised communities in mainstream media. That position needs to change.

The connection between the role perceptions of journalists in Western mainstream media and its inability to recruit journalists from marginalised communities is not often made.

Over the last couple of decades, research has been done into role perceptions. One classification (researched and described by Thomas Hanitzsch, chair and professor of communication at LMU Munich) is particularly interesting when it comes to diversity. It distinguishes three other roles beside that of the detached watchdog: the populist disseminator, the critical change agent and the opportunist facilitator. The detached watchdog, Hanitzsch found, dominated the journalistic field in Western countries, while the critical change agent was more prevalent in two Middle Eastern countries he researched, Egypt and Turkey. In countries with a bad track record of press freedom or a dictatorial past – such as China, Indonesia, Chile and Russia – the group of journalists seeing themselves as opportunist facilitator is relevant as they are often supporters of power.

While the critical change agent emphasises the importance of advocating social change, influencing public opinion and setting the political agenda through journalism, the concept of impartiality is at the core of the detached watchdog. What the detached watchdogs in mainstream Western media fail to see, though, is that objectivity does not exist. Everyone looks at the world in a specific

≣ Objectivity does not exist. Everyone looks at the world in a specific way

way. It becomes even more difficult when you add race, class and gender into the mix and many newsrooms in Western countries remain the preserve of white, older men.

In my own country, the Netherlands, the editorial floors of nine mainstream media (both papers and TV) have changed – but not very much. The daily newspaper NRC Handelsblad went from having 96.8% white staff in 2015 to 94.6% in 2018.

It's not only about race, it's about class. In the UK, according to the Social Mobility Commission's State of the Nation report in 2016, 11% of journalists were from working-class backgrounds, compared with 60% of the population.

There are at least some new initiatives to tackle this problem in the UK, such as PressPad and the Journalism Diversity Fund. In the Netherlands, there is none.

One of the changes NRC Handelsblad found was that editors were increasingly acknowledging that it was important for the quality of journalism to have reporters from a wide range of backgrounds.

This is not a problem which relates just to opportunities. It makes a difference to the sorts of stories that get reported – and how. White glasses, so to speak, are tinted glasses, too. And these are exactly the same as the ones worn by those holding power. Describing themselves as detached is in itself proof that they don't see their position. This is a problem because isn't it journalism's core task to hold power to account?

But while this role perception may be dominant amongst many journalists, it is less dominant among journalists from marginalised groups. A lot of these journalists are detached from power simply because they are not the dominant group in society, but they know power very well, merely by dealing with it on a daily basis. Wouldn't that be exactly the angle needed in the newsroom? You could even argue these journalists may be the actual detached watchdogs.

White glasses … are tinted glasses, too. And these are exactly the same as the ones worn by those holding power

I myself transitioned from self-proclaimed detached watchdog to critical change agent in the decade that I worked on the ground as a correspondent in Turkey and Kurdistan. I was forced to change my perspective by the work of Kurdish colleagues and the testimonies of the countless citizens I interviewed. What I saw were marginalised communities who knew dominant society better than the dominant society knew itself; Kurds, for example, who knew Turkish society and state power better than Turks. These journalists didn't strive or claim to be detached, and for that their Turkish colleagues would call them (at best) activists. But I can tell you their reporting was truthful and Turkish media were missing stories.

I started looking differently at my own country and the journalism that I knew. If I had got to know Turkey so much better and managed to write stories so much more sharply while looking through the marginalised lens, wouldn't the same count for journalism in the Netherlands?

Ethiopian-Dutch journalist Seada Nourhussen, editor-in-chief of magazine One World, has been a journalist for two decades and wrote a column about often being called an "activist".

She wrote: "I think it is my duty to explain and fight injustice and abuse of power. That's the reason I wanted to be in journalism. To bring stories to light that others didn't see, didn't want to see or told incompletely. To give space to underexposed perspectives in a profession that is dominated by a too homogenous group of privileged people."

Zoë Papaikonomou, who is Greek-Dutch, interviewed more than 50 bicultural journalists about their professional experiences. She told me: "[Many] of the interviewees said they had chosen to be in journalism because they missed stories from the perspectives of their communities in mainstream media. They felt a responsibility to help change that."

These journalists are, no doubt, critical change agents. Without more of them, stories will remain untold. An example in the Netherlands is the child benefits scandal (more than 20,000 families were wrongly accused of fraud) which eventually surfaced in mainstream media in 2018. Lawyer Eva Gonzalez Perez, who had been fighting for victims for years and couldn't get the attention of the media, said she eventually decided to put journalists in touch with white victims, even though most of her clients were black, because she knew journalists would identify with them more easily. Would that have been necessary if the newsroom had been less white?

So here is a proposal. Let's upgrade the critical change agent role to be the default setting. Journalists would become better at disseminating power dynamics. And journalists from marginalised groups would not be considered "too activist" but would be rightly recognised as examples to live up to. It's not the newcomers in the profession who have to adjust, it's the old guard. It is not too late to live up to journalism's promise to genuinely hold power to account. It's high time to ditch the detached watchdog. ✖

Fréderike Geerdink, based in the Nether-lands and Kurdistan, is a freelance journalist who writes about power and those who want to break it down

51(01):140/141|DOI:10.1177/03064220221084524

GLOBAL VIEW

A light in the dark

Index Chair **TREVOR PHILLIPS** reflects on some of the magazine's achievements, ranging from dominating the news agenda to the smaller acts that have kept people going when everyone else has overlooked them

"The most powerful weapon is not the bomb. It is the truth"
– *Andrei Sakharov, Nobel Laureate 1975*

ALWAYS THOUGHT IT one of the great ironies of the age that Andrei Sakharov, the father of the Russian hydrogen bomb, won the Nobel Peace Prize. Yet he deserved it for his lonely fight to give voice to the dissident movement in the USSR, when thousands of artists and writers had disappeared, their voices virtually unheard. Whilst the authorities could destroy the works of artists and writers, it was harder to silence the nation's most garlanded physicist, winner of both the Stalin and Lenin Prizes, and one of the greatest assets of the Soviet military establishment. But they had to try.

Just three years before our first appeal was launched in the pages of the Times Literary Supplement, the great physicist had published a stunning cri de coeur calling for creative and intellectual freedom everywhere. His advocacy made him a cause celebre to young scientists like myself. It also guaranteed his eclipse by the Soviet authorities. Within a decade of the launch of Index, even he had been locked out of his laboratories and denounced by official scholarly bodies. He was eventually exiled to Gorky, a closed city, where authorities hoped he'd be forgotten.

His example taught me lessons that still, in my view, inform the work of Index. First, that no-one, however distinguished and revered, is safe from persecution. If Sakharov could be muted, so could anyone if the authorities were determined. Second, that in the mind of authoritarians, truth is the most dangerous enemy. Third, freedom dies every time someone opts for silence in the hope that it will protect them from repression. And last, that tyranny never really gives up its assault on truth – it simply changes its flag and its anthem.

No one should have to be a hero in order to point out that everyday reality is separate from authoritarian fantasy. But for the past 50 years that is exactly what the many individuals have been struggling to do through their writings, art, satire and journalism. Index on Censorship, operating in the relative freedom of the West, has amplified their voices to the world – sometimes starting with nothing more than a conspiratorial whisper or a smuggled verse.

Written after leaving prison in 1983, the banned Czech playwright Václav Havel's Mistake responded to Samuel Beckett's Catastrophe; both appeared in our magazine. In 1989 we published the Hunger Strike Declaration by leaders of the Tiananmen Square protests. In 2002, the journalist Anna Politkovskaya gave us one of the first investigations of the Russian war in Chechnya. She was assassinated four years later. All of these stories gained global prominence.

But Index has never lost sight of the people whose stories are not worldwide news. For those who lose the right to speak, silence is total. The fact that someone, somewhere noticed made a difference. The disappearance of the Shah's opponents in the 1970s would have gone unremarked by many who entertained his generals both in London and in Tehran if it were not for Index's reports of their torture and disappearance. The arrests of journalists in the Maldives may not lead the headlines in London, but our coverage is no less important for those who are locked up or locked out. To the media organisation promoting LGBTQ rights in Uganda, or the radio station taking on drug cartels in Latin America, the fact that their struggle is not conducted in total darkness can make the difference between life and death.

The best thing would be for Index to have no reason to exist. But based on what we've learned over the past 50 years we have no plan for that eventuality. We know that those who have no answer to a question will still do their best to prevent it being asked. Those who cannot persuade others will still try to intimidate them. And those who find a diversity of views inconvenient will attempt to obliterate every version of the truth but their own. That is why Index has been here for half a century and why it won't stop being needed any time soon. ✘

Trevor Phillips is Chair of Index on Censorship

For those who lose the right to speak, silence is total. The fact that someone, somewhere noticed made a difference

51(01):142/142|DOI:10.1177/03064220221085927

Our work here is far from done

Index CEO **RUTH SMEETH** pays tribute to the organisation's past work and promises those efforts will not cease in the next 50 years

NDEX ON CENSORSHIP was founded to be a voice for the persecuted. A bastion for freedom of expression as a liberal democratic value that must be afforded to everyone on the planet, to shine a light on the actions of authoritarian regimes and to publish the works of those that the dictators sought to silence.

Even in the early 1970s, Stephen Spender considered the issue of censorship in the round – not just through the prism of the Cold War.

In his launch op-ed for Times Literary Supplement, he raised the spectres of censorship, surveillance and emergent technologies. He highlighted the fact that threats to free expression were not solely the purview of tyrants and cautioned all of us fortunate to live in democracies to keep an eye on the actions of our own governments.

His words continue to resonate today. As much as I wish the role of Index were unnecessary 50 years after our launch, the reality is that we have never been needed more.

On the pages of this anniversary edition, many writers and scholars have outlined the historic challenges to free expression over the last 50 years, as well as those which we continue to fight against – from the USSR to the CCP.

As the current custodian of this special and quirky organisation with an extraordinary heritage, the determination of what should be our future focus falls to me and our dedicated and brilliant trustees, led by the exceptional Sir Trevor Phillips.

There are too many issues that we could, and should, campaign against; too many tyrants who need to be exposed and too many brave writers, artists, academics and journalists who need our help. We will never be able to fix everything, but we must help and intervene where we can do the most good.

In the coming years, Index will continue to refocus our efforts on being a voice for the persecuted. We will go on building on our heritage in eastern Europe, China and South America; publishing the works of those whom governments seek to silence; celebrating the bravery of those who have faced appalling mistreatment for the "crime" of speaking, drawing or writing truth to power; and defending the rights of those whose views may be in the minority. It is in this tradition that we will embrace the ongoing threats to free expression by both authoritarian regimes and those that consider themselves to be democratic in nature.

At the heart of our challenges in the next 50 years will be AI, new technologies and new ways of communication.

The challenge won't be the tech itself but how democracies seek to regulate it and how dictators attempt to manipulate it. Technology has both facilitated greater freedom of expression and had unexpected consequences, from an increase in hate speech to threats to "cancel" people rather than debate the pertinent issues at hand.

Tech has also enabled the most repressive regimes to control every aspect of their citizens' lives. Our online presence and how we protect ourselves will be at the heart of Index's work in the decades ahead.

While we continue to analyse and shine a light on how repressive regimes are seeking to silence their own people within their borders, we will focus on how they are using their resources to control how the rest of the world responds to them – whether that's through academia, the arts or more traditional propaganda.

As we move into our sixth decade our work has never been more vital and it is this proud heritage that we will build on in the coming years.

It would be remiss of me not to thank every current and former member of staff and the wider Index family who have been part of our story so far. Their commitment and dedication have changed the law in numerous countries, provided support to some of the bravest people in the world and affected how we collectively consider some appalling regimes. Their work, under the banner of Index, is why we're still here today, and we are in their debt. ✖

Ruth Smeeth is CEO of Index on Censorship

51(01):143/143|DOI:10.1177/03064220221085929

We will never be able to fix everything, but we must help and intervene where we can do the most good

'a long overdue window'

MALIKA BOOKER

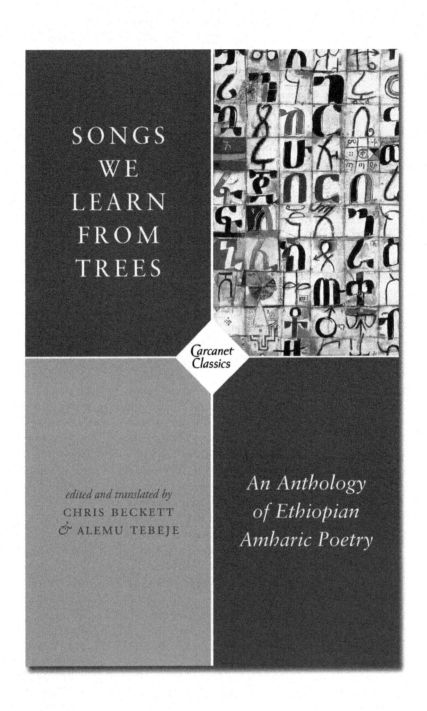

SONGS WE LEARN FROM TREES

AN ANTHOLOGY OF ETHIOPIAN AMHARIC POETRY

SONGS WE LEARN FROM TREES

Carcanet Classics

edited and translated by
CHRIS BECKETT
& ALEMU TEBEJE

An Anthology
of Ethiopian
Amharic Poetry

£18.99 / 978 1 78410 947 9 / CARCANET CLASSICS

CARCANET

CULTURE

"The place of writers is not within the state machine," Kuznetsov reproves. "Loyal outsiders, expressing the spirit of Marxism Leninism. The bird of freedom must live wild, or it is just a pet"

NICK HARKAWAY'S PLAYFUL REIMAGINING OF THE EARLY DAYS OF INDEX | ANYA'S BIBLE P147

In vodka veritas

NICK HARKAWAY talks to **JEMIMAH STEINFELD** about the story he has written based on the early days of Index and bars in Moscow

LEFT: The author Nick Harkaway (Cornwell), who is known for his mind-bending looks at the ills of modern society

CONVIVIAL AND WITH a mind that leads conversations off in tangents, Nick Harkaway is the kind of person who'd be great to have a drink with, which is fitting given his short story is set in a bar. In an Index exclusive, the award-winning author has reimagined the early days of the magazine when its content – and the magazine itself – would be smuggled across borders. In Harkaway's story a motley crew congregate in a dark, sweaty bar somewhere behind the Iron Curtain sometime in the 1970s. Harkaway, nom de plume of Nick Cornwell, says he was inspired by a trip he made to Russia years back and by the "smoky room craziness of the Writers' Union".

Harkaway went to a different writers' club when in Moscow, which was in "a dismal basement selling terrible food" and "was duly obliterated with vodka".

"It clearly had that history of having been exactly the same place doing exactly the same thing for about 100 years and having had to wear different hats in order to be allowed to do that. It was a club, it was a library, it was a union headquarters, it was a this and a that, but it was always a bar with

> ≡ The creeping rise of totalitarianism has persuaded Harkaway to pivot away from darker material

terrible food and too much vodka." Most significantly, it was somewhere people could speak more freely.

"It doesn't matter what the world is doing – there is always a bar where people can go and get drunk and say rash or inappropriate things they might not otherwise be able to get away with," said Harkaway.

His story reads like a thank-you to Index. "Essentially I just thought the original Spender letter was extraordinary," said Harkaway, of Stephen Spender's 1971 letter in The Times Literary Supplement that outlined the reasons for and ambitions of the magazine. Harkaway also has a personal connection to Index. He briefly worked at Article 19, which has close ties to the organisation, and his father, the late David Cornwell (better known as John le Carré), contributed to the magazine.

When he was writing the story for Index, he "thought about doing a full-on smuggling story – trying to get a document out or get something in", but decided against it. He feared that would feel like "a budget, espionage tribute to my dad".

Harkaway's background has clearly informed his writing, and not just when it comes to Index. His fourth novel, Gnomon, is a detective story set in a dystopic future of total surveillance. He started writing it in 2014. He wanted to write a short, literary book in which he warned "about the dangers of creeping totalitarianism and the possibilities of totalitarians popping out of the woodwork". It wasn't published until 2017, by which stage Donald Trump was president in the USA.

"I took a little bit too long over it to be prescient... When the book came out that was already happening," he said.

The creeping rise of totalitarianism has persuaded Harkaway to pivot away from darker material. "Essentially I feel since then I have kind of gone off dystopian writing because dystopia has moved into the real world."

"One of the things I've noticed about the Trumps and the Boris Johnsons of this world is that you can't really shame them into doing the right thing. You can't hold up a mirror and say 'This is what you are' and have everybody suddenly decide that they'll be a good person or a better person. All you do is sort of feed their narrative."

Harkaway is currently working on something hopeful because for him being hopeful is "obligatory". To give in to despair is to lose, to yield the high ground.

"The thing that a lot of these new populists depend on is a sense that things cannot get better, there is no agenda that can save you, there is no way that we can make things work for you so you may as well forget about it and let us get on with ruling you, which I find really depressing," he said.

"And actually there is hope, there are solutions, there are people who are working on answers and some of those answers are not just structurally interesting, they're also beautiful."

Plus, says Harkaway, we have moved forward on some conversations. Privacy, for example. He has noticed a change in attitude around surveillance in just the last few years, especially in terms of corporations harvesting data. People used to be indifferent whereas now they are more concerned. Harkaway talks about "intangible

CREDIT: Nadav Kander

bads", which are things you know are bad but you can't actually see them and touch them. Surveillance falls in this camp.

"What I hope is that we're getting better and better at dealing with ambient bad effect and recognising that they do have causes and you can take precautions against them because otherwise we really are in deep

trouble," Harkaway said of this.

If we are in deep trouble we'll have to hope there are bars still open where we can talk without fear, even if the food is terrible. ✖

Jemimah Steinfeld is editor-in-chief at Index on Censorship

51(01):146/151|DOI:10.1177/03064220221084526

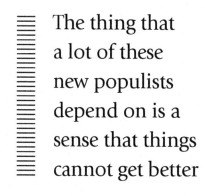

The thing that a lot of these new populists depend on is a sense that things cannot get better

Anya's Bible

By NICK HARKAWAY

THE RUSSIAN POET has Robbie in a headlock and is telling him he's a genius: he, Robbie, is a genius, a great genius to rival Eliot and Pound (who were both very Russian, for complex reasons which will have to be explained later) and the poet knows this because the poet is himself a genius of astonishing proportions, as yet unacknowledged by a society which - though masquerading as an egalitarian and socialist one in which the means of creativity have been reclaimed by the proletariat - is for now still blind in an almost American way to the scale of the genius which has been given life within its borders.

"Hi," Robbie says, to the poet's armpit. "I'm Robbie."

"Yes, you are!" The armpit agrees. "Robbie Malone, genius! I am Kuznetsov. It is to be a blacksmith, but I make words which are stronger than iron. In my cradle I was kissed by Ahmatova. In this I am enviable but also by this I was touched with poetry. Call me Dima, I will call you Robbie: we need beer and vodka."

Whether they do or not, it's coming, and though Robbie was broadly prepared for it, the arrival is still formidable: a tall glass, European style, full of yellow Czechoslovak lager, and with it not the decorous shot glass of clear

Russian booze he'd been anticipating, but a wide-bottomed tumbler into which his new friend pours a generous slosh which brings with it immediate condensation. Alexeev, Robbie's state interpreter and politely acknowledged watcher, shakes his head.

"Oh, shit," he says in English, and lifts his own glass. "Get some food as well, Mr Malone."

Kuznetsov nods vigorously. "Only the best food for genius. The best food and the best drink. We have already ordered for you."

Robbie says thanks, and receives as his comeuppance a scalding metal pan which he takes at first to be something like a Greek moussaka, but in fact contains button mushrooms and snails in a thick savoury custard or béchamel. Alexeev shakes his head.

"We should have gone to the Writer's Union," he says, with authentic gloom. "They have venison."

"The place of writers is not within the state machine," Kuznetsov reproves. "Loyal outsiders, expressing the spirit of Marxism Leninism. The bird of freedom must live wild, or it is just a pet."

"And it must eat really horrible crap," Alexeev murmurs, as Kuznetsov turns away to say something to a woman with thick hands and a severe grey dress, "this is vital to the creative process."

Sitting around the end of the refectory table, they're a curious trio: Kuznetsov, huge and hirsute, smelling strongly of sweat and the inside of a hunter's fur gilet he declines to remove even in the hot underground of the Library; Alexeev, ➔

→ prim and tweedy, his English note-perfect down to the spiteful asides, as if he learned the language from Robbie's seriously disapproving sister, whose finger can find dust on any mantelpiece either side of the Iron Curtain. Not that she'd ever come to Russia, after the way they treated their royalty. Robbie, who took a second class degree in history, feels more tenderly towards doing away with monarchs, but draws the line at heirs and infants.

He looks around, soaking it in: blue tobacco smoke, tart and rough; a low ceiling and two wood-burning stoves, one at either end of the basement room. Stone flagging that must be two hundred years old, could be eight. Books on the panelled walls – the place was a club in Tsarist times, then immediately an independent writers' union after 1917, then a library, and more recently notionally still a library, serving food and drink to those who live by the pen. According to Alexeev, almost nothing has changed across each of these incarnations. "Especially not that," Alexeev says, nodding to Robbie's congealing bowl.

The severe dress sits down at Robbie's other side. He realises dimly that the vodka has already had an effect. How long has it been? Twenty seconds? Twenty minutes? Jesus, has Kuznetsov been topping up his glass? Too late to worry about that now. He smiles shyly in the direction of the grey wool. Everyone here wears muted colours. Dyes, he supposes, are expensive and frivolous, but he can't shake the feeling that the uniform pastel and granite tones are also protective colouration. Standing out is not encouraged, even here in the interior, where the policing is less enthusiastic than hard by the border.

Grey dress looks back at him, expectant. He's forgotten something.

"Am I drunk?" he asks Alexeev.

The little man shrugs. "That probably depends on your points of reference."

Robbie decides that means yes.

"Elena," the dress says kindly, "Semenova."

His host, Robbie realises, and the whole reason he's here. They met in his publisher's flat in Primrose Hill, an area his mother warned him was where rich men kept their mistresses. He stands up, which leaves Elena Semenova sitting down and looking up at him. Kuznetsov gets up too, so now it's an occasion. There's a ragged cheer from the other tables.

"The poet Malone," Kuznetsov bellows, "'Red Fire In The Heart'. London, 1972."

Another cheer, and someone starts reciting the title poem. Robbie, when he reads it, does so with a hushed intensity he hopes is almost sexual, though evidence of this effect is scant. The woman by the stove now giving voice to his work is treating it like a pulpit oration, and the rhythms in her mouth are richer and surer. When she names the organs where the fire burns, he becomes acutely uncomfortable. They warned him at home: poetry in Russia is not poetry here.

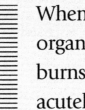

When she names the organs where the fire burns, he becomes acutely uncomfortable

Vodka and eye contact and blunt force eroticism. He looks away.

The severe dress is still waiting, indulgent of his un-Russian frailty.

"Robbie Malone," Robbie says. "A pleasure to meet you."

Elena Semenova tilts her head back to take him in. She is nearly sixty and famously beautiful, or at least beautiful and described that way in discussions at home, with silver hair arranged in what he thinks of as a Katharine Hepburn bun. Not a dissident, but a tolerated friend of dissidents, as any good organiser of literary exchanges must be. Not an informer, either, but too close to the state establishment to be entirely comfortable. Alexeev, on Robbie's right, relaxes a little, as if her presence absolves him of one →

→ layer of paranoia.

Don't get into it, Robbie reminds himself sternly. If you start trying to work out who's spying on whom, you'll go nuts. They all are, in every imaginable direction, and no one, but no one, actually knows what's going on.

"Welcome," Elena Semenova says. "To the great literary superpower that is my home."

"Not only literary," Alexeev says, and Elena snorts as she raises her glass: ballistic nuclear explosives are evidently *infra dignitatem*, and he should know better.

"You should take a lover," Semenova says, though whether to Robbie or to Alexeev is unclear.

The actual festival is very short, at least from Robbie's point of view: direly hungover, he reads Red Fire and realises as he does so that it is appallingly sophomoric. Meeting the glassy yellow eyes of Kuznetsov, still in his pungent gilet and unrepentantly living on black cigarettes which stink of clove, he finds himself reassessing his benign and pastoral British socialist verse in the knowledge that his new friend is deeply moved precisely because the poem describes nothing recognisable. When asked to connect Freud and Nechaev with the leitmotifs from After Pessoa, all Robbie can think of to say is that he hopes he was successful in emulating Pushkin, which is as close to a safe answer in the context as can be imagined, and is met with polite acceptance. They move on to questions, with Kuznetsov translating and Alexeev sulking in the corner because this was his big moment and the other man has somehow finessed it away from him. A long first question, clauses complexly subordinated. Robbie recognises the type from innumerable events in the Home Counties: a long preamble intended to show the questioner has done the homework followed by one of the standard queries couched in highfalutin terms. With due respect to Shakespeare and Marlowe's use of iambic pentameter and recognising the inferiority of the Patrarchian sonnet in the modern discourse, where do you get your ideas?

"Please," Kuznetsov says, "the question is: do you believe that the Black Flag of Mosleyite Fascism will ever fly over the British Houses of Parliament and in this eventuality what action will you personally take to restore the Historical Process and midwife the socialist imperative?"

"Oh," Robbie says, "right."

When he's answered that, plus a few other simple little gems, he's free to go. Elena Semenova tells him he's been perfect. He doesn't know what that means and he isn't convinced she does either. Alexeev takes him on a tour: architecture, historical interest, industrial and cultural superiority, then drinks. He shakes hands with a senior party member who tells him to come back soon. An American cultural attaché apologises for being unable to make the reading.

"I hear you were great."

Robbie nods, hoping that the CIA doesn't really believe that, or everyone's in trouble.

"You were not great," a voice says, and someone takes his arm. "You were ordinary." The woman from the Library, the one who recited Red Fire, smiles up at him. "Anya."

Robbie nods, afflicted with an instant form of panic he recognises as schoolboy infatuation.

She has brown hair and a wide face with a wide nose, a blue jacket and work trousers in the Land Girl mode, rendered stylish through an alchemical combination of needlework and confidence. Anya. This is Anya. This is what Anya looks like, the shape she makes in the world.

"I thought so too," he tells her. "Or maybe just bad."

"No." Very definite. "Not bad. You gave what you had, with integrity. To imagine it does not possess quality is to submit to a mystification of the process of art. A hierarchy of poetry. Your work is naive. Tomorrow it will be less. We are all the product of our days."

"Thank you."

"You are polite."

"Yes."

She shrugs. "That also is a mystification."

"Perhaps a permissible one, when a gentleman is speaking to a lady."

The ghost of a smile. "What is your opinion of Evelyn Waugh?"

Robbie has no poetic nonsense left, and even if

he had, he wouldn't use it now.

"He's fine. Studiously miserable. Everyone works hard to produce the most awful outcome imaginable. I rate the quality but I don't enjoy him."

She considers that. "Yes." A passing grade. "We should enjoy. That is true. Pleasure is not a mystification. Are you a religious person?"

Robbie considers saying that religion is hardly compatible with modern dialectical Marxism, but doesn't. He's not a modern dialectical Marxist. He's a poet, however lousy in his own internal reckoning. His poetry enforces his compassion, his compassion tells him unfettered commercial activity will not produce the kindly picket-fenced Utopia of advertising campaigns. But poetry about incremental change doesn't stir, so he writes what he writes and does not entirely believe it.

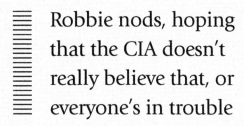 ## Robbie nods, hoping that the CIA doesn't really believe that, or everyone's in trouble

"No, I can't say that I am."

She smiles and reaches inside the work jacket. The process is captivating. She laughs at him, but not unkindly, and passes a small paper-wrapped object the size of a deck of cards. On the paper – not sealed, just folded – is written "return to sender" and under, what he takes to be the same message in Cyrillic. "For your Archbishop of Canterbury. It is his pleasure to send many Bibles to us, by many different routes. It is banned, of course. This one is the English Standard Version, made to look like a deck of cards. That way, it is to appear quite harmless." She leans closer. "They are the wrong cards. To play Preferans, one needs only the Piquet deck. The design is from Las Vegas. Your Archbishop needs better spies. Also the language is impoverished by contrast with

the grossly inaccurate King James." Her hand grips his shoulder so that she doesn't have to raise her voice. She's laughing at the Archbishop of Canterbury, and he could touch his face to hers merely by bending his neck.

"An appropriate cultural gift, no doubt," Alexeev says. Robbie, miraculously, does not murder him.

"Not at all," Anya says. "It is a contraband Bible. I have defaced it with pornographic sketches so that it cannot be returned to the Motherland."

Alexeev, in the act of reaching out to examine the little parcel, snatches his hand back again. "You have not!"

"No. I cannot draw."

"What can you do?" Robbie asks her. "Are you a poet? An actress?"

She sighs. "I am a writer of technical manuals. Do you know how to replace the cylinders on the Stalinets S-65? I can show you."

"I'd like that," Robbie says, which makes her laugh again, and Alexeev rolls his eyes.

"Oh, my God," he says. "Sex?"

"Not yet," Anya says. "In about an hour, maybe."

Alexeev goes a little pink. "Don't keep the Bible," he tells Robbie. "If the Border people feel like it, they can put you in prison for having one of those."

But he forgets, courtesy of Anya's quite accurate prophecy, and then in a whirl he's back on the home side of the Curtain with his unintended contraband, unpacking in Lady Margaret Road, holding the thing up and looking, as if the Russian watchers are still peering over his shoulder, to see whether Anya really did draw a frank self-portrait on Proverbs 5:18.

And finding instead a letter addressed to Stephen Spender, care of Malone.

To you, Dear Friends, who speak for no organisation, but see our need and extend your support, we are forever grateful.

Nick Harkaway is the pen name of the award-winning writer Nick Cornwell. He is the author of six books and lives in London

A ghost-written tale of love

The links between the past, present and future are important and hard to break, **ARIEL DORFMAN** tells **JEMIMAH STEINFELD**

AS HE APPROACHES his 80th birthday, Ariel Dorfman is interested in ghosts. His 2018 novel – a meditation on how the crimes of our ancestors reverberate for generations – even referenced them in its title, Darwin's Ghosts.

Now, in an Index exclusive, the playwright, novelist and activist has written a short story which, once again, examines the idea of continuity and confrontation with the past.

"As I grow older, I have found myself increasingly obsessed with the question of how the dead persist among us," he said.

"Mostly, this preoccupation has been made manifest in a series of poems that feature voices from the other side of death, warnings for those who are alive (like Dante foretelling Trump what awaits him beyond the beyond), words that are collected in a forthcoming volume of my verse."

But there is also a personal element to Dorfman's fascination.

"I worry, as an atheist, about how to bridge the abyss that death will excavate between myself and my wife, Angélica – to whom I have been married for almost 60 years."

Mumtaz takes us into the mind of Shah Jahan, the fifth Mughal emperor of India who reigned from 1628 to 1658 and famously built the Taj Mahal as a token of love for his deceased wife, Mumtaz. Dorfman was inspired when he visited the monument. He says his "search for ways in which love endures despite the physical absence of the partner's body was answered one morning when, sitting with Angélica, hand in hand, for hours on a bench facing the Taj Mahal, I was struck with the revelation that here was a story I would pursue until it was ready to be told, when the marble in love would speak to me in words and not stone".

He says that Shah Jahan came to him recently and dictated the story.

Dorfman is known for his exploration of trauma and injustice. His 1990 play Death and the Maiden – first published in English in Index and later turned into a film by Roman Polanski – follows the story of a sadistic doctor who rapes a political prisoner.

And so, in Dorfman style, this is not a straightforward love story.

Instead, we meet an anguished Jahan, nearing the end of his life and consumed with both his love for Mumtaz and a lingering suspicion that this love has led to bad decisions. Not that he says these words as such. In this story, to speak of this would waste words not on Mumtaz. Jahan is not so much censored by society as by his own mind, trapped in his love for his wife.

"It's paradoxical that if Shah Jahan had been less fixated on keeping his wife alive through the tomb he built for her, he would have probably been a better ruler and would have avoided the worst of his offspring taking over the throne," said Dorfman. In the story, as in true life, his son Aurangzeb usurps him.

Dorfman said that Aurangzeb "is his creation (the loins of Shah Jahan are social as well as anatomical: he is the 'author' of the usurper)".

"The 'villain', then, could perhaps merely be humanity, our collective that has not yet been able to figure out historical ways to envisage a future where beauty and justice are not at odds," he said. "Nevertheless, it is this extremely confused, stumbling humanity that has gifted us the consolation of a temple which urges us to never stop seeking the foundations of enduring love inside others."

For Dorfman, ghosts are reminders of past mistakes that we are destined to repeat. "That such a love-monument cleanses us is undeniable, but if we do not carry its message into the world, truly recognise that beauty, then the sins will continue to infect society," he said. "It's the case of India (and not only India) today. And yesterday. The narrator's own son is unable to comprehend what his father is doing."

That Dorfman is drawn to the themes of conflict and resolution is no surprise. His family has lived through some of the most tumultuous events of the 20th century.

The son of Jewish immigrants from Eastern Europe, he was born in Argentina but moved to the USA as a child after his father fled president Juan Perón's soldiers. McCarthyism later forced them out of the USA and they settled in Chile.

Dorfman worked as a cultural adviser to Salvador Allende, then president, in the early 1970s. But after Augusto Pinochet's coup in 1973, Dorfman was →

As I grow older, I have found myself increasingly obsessed with the question of how the dead persist among us

He says that Shah Jahan came to him recently and dictated the story

→ once again exiled. He lived in Paris, the Netherlands and later the USA. Today he splits his time between the USA and a now democratic Chile. When we speak he has just touched down in Santiago.

"I'm transfixed with hope at the resounding victory of [president-elect Gabriel] Boric, the possibility that his government could set an example for how to fight neo-liberal inequities and longstanding discrimination against women, indigenous peoples, the underserved," he said with optimism, before striking a more cautious note.

"But, as I wrote in a recent comment in The Guardian, the shadow of General Pinochet still darkens a Chile where 44% of the electorate voted for a crypto-fascist like [ultra-conservative candidate Jose Antonio] Kast. That minority, fearful of any deepening of democracy, retains enormous power and influence and will try to deter radical change."

When Dorfman was last interviewed by Index, Donald Trump was in power in the USA and Dorfman was incredibly worried about freedom in the country. Joe Biden's presidency has not quelled these concerns. In fact, he's concerned "more perhaps than before".

"Trump is a symptom of a deeper excrescence and malaise in America, the consequence of that country not having dealt with what has been corroding it since its inception, ghosts that do not only come from its own history but a situation I delve into in my novel, Darwin's Ghosts," he said. "Note, for instance, how the migrants of today come from the countries that not such a short time ago were aggrieved and colonised and twisted into places that are not havens for their own people."

We are back to those ghosts. We end, though, on a positive note – a discussion of Index on the magazine's 50th birthday.

A long-time contributor, Dorfman calls the magazine "a unique, essential, wondrous voice in a world where the temptation to silence dissent and free discussion is on the rise".

He added: "I am particularly taken with how the magazine devotes so much attention to countries that are generally neglected in the mainstream media. Gabriel Boric's peaceful battle cry 'Seguimos' applies to Index: 'We go on'."

Indeed, we go on. ✘

Jemimah Steinfeld is editor-in-chief of Index on Censorship

51(01):152/157|DOI:10.1177/03064220221084525

Mumtaz

Ariel Dorfman

I AM SHAH Jahan, once king of the Universe, conqueror of Kandahar and builder of the gardens of Shalimar, I am and once was Shah Jahan and now I am dying, I die as I look at her, the crown that was Mumtaz, I am already dead.

To describe her is to sin.

To refuse words is an even greater one.

One word, then: alive.

She was more alive than any bird is now–and now, now as well, even as I look upon the living light of her tomb – more alive than all the birds that I have seen in seventy-six years of life, than the birds that flock the air above and between and below and again above her four towers, more alive than I will ever be, ever have been, changing with each ray of sun and cover of cloud and nightfall and dawnrise, eternal in each moment, eternal and serene.

I would rather have lost my kingdom than have lost sight of my lost love.

I am Shah Jahan, son of Jahangir and father, alas, of Aurangzeb, seizer of the world, and sixth Emperor of this Mughal dynasty, I am and once was Shah Jahan, the king who lost his kingdom and has but one regret.

For twenty-two years, I watched the prophecy of mounting stones, one after the other. The first thing I saw in the morning when I rose, the last thing I saw at night when I went to sleep – like now, like now as I lay dying in the arms of

Jahanara, one daughter at least, one child who shared the womb of Mumtaz, one at least, who did not forget this old man.

Stone upon stone, what I saw every day, better to watch that mansion for the dead rising up than to risk the mother of my fourteen children visiting me in my dreams. Sweet to have her again and the same smile with which she greeted me the first time – I was fifteen and she a year younger. Betrothed for five years, five years she told me, we should wait five years so she could slowly cease to be Arjumand Banu and ease into becoming my Mumtaz, five years so the next twenty would be forever years, so there would be no one but her. Sweet, so sweet and wise, the dream and her body in the dream, but more bitter to awake and find her gone. With this recurring consolation: from my bed to witness the breathing white marble of her mausoleum as it shimmered up. Every day I could spare and so many I could not, spent on her memorial and memory and memories of her. Each gem selected personally by me, a homage. Each arch of Jali approved personally by me, a vow. Each scroll of Persian script read personally by me, a promise. Surround her with gates of light, the four rivers of paradise. So, she would remain with me while I remain, so she can be here now as I die, here and there as I feel darkness seep into me, so she will be waiting, saying goodbye and also waiting on the other side, when I join her, the resident of paradise.

I am Shah Jahan and I will soon walk into the Banquet Hall of Eternity.

O Noble, O Magnificent, O Majestic, O Unique, O Eternal, O Glorious, will you deny me the sight of her one more time?

I will never more wake up and see once more stone set upon stone, across the river and the plain of Agra, never again awake in this room in the Red Fort on this hill in Agra, never again examine through the frame of this window – all other rooms are forbidden me by my son – the granite from Bukhara and turquoise from Tibet, the jasper and malachite that inlayers came to prime, the flowering lattices as white as her soul, so the poets said – though they lied as poets lie,

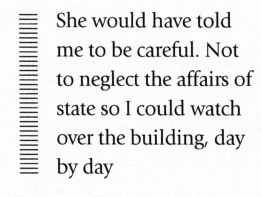

She would have told me to be careful. Not to neglect the affairs of state so I could watch over the building, day by day

as nothing was and is and can be as white as her soul. Slant the minarets thus, I said to Ustar Ahmad Lahauri, slant them slightly outward. So if they fall (as I must fall and die and decline, even I, Shah Jahan, once King of the Universe), so if they fail and fall, they will not fall upon her, my Mumtaz. May nothing but honey fall on her. May only milk and honey fall on her from the sky. May the stones turn all light into milk and all rain into honey. May the stars compete with the moon in their envy of her ravishment in the night. Reject the stone that is not perfect, that does not absorb and reflect and reject and subsume the bright. Refuse the slab that does not fit, make sure the soft fire of colour is both rose and white, so the sun will stay with her and keep her warm even in the winter of her bones and my bones, now that I could not rub her feet when they grew cold, make sure each last carving is flawless so she will have company while she waits for me, the ninety-nine names of God to guide her while I wait.

I would rather have lost my kingdom than have lost sight of my lost love.

This is true. But she would have told me to be careful. Not to neglect the affairs of state so I could watch over the building, day by day, afternoon through night, cloud and rain and summer beating down. That's what she would have whispered. If she had been there.

I looked at the men working day in and out, spring and fall turning, for twenty-two years I watched the stones rise seamlessly and then the gardens, I looked out onto my Mumtaz and ➔

→ turned my back on taxes except to demand more for her casket and tomb, I turned my back on wars, except to wage those which would bring me more translucent marble from Jaipur, more craftsmen from Baluchistan and artisans from Persia, I tried not to listen to disputes and petitions and petty power. I only had eyes for the mosaic of my love. I worshipped each shining amulet of rock and every curl and curve of the calligraphy, I asked Allah, may his name be blessed, to grant me time to complete her tomb and mine, so she could be there for all those young who have yet to discover love and all the old who still hope to love beyond this life.

I did not have eyes at the back of my head.

Behind me, as I watched the labourers and masons into the night, behind me, he was talking to the generals, he was conspiring with the courtiers against his father and his brothers, behind my head he was consulting the imams, Aurangzeb, whose name I shall not bite bitterly.

He came from inside her.

I shall not deign even to damn him, the son who did what needed to be done, what his brothers would never have done and thus will not rule over one inch of the Empire, he did to me what needed to be done to a father so in love with the dead that the living were forgotten.

He does not, did not, will never understand what it means to be in love, that word love, that word alive, what rolls in his mouth like the corpse of a tongue, he understands nothing. He understands nothing, and this is his punishment.

You understand nothing, Aurangzeb, even if you spent nine months inside the temple of your mother, a place more beautiful than Samarkand, more luminous than the tomb of Timor. This is all you knew: that I had no eyes at the back of my head, this he understood as he bent his knees and twisted his soul towards Mecca. So little that his prayers taught him: to insinuate, when he rose from bowing to God, at first merely to insinuate, then suggesting between clenched teeth, then more than murmuring, then finally bursting the saliva of his thoughts into a word.

Not the word, alive, that he does not understand, will never know what it means.

Sacrilege, that word. His favourite word.

For a woman, to do all this for a woman. Haram for our religion, a betrayal. Idolatry. Mortal man cannot represent the human figure. God alone, may He be blessed, only God can do this with the clay of our flesh. And my father, Aurangzeb said, first thought and then said, my father, Shah Jahan, is doing something worse than blasphemy, making of a mere human figure – a woman, a mere woman, even if she was my mother – making her into a goddess. Aurangzeb, her son and mine, gathering armies to defeat his brothers, gathering jailers to imprison his father, gathering his haunches to mount the Peacock Throne.

I did not see him.

I did not hear him.

My back was turned.

She was not there, my Mumtaz, to provide eyes.

I can say over and over that she is more alive than I am, than birds blessing the sky, but she was not there, my Mumtaz, not here by my side.

She was not here, my Mumtaz, my crown, to provide ears.

I can say she is more alive than ever, but she did not whisper in my ear, she did not say beware, beware, Jahan, beware.

She was dead.

How can I say this, dare as I die in this month of Rajab to decree this, that she is dead.

She could not receive news from the eunuchs, she was not there. She was not there to stare down into the courtyard and read his lips, see

Behind me, as I watched the labourers and masons into the night, behind me, he was talking to the generals

I smelled jasmine and only smelled her, I plucked the violets and the roses and it was her, always her

our son walking around the fountain, his head haughty as he cast his eyes down, waiting to pounce when I fell ill.

She was not here, my beloved, to tell me what to do, who to fear, who to punish, who to trust, how to stop him.

She was in the shrine I was building for her and for me. She could not be my eyes and ears, could not be my hands and feet, my skin, her skin.

I was blind and deaf without her.

My back turned on the affairs of the world until every last stone was in place, each juncture of each stone with stone like her body and mine, each stone making love to the stone above and the stone below and the stone to the west and the stone to the south until the dome designed by Ismail Afandi went up. I conquered provinces and levied taxes and issued edicts, oh, I pretended to rule, I planned and built the Garden of Grapes, I designed the Pearl Mosque and the red sandstone of the Vazir Khan Mosque at Lahore, I met Sultan Murad the Fourth in Baghdad but only so I could steal his main Ottoman architect, I visited my summer residence in Kashmir but all I saw in the spring near Srinagar was the water of my Mumtaz, I smelled jasmine and only smelled her, I plucked the violets and the roses and it was her, always her, urging me to hurry back and make sure nothing went wrong with what was to be her final resting place, like the resting places I built while she was alive so that travellers would not be weary, like the hospitals she had me foster so that the sick would be cared for, so that other women would not watch their blood flowing

from the source and centre of their life as the blood flowed from inside her as she died, do I dare to decree that it is true, that she really died?

My back was turned on the kingdom and my eyes existed only for the memory of Mumtaz.

While Aurangzeb prepared my prison and his palace, his palace and his haunches for a long reign.

Do I have regrets?

Only that she is not with me now.

Do I repent of what I did?

I would do it all over again, every first and final lotus minute.

I say this, Shah Jahan, once Lord of the Universe, Shahanshah Al-Sultan al-'Azam Wal Khagan al-Mukarram, I say this, as I lie dying in the arms of my daughter, the girl my wife gave to me so she could care for this man who is so alone and yet never alone, like the sun and the stone, like the stone and the stories, the girl her mother left me so I would not be alone.

Though I will always be alone.

Until I cross the river of death and find her.

I say this, Shah Jahan, once and no longer Lord of the Universe, Shahanshah–E-Sultanat Ul Hindiya Wal Mugahliya, grandson of the great Akbar and son of Jahangir, I dare to say, I who was the fifth Emperor of the Mughals, I dare to say that I am alone now that my eyes are closed and I cannot see her over there, across the river Yamuna and the plain of Agra, I dare to say that like all men on this earth I must die alone.

Ah, but behind me.

Behind me then, behind us, she and I, look, come and look, behind us we left behind so others can understand, so young and old lovers tomorrow and beyond, we leave behind an asylum where all past sins and weary eyes are to be washed away, we leave behind so you can try and understand, we leave behind us, Mumtaz and I, come and look and try to understand, we leave in front of us and behind us the solace of the Taj Mahal. ✖

'Threats will not silence me'

As the authorities in Kashmir crack down on critical writing, **BILAL AHMAD PANDOW** talks to the poet **MADHOSH BALHAMI** about his 30 years of resistance

LOSING BOTH PARENTS at an early age was extremely painful for Madhosh Balhami, who took to writing to vent his pain and suffering. Born in 1966 in Balhama, a village 12km from Srinagar, in Kashmir, he was named Ghulam Mohammad Bhat but writes under his pen name of Balhami.

He has worn many hats; a saffron cultivator, a former press secretary and a poet who started writing poetry inspired by love and grief, and soon moved to pen political themes in the 1990s.

"Mass rigging in the 1987 elections in Kashmir and subsequent political events in the late-1980s shook my faith in the elections and the democratic process. That proved to be a turning point for me," he lamented in an interview with Index.

Balhami is known in the Kashmir valley for his recitation of elegies, which he used to write for the funerals of slain militants. As the number of militants who were killed grew, he wrote a poem dedicated to them as a group. It was written from the perspective of a victim's mother and became a sort of anthem, turning Balhami into a household name.

As a result of this, he spent nearly three years in jail.

"I was sent to jail in 1993 for a couple of years on the ruse that I was an upper ground worker for militants; however, in reality, I was taken into custody for my political poetry," said Balhami, adding: "I was picked up by the Indian army again and sent to jail in 1998 for 11 months."

The detentions did not deter Balhami, who kept writing during his confinement. "I wrote huge volumes inside the jails of the valley. The authorities could confine me physically but not my thoughts," he said.

In fact, prison helped him develop as a poet.

"I started critically looking at everything, including militancy," he said.

Throughout his 30-year career as a poet, Balhami has stayed impartial. Today he has two books of poetry to his name: Sadaye Abu Zar and Dard-e-Furqat.

But his troubles have not ended. On 15 March 2018, Balhami's home, which was built by his father in 1967 and was home to his collection of poetry, was destroyed in a fire during a gun battle between the Indian army and rebels.

"I can rebuild my home brick by brick but I lost most of my work," Balhami said. He recited two powerful lines about his loss:

Tell me what crime I commit if I demanded my rights
In a flash of a moment this paradise-like city was reduced to rubble

Balhami's experience is part of a wider trend of writers losing their work in Kashmir.

LEFT: Kashmir poet Madhosh Balhami outside his house that was bombed in 2018, which resulted in the loss of his work

LEFT: The poet Madhosh Balhami continues to write despite the harassment he faces in Kashmir

In a flash of a moment this paradise-like city was reduced to rubble

Local reporters have spent years recording the daily hardships of living in the Kashmir conflict with unprecedented detail. Their work contributes to a vital record of widespread human rights atrocities involving the Indian military, including rape, torture, killings and the disappearance of hundreds of political activists and civilians.

The work of these journalists has started disappearing from the archives of local media outlets, which many believe the Indian government is attempting to erase. Along with the digital archives of regional newspapers such as Greater Kashmir, Rising Kashmir, and Kashmir Reader, many Urdu language journals have been either partially or entirely destroyed, especially since 2019.

Broadly speaking, the state heavily censors writers in Indian-administered Kashmir. The situation is alarming and has become worse since the abrogation of the quasi-autonomy of the region in August 2019.

The physical assaults of writers, especially journalists, have become the norm. The list of recent abuses feels endless.

One example was when Obaid Dar, a photojournalist, was assaulted at work in October. A security guard at a university hit him and he had to have stitches.

Meanwhile, the authorities are forcing editors to make changes to their style sheets. The editors claim the government is compelling them to change their terminology, such as using "terrorists" in place of "militants", which has been used for decades.

Staff in newsrooms find it challenging to use such a loaded word, especially in a conflict zone such as Kashmir where it can have serious repercussions. It is the first time that a word such as "terror" has appeared in local newspaper front-page headlines.

While journalists are particular targets, no critical writers are spared. In an interview with The New York Times, more than a dozen poets said that increased surveillance had left them with no choice but to stop writing.

"We are not allowed to breathe until and unless we breathe as per the rules and the wishes of the government. The silencing of voices, the freedom to speak and vent grievances, all is gone, and it is suffocating," said Zabireh, a Kashmiri poet who uses only one name.

Balhami still has enough poetry to complete a third volume, but he is frightened to publish it as it takes aim at the Indian state.

He told Index: "I've written the stuff that can get me killed. Also, because of the current political situation in Kashmir, no one will publish it." He added that he was old enough now to be afraid of these threats, but said: "I have toned down my language to some extent but will never stop writing."

On an optimistic note, Balhami believes that his writings will live on after his death because what he writes is for people and not for himself. "My writings will bear witness to historical occurrences in Kashmir." ✖

Bilal Ahmad Pandow is a researcher and freelance writer based in Kashmir

51(01):158/159|DOI:10.1177/03064220221084527

The dark age

by Madhosh Balhami

The dark age of freedom of expression
Through an extreme stone-hearted approach,
Delhi has rendered Kashmiris helpless through reproach;
Remediless! And full of pain,
That is what people have to confront and sustain;
To speak is a crime and so'tis to write
Even a whisper is punishable;
The dark age of freedom of expression
The heart consuming and enduring suppression;
No one moans even under extreme pain
And death keeps guard at every door;
The massacre of humanity if one might witness
Must know to act blind and not to express;
Must turn his gaze away from daylight murders
That constitutes the art of living on bloody Kashmir shores;
Labelling stark darkness as broad daylight
May help one survive the wrath of the kingly might. ✖

END NOTE

Classic case of cancel culture

If you thought the 21st-century scourge was a modern phenomenon, remember how Socrates met his end, writes **MARC NASH**

PICTURED: Socrates chose to take his poison rather than be exiled from Athens, where his statue stands today

T'S NOTHING NEW. As his death sentence, Socrates, freelance academic and philosopher, was ordered by an estimated 500 of his Athenian citizen peers to quaff hemlock. The charge? Impiety and corrupting Athenian youth.

The specifics of the accusations were that Socrates denied the gods of Athens and instituted his own in the form of the daimons, or tutelary spirits, which he claimed guided him and his ideas. At trial, one of his accusers denounced Socrates as an atheist, which he denied, pointing out the contradiction between introducing new divinities and being an atheist. It didn't do him any good.

His other main argument was that, unlike other philosopher teachers who charged for attending their schools, he worked for free. Therefore students weren't bound to attend his teaching, but could come and go as they pleased. Thus he was hardly "corrupting their minds" in any systematic way. It's an interesting take on academic freedom, whereby Socrates was accentuating freedom, not in him expressing his ideas so much as whether his audience wanted to listen to them.

It was his student Plato who kept Socrates' teaching alive through his own published work centring on Socratic dialogue and thought. Indeed, one of the main accounts of Socrates' trial comes from Plato's pamphlet Apology. Plato called his philosophy school The Academy, named after Academus who provided the land where philosophers gathered to discourse. The word has passed into our language.

Socrates was found guilty by a similar margin to that of the Brexit referendum. He claimed such a narrow vote ought to mitigate against the death sentence. However, the punishment phase of the trial saw a greater margin in favour of a death sentence. This suggests that the trial was not really to do with impiety.

Socrates had made many political enemies during the short-lived puppet regime instituted in Athens by its enemy Sparta. Socrates was tarred with having taught some of the key players behind the regime and being sympathetic to their anti-democratic beliefs. Socrates denied this, pointing out that he had refused to carry out an order given to him by the regime, to form part of an arrest squad for one of its enemies. This should not have formed part of his trial, since there had been an amnesty on any charges associated with the time of

Socrates was a speaker of truth to power and it was probably this that proved fatal

Sparta's control. Hence any resentment towards Socrates had to be channelled through the religious indictments.

The trial was a battle over definitions of democracy. Socrates himself said he attached himself only to the city of Athens "in order to sting it". Socrates was a speaker of truth to power and it was probably this that proved fatal.

It was expected that those sentenced to death would go into exile, but Socrates refused to do this and took his poison. He, his ideas and his school were summarily cancelled in 399BC. ✖

Marc Nash is a writer who lives in London. His latest book is Stories We Tell Our Children (Lendal Press, 2021)

51(01):160/160|DOI:10.1177/03064220221085926